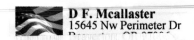

PATTON'S THIRD ARMY

PATTON'S THIRD ARMY

A Daily Combat Diary

Charles M. Province

HIPPOCRENE BOOKS
New York

For information, address:
HIPPOCRENE BOOKS, INC.
171 Madison Avenue
New York, NY 10016

Library of Congress Cataloging-in-Publication Data is available.

ISBN 0-87052-973-0

Printed in the United States of America

For my father, Herman H. Province, Sr.
He was a pretty good old guy.

Headquarters
THIRD UNITED STATES ARMY
Office Of The Commanding General
APO 403

Regensburg, Germany
15 May, 1945

   With the termination of hostilities, the
Third Army and its inseparable
comrade-in-arms, the XIX Tactical Air Command,
completed 281 days of constant battle during
which we have engaged in every type of combat
except defensive. In each type of fighting
successful solutions have been evolved.
   This report describes in considerable detail
the various situations which developed and the
tactical combinations utilized for their
successful solution.
   It is noteworthy that while our operations
in pursuit or exploitation have at times
developed phenomenal speed, they have always
been preceded by bitter and sometimes
prolonged assaults. This is particularly true
in the initial breakthrough at St. Lo in July,
in Lorraine from November 8 to December 19,
and in Luxembourg and Germany from December 22
to March 5.
   The success of all our operations has been
due to teamwork and mutual cooperation, to the
untiring efforts of a devoted and experienced
staff, to the ability of commanders from Corps
and Tactical Air Commands to platoons and
individual pilots. But above all to the
fighting heart of the American soldier.

G. S. Patton, Jr.
General

Contents

The Third Army

1918 - 1941
The Early Years

The United States Third Army was officially created on November 15, 1918, four days after the signing of the armistice which ended the First World War in Europe.

Originally encamped at Ligny-en-Barrios, France, Third Army was later moved to Koblenz, Germany where it served as an army of occupation. On July 2, 1919, Third Army was deactivated and its units and personnel were renamed *American Forces Germany*.

It was the original job of the Third Army which gave rise to the design of its shoulder patch. The patch is a white **A** on a round, blue background with a red circle around the **A**. The meaning of the patch was originally Army (white A) of Occupation (red O).

Thirteen years later, in 1932, the Third Army was reorganized within the continental United States. This army-wide reorganization divided the United States into four sections, with one army located in each section. The Third Army was located in the southeast, with its headquarters alternating between Atlanta, Georgia, and Fort Sam Houston, Texas.

1941 - 1943
Lt. Gen. Walter Kreuger

From 1941 until 1943, Third Army was commanded by Lt. Gen. Walter Kreuger. General Kreuger was born in Germany and immigrated to the United States when very young. He had viewed army command from both sides of the fence, serving as a doughboy before he was commissioned as an officer in 1901. Kreuger served in World War I and was known as a tough, gritty commander who demanded the best from his soldiers. He also was known as a fair-minded man, and his leadership made the Third Army one of the best *training* armies in the United States.

It is interesting to note that in Kreuger's command there were two relatively unknown officers who would later make their mark in world history. One of them was Dwight D. Eisenhower. The other was Major General George S. Patton, Jr., who would later achieve the commander's position that Kreuger held.

Although Kreuger was beyond the age limit set for combat commanders by General George Marshall, Kreuger was luckily a friend of General Douglas MacArthur. It was due to the personal intervention of General MacArthur that Kreuger was given command of the Sixth Army in the Pacific Theater of Operations in January 1943.

1943 - 1944
Lt. Gen. Courtney H. Hodges

Lt. Gen. Courtney Hodges commanded the Third Army from 1943 until 1944. Like Kreuger, Hodges had risen from the enlisted ranks to become a general officer. He, too, had combat experience as an infantry battalion commander during World War I. Also, Hodges, like both Patton and Eisenhower, had served under Kreuger's command in the Third Army.

After a major reorganization of the army in the late 1930s, Hodges had been reorganized out of a job. His position in 1940 was Chief of Infantry until it was abolished. He then was assigned to command a corps in Kreuger's Third Army. After Kreuger left to command the Sixth Army, Hodges assumed command of the Third Army.

It has been reported by Robert S. Allen, in his book, *Lucky Forward*, that Hodges, unfortunately, was not as much interested in the training and maneuvers of the Third Army as was Kreuger. He left many of his duties to his subordinates, especially his chief of staff.

Because of this laxness, Hodges failed to keep a firm grasp on the policies and decisions, which greatly affected the attitude and ability of Third Army. It also has been reported that Hodges' chief of staff was a rather abrasive individual who failed to get along well with the other members of the general staff. It was most probably this demonstrated lack of strong command ability which caused Hodges to be removed from command of the Third Army, although the official reason was kept secret.

Officially, the Third Army was changed from a training army to a combat army on December 31, 1943.

The Beginning
England

On January 1, 1944, the alert was sounded. Third Army was ordered to prepare for overseas movement to the European Theater of Operations.

An advance party of thirteen officers and twenty-six enlisted men left Fort Hamilton, New York on January 12 on board the HMS *Queen Mary*. Upon arrival in Glasgow, Scotland, on January 29, they were met by the new commanding general, George S. Patton, Jr.

The small group of men then had their first ride on an English train. They arrived at Peover Camp and began preparations for the reception of the main body of troops of the Third Army.

The main body of headquarters troops arrived on March 21. They, too, had been met and addressed by their new commanding general. He spoke to them of the standard of performance that he expected from them, his policies, and what was to be expected of the Third Army in its mission in Europe.

On March 12, before the headquarters contingent had arrived, a group of staff officers met with First Army's Group G-3 to discuss the Third Army's participation in Operation Overlord, the invasion of Normandy.

Third Army's G-2 Section set up their War Room in Peover Hall and General Patton immediately started daily staff conferences to brief the section chiefs on security instructions, G-3 Section operational plans, G-2 Section estimate, and staff policy. Third Army was one of the first commands to use the war room concept, not only in planning in headquarters, but also in the field of combat. Supreme Headquarters directed a new document classification of Top Secret which was to be controlled by the Adjutant General Section.

One of the primary problems that had to be solved by the G-3 Section was that of finding suitable training areas and accommodations for the Third Army units that were beginning to arrive from the United States. They also were deeply involved in planning the continuing training of new units as they would become combat ready on the continent.

The work of the G-4 Section was initially oriented toward requirements for new equipment. Plans were started for the organization of a Transportation Section to operate and control all motor, rail, water, pack and civilian impressed transportation of army agencies.

The Engineer Section began their job of analyses of bridge requirements, river crossing sites, road studies, traffic circulation plans, computation of supply requirements, and survey and mapping plans. The immediate area of study was that of north and northwest France, where the Third Army would become combat operational in August 1944 after the establishment of a firm beachhead.

The Signal Section started their planning of the extensive and complex network of communications. This initially involved the mapping of wire circuits and radio nets, but as it later developed, it involved the planning for all of the Third Army's communications facilities for the gathering of intelligence, the establishment of security, and the procurement of signal supplies and personnel sufficient to adequately meet the upcoming operations.

The Quartermaster Section was reorganized, with the creation of a new division called Field Service. The old Transportation Section was dropped by Quartermaster Section and taken over by the G-4 Section.

The Medical Section began a series of special conferences and detailed inspections, which were to become almost daily occurrences. Fortunately, there were no major personnel shortages in the Medical Section as there were in almost all of the other service sections. Formal training was initiated for the medical troops to insure their ability to perform adequately in a combat situation.

In March, the chaplain initiated plans for complete religious coverage of all units and all denominations.

During all of this preliminary planning, General Patton was busy making impromptu, personal inspections of all units. As usual, he would show up out of nowhere, poking and probing into the problems which would arise. He took the time, as he always did, to speak personally and individually with officers and noncommissioned officers to find out for himself what was really going on at the lower echelons.

The systematic, detailed planning for Third Army's operations on French soil continued unceasingly throughout the months of March, April, and May, right up to the actual Allied invasion of Normandy on June 6, 1944.

Under the command of the Twenty-first Army Group, Allied forces made airborne and seaborne landings on the coast of France. The 82nd Airborne landed in the vicinity of St. Mere Eglise, while the 101st Airborne landed near Carentan. British forces parachuted into an area near the city of Caen. The entire operation was strongly supported by naval and air bombardment. Landings were made by the V Corps at Omaha Beach northwest of Bayeux. The VII Corps landed and gained a beachhead at Utah Beach east of St. Mere Eglise. British forces landed to the north and northwest of Caen. The whole operation came as a complete surprise to the Germans.

They had been expecting General Patton to land his army in the Pas de Calais area.

The United Kingdom planning phase for the Third Army came to a close during the period of July 5 through July 7. Third Army's Forward Echelon, named Group X, sailed from the city of Southhampton and headed for France. General Patton and his chief of staff, General Hobart Gay, flew to France to join the headquarters unit which now was reported as having a strength of 264,843 men.

Their new headquarters was a canvas tent in the orchards of Normandy. In front of them were the famous hedgerows. The stage was set for one of the greatest human endeavors in the history of the world.

Pre-Operational Phase In Normandy

When the Third Army Headquarters landed on French soil, the first thing done was to insure absolute security. In accordance with the plan of Overlord, the presence of the Third Army was to be kept secret as long as possible. The idea was to keep the German High Command guessing as to the whereabouts of General Patton.

During these first days in the Allied invasion, the XIX Tactical Air Command, whose primary job was aerial support for the Third Army, established its own headquarters adjacent to the army headquarters. Their detailed planning then started with high hopes for quick destruction of the Germans.

The G-2 Section of the Third Army made an in-depth report on enemy capabilities.

It was the immediate concern of Third Army Headquarters to receive and prepare their arriving troops, who were coming in via control points established at the Utah and Omaha beachheads. During the month of June, over five hundred units of the Third Army were moved over the small roads of the peninsula.

With these troops arriving daily, Patton was in a hurry to get going. He was fearful that the war might be over before he could get into the battle, since battle reports had indicated that First Army alone had, by July 7, taken 46,219 prisoners of war (POWs) and killed 4,739 of the enemy.

On July 22, General Bradley issued a directive from Twelfth Army Group indicating that the Third Army could become operational by July 24. Operation Cobra, Bradley's slightly changed version of Patton's breakout plan, was originally to start at 1300 hours on July 24, with VIII Corps to join in at 0530 hours on July 25. In each case, the D-Day and H-Hours were advanced a full twenty-four hours due to bad flying weather, which prevented the scheduled aerial bombardment.

Finally, champing at the bit, Patton was given verbal orders on July 28 that he would, indeed, assume operation control of the Third Army. As Acting Deputy Commander, Patton hit the enemy with the VIII Corps, quickly followed by the 4th and 6th Armored Divisions. Bringing up the rear were the 8th and 79th Infantry Divisions. The lightning-quick blow thoroughly upset and hurt the Germans. They began a rapid retreat which would become the normal course of events for the next nine months.

The Forward Echelon of Third Army Headquarters, named Lucky Forward by General Patton, made their first of many moves to a position five miles west of Coutances.

Third Army Staff

1200 Hours, 1 August, 1944

Commanding General	Lt. Gen. G.S. Patton, Jr.
Chief Of Staff	M.G. General Hugh J. Gaffey
Deputy Chief Of Staff	B.G. General Hobart R. Gay
Deputy Chief Of Staff (optns)	Col. Paul D. Harkins
Asst Chief Of Staff G-1	Col. Frederick S. Matthews
Asst Chief Of Staff G-2	Col. Oscar W. Koch
Asst Chief Of Staff G-3	Col. Halley G. Maddox
Asst Chief Of Staff G-4	Col. Walter J. Muller
Asst Chief Of Staff G-5	Col. Nicholas W. Companole
Adjutant General	Col. Robert E. Cummings
Antiaircraft Artillery	Col. Frederick R. Chamberlain
Artillery	Col. Edward T. Williams
Build Up Control Organiz.	Col. Redding F. Perry
Chaplain	Col. James H. O'Neill

Chemical Warfare	Col. Edward C. Wallington
Engineer	Col. John F. Conklin
Finance	Lt. Col. Charles B. Milliken
Headquarters Comndnt.	Col. Rufus S. Bratton
Inspector General	Col. Clarence C. Park
Judge Advocate	Col. Charles E. Cheever
Medical	Col. Thomas D. Hurley
Ordnance	Col. Thomas H. Nixon
Provost Marshal	Col. John C. Macdonald
Public Relations	Col. Charles C. Blakeney
Quartermaster	Col. Everett Busch
Signal	Col. Elton F. Hammond
Special Service	Lt. Col. Kenneth E. Van Buskirk

CHAPTER 1

August, 1944

August 1
D-Day +56

The Third Army became operational at 1200 hours on August 1, 1944, a warm, clear day. It was perfect weather for the type of mobile war that General Patton loved to wage.

Under Patton's command were the VIII Corps, commanded by Troy H. Middleton; the XII Corps, commanded by Gilbert R. Cook; the XV Corps, commanded by Wade H. Haislip; and the XX Corps, commanded by Walton H. Walker, one of Patton's favorites. Patton once said of Walker that "He will apparently fight anytime, anywhere, and with anything that I will give to him." That was the type of commander Patton liked.

At the same time and day, the XIX Tactical Air Command became operational under the command of General O.P. Weyland.

The operations of August would develop into five distinct phases:

1. The conquest of Brittany;
2. Encirclement of the Seventh German Army at Argentan-Falaise;
3. The rapid advance to the Seine River, including the envelopment of enemy forces from Mantes Gassicourt to Elbeuf;
4. The enemy evacuation of southwestern France;

5. The chasing of the Germans across the Marne, Aisne, and Meuse Rivers.

G-2 Section made estimates concerning two separate fronts. The first estimate was for enemy elements in the Brittany peninsula, and the second was for enemy elements in central France opposing the Third Army's advance. It was decided that at the current time the enemy would be in too fluid a situation to formulate any specific enemy capabilities, so the order was given simply to find the enemy and engage them, in battle. While the VIII Corps was exploiting to full advantage the breakthrough at Avranches, the XIX Tactical Air Command (XIX TAC) provided armored column cover and flew armed reconnaissance in the afternoon.

August 2
D-Day +57

Air reconnaissance reported possible enemy reserves in fifty small ships at Cancale and Pont-du-Grium. Patton ordered the XV Corps to occupy and hold the general line from St. Hilaire-Du-Harcouet to the city of Rennes. After this had been accomplished, the objective was the Quiberon Bay area in Brittany. St. Malo was to be bypassed and contained if its capture took too large a force. Task Force "A," commanded by General Herbert L. Earnest, was formed with the purpose of clearing the enemy from the northern Brittany route to Brest. Spearheads of the Third Army made considerable progress to the south, southwest, and west while the XV Corps prepared for battle. Lucky Forward moved to Beauchamps, eleven miles north of Avranches.

August 3
D-Day +58

The Germans, uncertain of what to expect from Patton's Third Army, were unable to present a cohesive front line. They established defensive perimeters with well-emplaced, dug-in 88mm guns and assault guns. POWs indicated that there was a shortage of gasoline and what they did have was reserved for use by heavy tanks and officers inspecting troops.

In spite of bad weather, the XIX TAC covered the advancing armored and infantry columns. The city of Rennes was captured and armored elements reached Loudeac.

August 4
D-Day +59

The Germans remained unorganized and only offered limited use of delaying tactics, usually by small groups employing roadblocks, demolitions, and mine fields. Snipers hindered the movement of supplies. Enemy aircraft—what there was of it—attacked the Third Army's supply lines.

Orders were given to VIII Corps to continue clearing Brest and securing ports to be prepared for operation by Allied forces. The XII Corps was to go as far south as the Loire River, advance as quickly as possible to the immediate east, and protect the south flank of the army. The XV Corps captured Mayenne while keeping in contact with elements of the 1st Division of the First Army. A company of 150 Special Air Service Troops, British troops, were parachuted behind enemy lines to assist the Forces Francaises de l'Interieur in protecting railroad trestles in the Morlaix vicinity.

At this time it was possible to issue news flashes of the Third Army activities for the first time. For security purposes, the name "Third Army" still was not to be used.

With French authorities beginning to restore their power, the problem of civilian circulation control began to become visible to Third Army personnel.

August 5
D-Day + 60

The swift and aggressive tactics of the Third Army resulted in a widespread disorganization of the German forces. The XV Corps secured the city of Mayenne and Combat Command "A" captured Vannes. As Mayenne was being secured, the retreating enemy destroyed bridges over the Mayenne River.

The XIX TAC kept the enemy away from the advancing columns while attacking motor vehicles, gun positions, and an enemy headquarters and performing fighter sweeps in the St. Malo area.

August 6
D-Day +61

G-2's estimates indicated a possible combining of defenses just east of the Mayenne River with the possibility of a counterattack in the Mortain area, the idea being to sever the Third Army's north and south forces and to make the latter logistically untenable.

Upon securing Mayenne, the Third Army, as usual, did not stop. Patton often had instructed his men that "Too many battles have been lost because of stopping on the wrong side of a river." If the Third Army would keep advancing continually, hitting the enemy with everything it had, the enemy would have no time to stop and organize an active defense.

Third Army units were again spearheading the advance and driving to the east, with Le Mans as the objective. Supply lines were lengthening rapidly and putting a strain on the truck companies.

Third Army's zone of operations now included a total of 119 towns and a population normally numbering 3.5 million French people. There was a scarcity of bread, but there was also a wheat harvest under way which would alleviate that situation.

During the night, a stick of bombs was dropped on the army headquarters at Beauchamps. Ammunition Depot No. 1, near Granville, was bombed, with a loss of approximately six hundred tons of badly needed ammunition.

August 7
D-Day +62

The only aggressive enemy resistance at this point was in the St. Malo peninsula. Mines, booby traps, antitank obstacles, and antitank guns all were in use. St. Malo was reported to be barricaded and locks in the harbor were apparently mined and prepared for demolition. All roads out of Nantes were heavily mined, as was the area outside the town of Angers. The bridges across the Mayenne River in the vicinity of Laval were reportedly blown up or mined.

Patton, anticipating a German counterattack in the vicinity of St. Hilaire-du-Harcouet, ordered the 2nd French Armored Division, the 35th Infantry Division, and all complete artillery battalions available to hold their positions.

The VIII corps continued its attack on St. Malo, using the 83rd Infantry Division. The XV Corps advanced to a point twelve miles west of Le Mans. The enemy offered only token defense and delaying actions to obstruct their advance.

The XII Corps continued its assigned mission of moving Third Army units from the beaches to selected assembly areas as they landed in France.

The XIX TAC raised its strength to a total of nine full groups of fighter bombers. The Luftwaffe, growing more aggressive, met the fighters of the XIX TAC and lost a total of thirty-three aircraft. The XIX TAC were responsible for the destruction of twelve tanks and five staff cars. They continued to cover all columns moving to the west, south, and east, while also attacking troops in Brittany.

During the night the enemy initiated a strafing and bombing attack on their own troops held in the POW enclosure at Marcey, killing twenty-one German Pows and wounding sixty-two. Due to this raid, the Third Army started a policy of lighting the prisoner of war enclosures only in emergencies.

The population of Rennes, around eighty-seven thousand, had begun to return to their city. It was up to the Third Army to insure that there were adequate medical facilities and personnel available to meet the local needs. With the returning citizens, ample labor was found and secured for the harvesting in Brittany.

August 8
D-Day +63

Per Twelfth Army Group instructions, Patton ordered an

advance to the towns of Le Mans, Aleçon, Sees, and Carrouges. The capture of the Brittany ports and the reduction of the peninsula were ordered to continue.

The VIII Corps consolidated its position on the outskirts of Brest, while Task Force "A" continued its drive toward the city along the northern route. The XIX TAC reached a new peak of activity by flying a total of 717 sorties, during which 29 locomotives, 137 freight cars, 205 vehicles, and 17 tanks were destroyed. Armed reconnaissance sorties were flown to gain aerial superiority, knocking out German airdromes north and east of Paris.

Le Mans was captured.

August 9
D-Day +64

G-2 estimates indicated five possibilities of enemy action:
1. Continued defense from Brest to St. Nazaire
2. Counterattack against Third Army's east flank around Mortain
3. Withdrawal from the Le Mans area to the north and east
4. Enemy withdrawal along the entire Allied front toward the east
5. Moving reinforcements from the Pas de Calais area and the Rhine River area to any portion of the Allied front to strengthen forces.

The XIX TAC flew 72 missions and 780 sorties, destroying 7 of 12 ME-109s encountered. A rocket-carrying squadron was placed into operation.

August 10
D-Day +65

Enemy resistance now centered in the Dinard peninsula across the Rance estuary from St. Malo.

Low hanging clouds failed to stop the XIX TAC from providing strong support of the army's operations.

The Mont St. Michel, an architectural antique from the eleventh century, was found to be intact, although the Germans had used it for observation posts and billets. Angers was captured and the Germans were cleared from St. Malo.

August 11
D-Day +66

The Germans were reinforcing the troops in the Le Mans-Alencon-Sees area while at the same time evacuating a large number of troops from Belle Island to the Quiberon peninsula. Increasingly violent enemy delaying action was encountered from infantry supported by individual tanks attempting to hold on to roadblocks. Patton ordered the XV Corps to push on in the direction of Falaise after the capture of Argentan. When Falaise was reached and captured, orders from Bradley were to contain the situation and wait for the British forces to close the gap, which they failed to do.

The ration situation was becoming critical, with all forward units outrunning their supply lines. Shipments of supplies were short and heavy withdrawals already were being made on the emergency reserves.

August 12
D-Day +67

The Germans were reported to have withdrawn eleven divisions from the Pas-de-Calais area and rushed them to the Seine River to plug growing gaps in their defense. It was estimated by G-2 that the Germans might withdraw behind the Seine, but that they would still attempt to hold on to northern France.

Patton now ordered the XII Corps into combat action for the first time. Its objective was to concentrate forces to the southeast of Le Mans; prepare to operate north, northeast or east; and protect the south flank of the army.

The XV Corps was ordered to assemble in the vicinity of Argentan; wait for the British to close the Argentan-Falaise Gap, and prepare for immediate and rapid advance to the north, northeast, or east.

Planes of the XIX TAC patrolled the Loire River area and prepared the way to the French capital of Paris.

An important telephone center at Rennes was restored under Third Army supervision and put into military use.

August 13
D-Day +68

Reports from the Third Army G-2 to Supreme Headquarters Allied Expeditionary Force were that the enemy withdrawal through the Falaise-Argentan Gap was well underway. Aggressive enemy delaying action included local counterattacks, using predominantly armored units.

The 90th Division relieved the 5th Division at Argentan to strengthen the shoulder at the south end of the gap. The Third Army waited in vain for the British, under Montgomery, to close the gap.

The XIX TAC gave heavy support over Falaise-Argentan, destroying 710 enemy motor transports. A force of thirty-seven P-47 pilots, attacking a concentration of between eight hundred and one thousand vehicles, claimed four hundred to five hundred enemy transports destroyed. The VIII Corps' heavy artillery showed its muscle against the concrete fortifications of the Citadel at St. Malo. In one attack, 185 rounds from eight-inch guns blew a ten by twenty foot hole in a turret built of 26-inch concrete backed with steel sheeting, blew a 20 foot hole in a concrete tower, and destroyed two 88mm guns in concrete turrets.

Air observations were used extensively, resulting in relatively high losses of both pilots and aircraft.

August 14
D-Day +69

In an effort to destroy as much of the enemy forces as possible, the Twelfth Army Group ordered the Third Army to hold at the south portion of the Argentan-Falaise Gap with part of the XXV Corps and the 80th Division, while at the same time initiating a rapid movement to the east to harass and confuse the retreating Germans. The XX Corps was ordered to alter its original objective from Dreux to Chartres. The 80th Division was to remain in the Argent-Falaise pocket and was to be used to take over that part of the front after it was cleared by the First Army.

In order to speed the capture of the whole Brittany peninsula, three divisions of the First Army were attached to the Third Army in that area. During a temporary truce, twenty thousand civilians were marched out of the besieged city of Brest by the German and were turned over to French authorities. A Third Army refugee camp was opened at Plabannec and relief supplies were brought from Rennes in captured German trucks.

Approximately four hundred enemy soldiers surrendered to the XIX TAC by waving white flags from their positions. Fighter control was given the locations so that the nearest ground troops could pick up the prisoners.

Lucky Forward headquarters moved to an area at La Bazoge, ten miles north and northeast of Le Mans.

August 15
D-Day + 70

The Germans seemed to be making a last stand in the Dinard peninsula, generally utilizing small groups of infantry supporting tanks and occasional antitank guns in that area.

Reports indicated that in the last two weeks of action, the Germans were losing about ten men killed, wounded, and captured for each Third Army soldier killed, wounded, or missing in action. Due to the rapid advance of the Third Army, the execution of a planned operation called Transfigure was not necessary. The area south of the Seine River from Paris to Orleans was already under control.

On this date, the SHAEF officially announced for worldwide news coverage the fact that the Third Army was operational on the continent under the command of Lieutenant General George S. Patton, Jr.

August 16
D-Day +71

G-2 estimates indicated that the Third Army had in its area of combat approximately 125,000 combat-effective enemy soldiers and 300 enemy tanks. Enemy forces in the Brittany peninsula were estimated at a total of 38,300 men.

The XV Corps captured Dreux and the 79th Infantry Division closed into concentration in the same area, establishing a bridgehead across the Aunay River.

The XII Corps captured Orleans, and despite strong delaying tactics by the Germans, the objectives of Châteaudun, Dreux, Chartres, and Orleans were attained.

August 17
D-Day +72

Patton ordered the XII Corps to hold Orleans with a minimum force, maintain an armored combat command in the vicinity of La Loupe, move the bulk of the corps to an area south of Janville, and push reconnaissance to the east.

The 2nd French Armored Division, the 80th Infantry Division, and the 90th Infantry Division all were detached from the Third Army and attached to the First Army to assist in the closing of the Argentan-Falaise Gap. The Third Army continued to wait for the closure of the gap.

The Third Army relieved the XV Corps of the responsibility for antiaircraft defense of Alencon and assumed that responsibility. In addition, the Third Army also took over the responsibility for four airstrips which were scheduled to become operational very soon.

August 18
D-Day +73

G-2 estimated that the German forces in the Third Army's operational area were capable of five possible moves:
   1. They could continue a determined defense of the major Brittany ports
   2. They could continue aggressive delaying action to cover their withdrawal across the Seine River
   3. They could mount small counterattacks from the northwest and northeast in the Argentan area
   4. They had the capability of establishing hasty defensive posi-

tions in the northeast sector of the pocket between the La Tonques and Risle Rivers

5. They could establish a defensive or reorganization position east of the Seine River, manned by an infantry force estimated at 250 thousand.

The Third Army secured bridgeheads at Dreux and Chartres and various units reached the banks of the Seine River. The Third Army was moving so rapidly that there was a tremendous strain on the supply of communications wire. To keep communications at their peak operation, a used wire recovery program was put into effect, utilizing specified artillery battalions to do the actual gathering of the wire.

August 19
D-Day +74

There was little change in the Brittany peninsula situation. Though the Third Army could go anywhere it wished, the Germans still had control of some ports and would retain that control for some time.

Major General Manton S. Eddy became the commanding general of the XII Corps, succeeding Major General Gilbert R. Cook. Cook was relieved at his own request due to ill health.

Armored units cut off possible enemy escape routes by establishing bridgeheads at the Seine River at Mantes Gassicourt.

The first supply shipment by air was received at the Beille airstrip three miles south of Tuffie, near Le Mans. Twenty-one C-47 transports landed and air evacuation of wounded was begun the same day, with fifty patients being flown out.

August 20
D-Day +75

The Argentan-Falaise Gap was finally closed, by the American First Army, trapping a total of ten thousand Germans.

The XX Corps launched an attack east of the Seine River after establishing bridgeheads there. General Patton issued a letter to all troops emphasizing the extreme punishment which had been and would be imposed upon those soldiers committing crimes of violence against civilians.

Lucky Forward moved to Brou, twenty-two miles southwest of Chartres.

August 21
D-Day +76

The 4th Armored Division captured the town of Sens while the 35th Infantry Division continued eastward to the vicinity of Boynes, six miles southeast of Pithiviers, with only sporadic resistance being encountered.

The XV Corps was having more difficulty, meeting strong resistance of both infantry and tanks in the vicinity of Champenard.

The Germans now altered their air operations. Previously almost exclusively night operations were now done during daylight hours. Repeated attacks in the Seine crossing area included bombings, strafings, and rocket firings. Antiaircraft of the Third Army beat back the attacks, and a total of sixty planes were claimed to have been shot down.

A supply plan for all future operations was prepared, stating seven recommendations:

1. That the Third Army be relieved of supply responsibility for units in the Brittany area
2. That aviation groups be attached to the Third Army for construction of airstrips for evacuation and supply
3. That necessary railway operating and construction battalions follow closely behind the army to provide speedy rail transportation
4. That minimum daily tonnages for supply and maintenance, less reserve buildup, be estimated at five thousand long tons per day
5. That additional truck companies be attached to the army;
6. That the operation could be supported provided the main effort for supply and evacuation by Communications Zone (ComZ) and its Advance Section be directed toward the Third Army's advance route;
7. In the event that VII Corps was substituted for XV Corps, all

Third Army supporting troops with the XV Corps should be reverted to the Third Army for support of VII Corps.

Arrangements were made to furnish diesel fuel to French civilians for their tractors during harvesting of crops in Brittany.

General Patton was visited by Under Secretary of War Robert P. Patterson and Commanding General of Supply Services Lt. Gen. Breton B. Somerville.

August 22
D-Day +77

G-2 reported that there were some indications that the Germans might be planning a strong stand in the area of Fontainebleau. In the area south of Orleans, there were reports of considerable troop, rail, and motor traffic by the Germans, possibly indicating a coming counterattack at that point.

Planes from the XIX TAC bagged another twenty German planes.

ComZ was notified that the tonnage scheduled for the Third Army had not been delivered and that the supply situation was becoming critical. Ten tons of German medical equipment were captured at Orleans, fifteen tons at Dreux, and twenty tons at Fontainebleau. Three hundred miles of German communications wire was captured in a cave near Chartres.

August 23
D-Day +78

General Patton issued a new directive outlining two distinct plans of operations. Plan A would move the Third Army in a northern direction while plan B would move the army in an eastern direction, according to the possible wishes of the Twelfth Army Group.

With only three corps, one of which was occupied in the Brittany peninsula, the Third Army captured Fontainebleau and Montargis while its armored spearheads continued their race eastward toward Germany.

The XV Corps was released to the First Army.

Gasoline shipments were short of the allotted daily requirements and a critical situation began to develop. Because no appreciable reserve of supplies had been established, ComZ established special trucking services from the beaches of Normandy to expedite the forwarding of supplies. This was the **Red Ball Express**.

Among the day's guests were ten representatives of American labor organizations.

August 24
D-Day +79

General Patton ordered that XX Corps and XII Corps execute plan B of the directive issued on August 23. He stipulated, however, that they still should be ready, if necessary, to fall back on plan A. Upon request from Twelfth Army Group, a small group of officers and enlisted men from the Third Army's Public Relations Section was ordered to Paris to assist war correspondents there in handling their news articles and photographs upon the liberation of the city, which was expected to be very soon.

August 25
D-Day +80

Orders were issued to both XII Corps and XX Corps to seize and secure bridgeheads from Reims to Vitry-le-Francois. In the XII Corps area, Combat Command A of the 4th Armored Division captured Troyes, but only after some difficult street fighting.

The enemy continued their withdrawal to the east, resisting stubbornly around the northern entrance to Melun and the eastern outskirts of the city where extensive mine fields, mortars, and antitank weapons were encountered.

Bridgeheads were consolidated across the Seine while armored spearheads continued their push to the east and toward Germany.

Gasoline shipments were again short, the daily request being 250,000 gallons, of which 197,450 gallons were received.

The 2d French Armored Division, detached from the Third

Army and now under the First Army, entered Paris and obtained the surrender of the City of Lights that afternoon.

Lucky Forward moved to Courcy-aux-Loges, eight miles south of Pithiviers.

August 26
D-Day +81

A Twelfth Army Group directive ordered the Third Army to cross the line of the Seine River and Yonne River to the line of Troyes-Châlons-sur-Marne-Reims, protect the right flank eastward from Orleans, and be prepared to advance rapidly on order to seize crossings in Germany of the Rhine River from Mannheim to Koblenz.

The XIX TAC encountered very few enemy aircraft while providing protective cover for army columns.

Gasoline continued to be in short supply, although eighty tons of critical medical supplies were received at the Bricy airstrip. Ordnance heavy maintenance tank companies were moved from support of armored divisions and placed at collection points in support of separate armored units other than divisions. The rapidity of the Third Army's advance made necessary this increased maintenance for both tanks and tank destroyer battalions.

August 27
D-Day +82

G-2 reports now indicated a very marked decline in the battle worthiness of enemy personnel. They were facing a serious manpower problem in addition to a moral deficiency. As the Germans were withdrawing to the east of Provins and Nangis, they were heavily attacked and strafed by fighters of the XIX TAC. The XIX TAC also conducted a rail-cutting project to sever a main enemy escape route south of the Loire River.

August 28
D-Day +83

An estimate of possible enemy capabilities was issued by G-2.

1. An attempt for a northward thrust from south of the Loire River to disrupt the Third Army's line of communications
2. A possible delay and defense operation to the east and counterattack from the south
3. A withdrawal of troops from the south to the northeast for use as reinforcements or replacements in the path of Third Army's advance
4. The enemy could mount small scale local counterattacks spearheaded by tanks in the area from Reims to Troyes to cover a possible withdrawal behind the Aisne and Meuse Rivers.

Indications were that the enemy was withdrawing beyond the Aisne and Meuse Rivers in the direction of Verdun.

Results of operations for the day were rapid progress and the liberation of Châlons-sur-Marne, Montmirail, and Épernay.

By now, the gasoline situation was not just critical, it had become alarming. The word from the Twelfth Army Group was extremely disappointing. The Third Army, the fastest, most successful fighting force in the European Theater of Operations might be forced to halt. The reason given was that all supplies would be going to the First Army. The real reason was that General Montgomery was being allotted all the supplies that he requested for his upcoming airborne attack focused on the city of Arnhem.

August 29
D-Day +84

Patton announced the next mission for the Third Army: seizure and securing of bridgeheads east of the Meuse River to be prepared for a further advance to capture crossings at the Rhine River. He told his men that with or without gasoline, the Third Army was going forward. If three tanks had to have their gasoline tanks drained to fill the fourth tank, then that would be done. He said that he had done it in World War I, it had worked, and it could be done now. When that fourth tank ran out of gasoline, the crew was to get out and walk forward. Under no circumstances were the soldiers of the Third Army to stop their advance.

August 30
D-Day +85

G-2 estimated that as the enemy withdrew, he would make a determined stand once his prepared fortifications were reached. That meant the Siegfried Line. There were reports that troops in the Maginot Line to Metz area were being reequipped and were preparing for attacks from the west.

The Twelfth Army Group informed the Third Army that there would be no gasoline available until September 3. The shortage was disastrous. With only 31,975 gallons delivered out of a requested 400,000 gallons, the Third Army, a modern force created on the concept of mechanized mobility, was virtually forced to halt in its tracks.

Lucky Forward moved to La Chaume, thirteen miles northeast of Sens.

August 31
D-Day +86

In the XII Corps area, the Fourth Armored Division advanced to the high ground east of the Meuse River in the vicinity of St. Mihiel, where General Patton had fought and almost bled to death from machine gun wounds in the First World War.

Verdun fell to Combat Command "A" of the 7th Armored Division in the XX Corps area, and the division established a bridgehead while Combat Command "B" moved to the town of Eix.

No gasoline shipments were received.

CHAPTER 2

September, 1944

Due to the acute gasoline shortage, the Third Army was almost at a standstill. Other supply shortages began to crop up. The gasoline shortage, coupled with worsening weather conditions, gave the Germans time to begin a defense build-up program.

September developed into four phases:

1. The slowing of the Third Army's offensive operations
2. The crossing of the Moselle and Meurthe Rivers and the German counterattacks against the north and south flanks of the Third Army
3. Developments along the Third Army's flanks
4. Termination of the Third Army's activities in the Brittany peninsula.

September 1
D-Day +87

German activity reached a fever pitch as they constructed defense devices in the Westwall sector between Metz and Saarbrücken.

The Brittany peninsula finally was reduced by the XIII Corps.

The XII Corps held high ground east of the Meuse River in the vicinity of St. Mihiel, while the XX Corps secured a bridgehead over the Meuse River at Verdun and the 5th Division advanced to the town of Cheppy, twelve miles west of Verdun.

The XIX TAC flew 492 sorties and destroyed 11 enemy planes confirmed, 6 probables, and 12 damaged. Thirty-three locomotives, 130 tanks and armored vehicles, and 817 motor transport vehicles were damaged or destroyed in the day's bombings and strafings.

The Twelfth Army Group was officially designated as Central Group of Armies.

A medical gas treatment battalion arrived fully equipped in the army assembly area, making a total of three such battalions, while the engineers began reproduction of topographic maps covering the Siegfried Line directly in front of the Third Army.

September 2
D-Day +88

The enemy was cleared from north of the Loire River to Orleans.

The XIX TAC reported that in 164 sorties they destroyed 47 railroad cars, 106 motor transports, 7 locomotives, and 7 tanks and armored vehicles destroyed or damaged.

The 7th Armored Division secured its bridgehead across the Meuse River and extended its reconnaissance to the east.

Out of a requested 750,000 gallons of gasoline, the Third Army received a total of 25,390 gallons.

French civilian authority was reported to be in excellent condition, with capable officials being appointed by the provisional government. They were cooperating efficiently in carrying out the wishes of the army commander.

Captured German foodstuffs—many tons of grain, flour, sugar and rice—and hundreds of carloads of coal were distributed among the French population. During the early part of September, fishing resumed along the north coast of Brittany.

September 3
D-Day +89

G-2 estimated that the current German capabilities would favor the attitude of defensive measures. The three possibilities considered were:

1. The Germans could defend and delay, supported by local counterattacks, to screen the withdrawal of his forces behind the Siegfried Line
2. The Germans could defend and delay in the army's zone of advance while establishing blocking lines south of the army's south flank to facilitate the withdrawal of his forces from the Loire River to the Rhone Valley
3. The Germans could defend and delay east of the Moselle River, while massing reserves from the Pas-de-Calais in France, Germany, and distant fronts.

This last possibility was to be considered if the Germans planned a large scale counterattack.

In an estimate of enemy strength, two Italian divisions were identified and a third division tentatively identified.

Estimates of enemy losses for the past week totaled 264,300 infantry and 120,000 Panzer troops. His estimated combat strength was 106,700 infantry and 78,000 Panzer troops.

The VIII Corps continued its attack on Brest, while the island of Ile-de-Cezembre surrendered at 0930 hours to the XIX TAC.

The 4th Armored Division and 80th Infantry Division of the XII Corps consolidated their positions east of the Meuse River and pushed patrols to the east. The XV Corps concentrated in the vicinity of Nangis. The XX Corps secured the Verdun bridgehead while pushing further patrols to the east toward Germany.

Fighters of the XIX TAC flew 38 missions with 510 sorties, but found very few targets. They destroyed 14 railroad cars and 45 military installations were either damaged or destroyed.

The Central Group of Armies officially became Twelfth Army Group.

Daily request for gasoline was 590,000 gallons with 49,930 received.

Engineers began a study of German terrain to determine suitability for mechanized operations.

September 4
D-Day +90

The Germans built up their defensive positions south of the Moselle River.

The Twelfth Army Group directed that the Ninth Army assume command of the VIII Corps. The 83d Infantry Division and 6th Armored Division were to be released to XV Corps of the Third Army upon transfer of the VIII Corps effective at 1200 hours, September 5. The Ninth Army was to prepare for action to the east on the southern flank of the Third Army.

The XX Corps was ordered to seize the city of Metz immediately, to advance east of the Moselle River, seize Mainz, and secure a bridgehead east of the Rhine River.

The XII Corps was ordered to seize Nancy and secure a bridgehead east of the Moselle River. An additional job was the protection of the southern flank of the Third Army until relieved by units of the XV Corps. XII Corps was to be prepared to move rapidly to seize the city of Mannheim and secure a bridgehead east of the Rhine River.

Artillery reports indicated that in the VIII Corps area they had fired 607 missions in the twenty-four-hour period ending at 0600 on September 4, including a total of 105 counterbattery missions and 263 harassing missions. A great number of duds were found in the enemy artillery.

The Forces Francaises de l'Interieur captured a bridge across the Moselle River and destroyed an enemy gasoline dump of 200 thousand gallons, which could have been put to good use by the Third Army. Patton ordered the Forces Francaises to assist in establishing traffic control in key cities on main supply routes to help control the movement of supplies.

The XIX TAC flew 159 sorties, destroying 77 railroad cars and 19 motor transports.

Gasoline receipts began to increase, with 240,265 gallons delivered out of 640,000 requested.

Lucky Forward moved to a bivouac area north of Marson, eight miles east of Chalons-sur-Marne.

September 5
D-Day +91

On the XX Corps front, the 3d Cavalry Group located strongly held positions from Nilvange to Uckange that were defended by tanks, antitank weapons, and infantry.

Against very stiff enemy resistance, the 319th Infantry Division was able to force part of one battalion across the Moselle River in the vicinity of Pont à Mousson.

The XIX TAC flew 389 sorties in and 31 missions dropping napalm tanks on enemy installations and troops. Also claimed were 19 railroad lines cut, 31 gun installations, and 46 military installations damaged or destroyed.

Gasoline supplies improved greatly. Of 560,000 gallons requested, 275,720 were received.

September 6
D-Day +92

The XX Corps' 7th Division crossed the Meuse River and advanced toward the Moselle River, while the 90th Infantry Division closed in an area near Foameix, two miles northwest of Etain, and the 5th Division continued to force crossings of the Moselle River against stiff resistance.

The XIX TAC flew 416 sorties in 37 missions.

Now that the gasoline shortage was being alleviated, a new crisis erupted. There was an increasing shortage of artillery ammunition. The XX Corps had a fair supply, but the XII Corps was very short of all types of ammunition and fuses.

September 7
D-Day +93

The 80th Division, in the XII Corps zone, was meeting with fierce resistance in an attempt to drive bridgeheads across the

Moselle River. The 319th Infantry secured a bridgehead across the river in the vicinity of Gondreville-sur-Moselle, four miles north of Toul.

A combined force of the 2d Cavalry Group and one 105 howitzer battalion met an enemy column. The cavalry fired on the front of the column while the howitzers fired on the rear of the column resulting in thirty-six destroyed enemy vehicles and a large number of enemy casualties.

Hundreds of Germans were killed and over one thousand prisoners were taken in the Ardennes sector by the Forces Francaises under command of the Third Army. (When this area would be taken over by the First Army; the laxness of the command would allow a breakthrough for a major German offensive which would be called the Battle of the Bulge.)

The XIX TAC flew 238 sorties in 16 missions, destroying 132 motor transports and 310 horse-drawn vehicles. Eleven gun installations and 11 military installations were either damaged or destroyed.

For the first time in September, the receipts of Class III supplies exceeded the requests as the first railway shipment of gasoline arrived at the city of Sommesous. Delivery of approximately 200,000 gallons arrived, which helped to build a reserve, but left receipts for the month 2,865,000 gallons short of total requests.

September 8
D-Day +94

Within the XX Corps zone, fighting continued on both sides of the Moselle River, with the enemy launching four counterattacks.

The XIX TAC flew 470 sorties in 39 missions. These missions concentrated heavily on the enemy's military installations, with claims of 28 gun installations and 136 military installations destroyed or heavily damaged.

There was an increase in the number of bridgeheads reported by Third Army units.

A new policy was initiated concerning Third Army hospitals. Previously having been totally under canvas tents, with large red crosses to ward off enemy bombings, they now were permitted to begin moving operations into captured buildings.

September 9
D-Day +95

An estimate of enemy capabilities by G-2 section indicated that he was still capable of only defensive operations. The most favored possibility listed was:

1. Defense and delaying operations east of the Moselle River, counterattacking with armor spearheaded assaults against the Third Army's bridgeheads to contain them and to impede their advance to the east.

Less favored possibilities included

1. Opposition of the Third Army's advance with local armor spearheaded assaults against the shoulders of the advance from Thionville to Nancy
2. Establishment of blocking lines south of the area from Langres to Neufchâteau to screen withdrawal to the northeast and the northeastern portion of his forces withdrawing before the Seventh Army
3. Defense and delaying tactics supported by counterattacks against bridgeheads over the Moselle River to gain time and bring up reserves from distant areas for the organization and manning of the Siegfried Line
4. Defense and delaying operations while launching counterattacks against the southern flank of the Third Army from Chaumont to Neufchâteau.

The 80th Infantry Division continued its difficult drive to cross the Moselle River. The 319th Infantry Division had taken and was holding only the northern half of Liverdun, six miles northwest of Nancy.

The Forces Francaises protected bridges and contained enemy pockets from Chaumont to Neufchâteau.

Artillery ammunition supply improved with greater amounts of all calibers delivered. The only exception was the 105 howitzer ammunition, which was still critically short. The XX Corps fired over twenty thousand rounds within two days. The enemy was making extensive use of the old forts around Metz.

The XIX TAC flew 308 sorties in 25 missions, claiming kills on rail installations, 88 motor transports, 200 locomotives, 27 gun installations, and 32 military installations. Thirteen tanks and armored vehicles were destroyed and 5 enemy airdromes were attacked.

The Third Army requested permission to be relieved of the responsibility of accepting the surrender of a German general and eighteen troops in the province of Loire. It was recommended that the Ninth Army be given this duty.

A total of 2.6 million pounds of frozen beef and 500 thousand pounds of canned beef were captured and immediately issued to troops at the front.

Four medical ambulance companies and one full field hospital were transferred from the Third Army to the First Army.

September 10
D-Day +96

On the XII Corps front, the Germans still had control of the Moselle River line.

The Germans continued their stubborn resistance and improved defensive positions in the Foret-de-Haye area, three miles west of Nancy.

The 2nd French Armored Division, attached to the Third Army, established contact with elements of the 1st French Infantry Division, attached to the Seventh Army in the vicinity of Sombernon. This contact was the culmination of the Seventh Army's landing on the Mediterranean coast of France. It firmly placed a barrier of friendly Allied troops between the Third Army's southern flank and the enemy. It also assured SHAEF of a continuous battle line facing the whole of the German frontier and trapped behind it thousands of enemy troops in southwestern France.

The XIX TAC flew 377 sorties and destroyed or damaged 32 enemy tanks, 33 gun installations, and 32 military installations.

With two tank destroyer battalions arriving on the continent, the Third Army was complete in its original assignment of field artillery and tank destroyer units.

Ammunition continued to be critically short, especially in the XII Corps. The weekly ammunition ration received from the Twelfth Army Group was about one-third that of a unit of fire per day in all calibers of artillery weapons.

All artillery groups stressed observed fires and held unobserved fires to a minimum in order to conserve their ammunition.

Air observation was found to be extremely effective for minimizing enemy artillery fire. The enemy would not fire when spotter planes were airborne for fear of being detected and fired upon.

September 11
D-Day +97

The XII Corps continued its attack to secure bridgeheads across the Moselle River. The 137th Infantry pushed seven companies across the river north of Bayon and made contact one mile up-river with Combat Command "B" of the 4th Armored Division.

The XX Corps continued to cross the Moselle River and establish bridgeheads.

The XIX TAC flew 411 sorties in 45 missions during the day's operations. They destroyed or damaged 32 military installations and destroyed 92 railroad cars, 46 motor transports, 44 gun installations, and 35 horse-drawn vehicles.

With only 65,348 gallons of gasoline delivered out of a requested amount of 300,000, the difference was taken from reserves.

September 12
D-Day +98

The XII Corps continued to enlarge and expand its bridgeheads across the Moselle River north and south of Nancy. After fighting its way across the river, the 317th Infantry gained control of the high ground south of Pont-à-Mousson, while the 4th Armored Division completed a movement across the river of both Combat Command "A" at Dieulouard and Combat Command "B" at Bayon.

The XV Corps had the 79th Infantry Division fighting forward with the 313th Infantry reaching Mirecourt and the 314th Infantry occupying the city of Charmes. The 315th Infantry captured the city of Neufchâteau.

The XIX TAC flew 388 sorties, downing 35 German planes confirmed and 7 planes damaged on the ground. The TAC lost a total of 8 planes. Other claims included 68 railroad cars, 129 motor transports, 13 locomotives, and 26 gun installations destroyed or damaged. Two enemy airdromes were attacked during the day.

The Third Army photo center opened for business in the vicinity of St. Dizier, the first time it was within range of the SCR193 radio.

A Third Army air evacuation holding unit was opened at Etain, in accordance with existing policy that the army set up these units as far forward as possible and as soon as airstrips became available.

A request was made that the entire airlift available to the Third Army be used for the purpose of supplying ammunition, which had been placed on a priority.

September 13
D-Day +99

It was estimated that the enemy strength in the Third Army zone of operations on this date was

1. The equivalent of 8 divisions, consisting of 67,500 troops and 90 tanks and assault guns
2. Immediate reserves were the equivalent of six divisions, consisting of 53,500 troops and 80 tanks
3. Strategic reserves were considered to be six divisions. Reports indicated that enemy reinforcements were en route from other fronts. It was estimated that by October 1 the enemy could bring the equivalent of three divisions with fifty tanks from Italy and four divisions from Denmark and Norway. Four other divisions were reported moving from the Scandinavian countries. Although no known reinforcements were coming from the Russian Front, it was believed that

the Germans had the capability of withdrawing an estimated three divisions and 150 tanks from the Eastern Front
by October 1, if necessary.

Elements of Combat Command "A" of the 4th Armored
Division reached the vicinity of Arracourt and crossed the
Meurthe River.

The 79th Infantry Division, part of the XV Corps, captured
Bettoncourt, four miles north of Mirecourt. Combat Command "L" of the 2d French Armored Division captured Dom-
paire and Damas, nine miles west of Épinal, while Combat
Command "V" advanced to meet the 79th Division at Mirecourt.

Combat Command "B" of the Seventh Armored Division
completed crossing the Moselle River in the zone of the 5th
Infantry Division.

XIX TAC flew eighty-two sorties in nine missions with few
claims for the day, only destroying five gun installations and
attacking three troop concentrations.

Due to a critical shortage of Class I supplies, the Third Army
headquarters began issuing German rations, numerous captured storehouses being emptied, and field bakeries began to
use captured German flour. The pipeline (PLUTO) to Chartres started operations with an expected gallonage of 100,000
daily. The air lift, which had been discontinued, was not to be
resumed until further notice, according to Twelfth Army
Group.

Military Vicar Archbishop Spellman of New York, arrived at
the Third Army headquarters and offered mass for the personnel of headquarters and adjoining units. He also made a
tour of the front lines.

September 14
D-Day +100

The XV Corps continued its push toward the east. The 79th
Infantry Division moved forward with its 315th Infantry capturing the city of Chatenois and advancing to the area from
Neueville to Sous. The 313th Infantry captured Remecourt,
two miles west of Mirecourt. The 2d French Armored Divi-

sion captured Mattaincourt, two miles south of Mirecourt, and then made contact with elements of the Seventh Army at Chaumont.

The XIX TAC was limited in its operations due to adverse weather, only completing 108 sorties in 6 missions with claims of 28 motor transports, 6 locomotives, and 7 tanks and armored vehicles either damaged or destroyed.

The first rail shipments of gasoline arrived at Lerouville, five miles northwest of Commercy. These shipments were a great help since truck haul distances were tremendously reduced and much gasoline was saved.

September 15
D-Day +101

Severe counterattacks against the 80th Infantry Division's bridgehead across the Moselle River were broken up and repelled. Fourteen German tanks were either destroyed or disabled by the division's artillery fire. A sound and flash detachment of the 14th Field Artillery Observation Battalion was overrun and fought as infantry for six hours, until relieved.

Concentrating on German rail activity, the XIX TAC flew 294 sorties in 23 missions during the day's operation. Claims for the day's activities were 22 railroad lines cut, 62 railroad cars damaged, 16 gun installations and 18 military installations damaged or destroyed.

At Vittel, 2,087 Allied nationals were found who had been interned for four years in hotels surrounded by wire barricades. Of these, 361 were U.S. citizens, 1,160 British, and the remainder were of 29 other nationalities. Food from captured German stocks was issued to them.

Lucky Forward headquarters moved to a bivouac area near Braquis, eleven miles east of Verdun.

September 16
D-Day +102

An extremely significant fact was confirmed on this day regarding the enemy order of battle. Out of four previously reported administrative divisions of the German forces, one of these was reported to be in combat contact with the Third Army. This information indicated the extremes to which the Germans were going in seeking manpower. POW statements indicated that these divisions, of strength estimated at not more than six thousand men each, were composed of cooks, bakers, clerks, and other normally non-combative elements. Several new and substandard Panzer and infantry divisions also were identified by G-2 Section. A further development considered very important was the information that General Von Rundstedt had been restored as the supreme commander of the German forces in the Western Front. Von Rundstedt's reappointment, only eight weeks after his ouster, was regarded by Third Army headquarters as an indication that Hitler had been forced to compromise somewhat with the wishes of the German General Staff.

German strength was estimated at 54 infantry divisions, with a combat strength of 565,000 men when committed, and an effective strength of 165,200. Sixteen Panzer divisions, with 199,500 men and 335 tanks total, were identified.

In the XII Corps, the 35th Infantry Division was still cleaning up pockets of resistance and the 137th Infantry advanced to Dombasle. By now, all elements of the 80th Infantry Division were across the Moselle River, with the exception of two battalions of the 319th Infantry.

The 3d Battalion of the 318th Infantry had been isolated for several days beyond St. Genevieve, fifteen miles south of Metz, and on this date was finally relieved. During the combat, a total of twenty thousand rounds of small arms ammunition had been dropped by liaison pilots of the 80th Division artillery.

A strong German counterattack was broken up by massed firing missions of the 80th Division artillery, coordinated with air support.

Two separate counterattacks against the 2d French Armored Division were stopped and pushed back by both the 2d French Armored Division's fire and assistance fire support of the 79th Infantry Division's artillery. The 79th Division encountered little or no enemy artillery opposition.

The XIX TAC flew 286 sorties in 21 missions with few claims being made. Fourteen gun installations, 7 military installations, and 8 small naval vessels were either damaged or destroyed.

A critical shortage of both clothing and individual equipment was developing. The quantities needed for immediate issue totaled 258 thousand items which were not available.

September 17
D-Day +103

The XV Corps was ordered to advance to the northeast on army order, echeloned to the right rear by the XII Corps. Its mission was to protect the southern flank of the army, maintain contact with the Seventh Army, be fully prepared to seize Mannheim, and then secure a bridgehead east of the Rhine River within its zone or else move through bridgeheads secured by the XII Corps or the XX Corps.

The last two elements of the 80th Infantry Division crossed the Moselle River against heavy enemy resistance, placing the entire division east of the river.

The XX Corps launched a coordinated attack on the city of Metz, with both the 5th Infantry Division moving from the south and the 90th Infantry Division moving from the west.

Metz had been the center of strong resistance, and the Germans were holding out in the ancient forts around the city which were virtually impregnable to artillery fire yet capable themselves of launching heavy and effective fire. Much of the artillery was emplaced so that a direct hit upon a relatively small opening was necessary for effective neutralization. The XX Corps allotted a 155mm gun battalion for the sole mission of maintaining continued fire upon this group of forts.

The XIX TAC flew 133 sorties in 17 missions with the following claims: two railroad lines cut, 23 railroad cars, 15 motor transports, and 23 military installations damaged or destroyed.

Due to a scarcity of transport planes, a new evacuation policy for wounded soldiers was initiated.

The Third Army was beginning to experience a growing problem with civilian refugees. Those encountered were of thirty different nationalities, mostly Ukrainian Russians. They began to filter back through the front lines. Civil Affairs detachments, augmented by Red Cross workers and uniformed volunteers of the French Secours National, were called to forward areas to take charge of these refugees. The Verdun center immediately housed a total of 2,200 on this date, with hundreds more moving constantly along the roads.

September 18
D-Day +104

The XV Corps launched an attack to the northeast and the 79th Infantry Division succeeded in driving completely across the Moselle River in the vicinity of Bayon, with the 313th, 314th, and the 315th Infantries advancing to Gerbeviller.

The 6th Armored Division (without Combat Command "B") moved to Neufchateau and relieved elements of the 2d French Armored Division to assist in the protection of the Third Army's southern flank.

Enemy artillery activity at Metz increased in volume, especially from Fort Jeanne D'Arc. It was discovered that even 240 howitzers from the XX Corps could do no more than temporarily neutralize the forts.

Eight-inch howitzers fired on and destroyed two enemy railroad trains near Metz.

The XIX TAC flew only thirty-two sorties due to bad weather.

September 19
D-Day +105

In continuing to delay the Third Army's advance, the Germans blew up bridges; constructed roadblocks consisting of mines and felled trees; and built trenches, bunkers, and anti-tank positions as they fell back.

Due to a threat which existed on their north flank, XX Corps ordered the strengthening of the Regimental Combat Team from the 90th Infantry Division and the cavalry currently covering their flank. This was done with tanks and tank destroyer units. The 90th Infantry Division was to contain Metz, while the 5th Infantry Division and the 7th Armored Division proceeded on their assigned missions.

Two hundred and sixty-two sorties in twenty-two missions were flown by XIX TAC, with only light claims made.

Supplies for Graves Registration were critical. Immediately needed, but unavailable, were two thousand mattress covers and three thousand personal effects bags. It was necessary to send trucks three hundred miles to the Normandy beach-heads to obtain these supplies and other items. The gasoline supplies were once again uncertain, receipts being short since September 17.

One hundred thousand pounds of green coffee were received at Lerouville, and available bakeries began to roast it immediately.

September 20
D-Day +106

An estimate of German forces in Third Army's zone was total effective combat strength of 8 divisions, consisting of 63,750 troops and 175 tanks or assault guns. In immediate reserves the estimate was 5 divisions, consisting of 42,000 troops and 150 tanks.

The Twelfth Army Group ordered the Third Army to advance to and secure crossings at the Rhine River at Mannheim and Mainz. If sufficient forces they were also available, also to establish a bridgehead at Karlsruhe.

The XX Corps continued its attack on Metz.

XIX TAC flew 165 sorties in 12 missions claiming 13 railroad lines cut and 30 railroad cars, 12 motor transports, and 11 locomotives damaged or destroyed. In addition, 5 marshalling yards were attacked with good results.

September 21
D-Day +107

Heavy fighting continued in the XX Corps area. The Germans were determined to hold on to Metz to the last man. Strong counterattacks delayed the 7th Armored Division in their crossing of the Seille River, to the south of Metz. The Germans were using dug-in tanks and heavy artillery, and they made small counterattacks all along the front line.

One German counterattack against the 5th Infantry Division was preceded by three hundred rounds of artillery preparation. A sound and flash base was installed east of the Moselle River in an effort to locate more easily the artillery which was firing on both the 5th Infantry and the 7th Armored Divisions.

XIX TAC flew 245 sorties in 19 missions, with heavy claims made, especially on rail transportation. Fifteen railroad lines were cut, 256 railroad cars, 14 locomotives, 47 motor transports, and 20 tanks and armored vehicles were damaged or destroyed.

Only small gains were accomplished over the whole of the Third Army's fighting front during the day's activities.

A shipment of twelve thousand gallons of gasoline arrived at St. Dizier, brought by bombers of the XIX TAC.

September 22
D-Day +108

The Germans continued to construct additions to the Siegfried Line fortifications. Along all routes of advance, German tanks were being used as artillery in dug-in positions.

G-2 Section estimated that the favored capability of the Germans would be to pivot at Metz to establish a general defensive line paralleling the Siegfried Line. Using Metz as a fortress stand, the Germans could impede the Third Army's advance and throw armor spearheaded attacks against the shoulders of the advance from Thionville in the north to Foret de Parroy in the south. Although the Germans were not considered capable of concentrating reserves sufficiently enough to start a major concerted offensive, they still were capable of massing desperate resistance in the Third Army zone.

The 6th Armored Division, originally ordered to the vicinity of Jallaucourt, thirteen miles north of Nancy, was directed to discontinue its movement in anticipation of a new and different mission.

The Third Army was ordered by the Twelfth Army Group to release the 7th Armored Division, which was to go to the First Army.

The XX Corps was to continue its present mission, give particular attention the protection of the city of Luxembourg, protect the north flank of the Third Army, and maintain contact with the First Army.

In the XV Corps area, the advance continued to the northeast. The 79th Infantry Division strengthened its bridgehead east of the Meurthe River and more elements of the 313th Infantry reached Moncel, three miles southeast of Lunéville. The 314th Infantry advanced to the edge of the Foret de Mondon, five miles east of Luneville, and the 2d French Armored Division went forward with Combat Command "V" to the Meurthe River at Flin and at Cheneivieres.

The XIX TAC flew 273 sorties in 23 missions with many claims against both enemy transportation and military installations. Twenty-one railroad lines were cut, 135 railroad cars, 120 motor transports, 13 locomotives, 4 supply dumps, 6 gun installations, and 22 tanks and armored vehicles were either damaged or destroyed.

Lucky Forward moved to covered billets in Etain, ten miles east of Verdun, marking the first time since arriving on the continent that they were housed indoors.

September 23
D-Day +109

The XII Corps continued its attack, using the 35th Infantry Division to reach high ground ten miles northeast of Nancy. The 80th Infantry Division straightened its lines and held its high ground between Montenoy and Jeandelaincourt. The

4th Armored Division repulsed a strong counterattack by the Germans.

The XX Corps attacked with only slight progress being attained. The 331st Infantry closed into an area in the vicinity of Esch, while the 90th Infantry Division was still stuck at Metz.

The XIX TAC flew only ninety-six sorties in which eighteen railroad lines were cut, and twenty railroad cars, twenty-seven motor transports, eleven locomotives, fourteen gun installations and five tanks and armored vehicles were damaged or destroyed.

There was very little headway in Third Army operations.

September 24
D-Day +110

Patrols began probing the outlying defenses of the Siegfried Line and met with strong enemy resistance from pillboxes and other types of strongholds.

Until the gasoline shortage suffered by the Third Army, the Siegfried Line was completely open and unprotected. When SHAEF took the supplies from the Third Army and gave full support to the Twenty-first Army Group to the north, they gave the Germans ample time to man and protect the Siegfried Line. Patton had written in his diary at the time, "Eisenhower keeps talking of the upcoming 'Great Battle of Germany,' but there won't be one if we just keep moving."

The XII Corps consolidated bridgeheads and made preparations to improve its positions. The 35th Infantry Division's 134th Infantry advanced to Armancourt, ten miles northeast of Nancy and contacted the 80th Infantry Division on the left and the 6th Armored Division on the right.

The XV Corps continued its aggressive patrolling beyond Lunéville and Badonviller. In the XX Corps zone, the remaining elements of the 83rd Infantry Division closed in on the vicinity of Esch and the 7th Armored Division began concentrating its forces west of Metz.

Two fighter groups of the XIX TAC (on very short notice and in extremely bad weather) flew close support of the 4th Armored Division during a counterattack by strong enemy armored elements and infantry units. They destroyed three enemy tanks and then bombed and strafed a section of wooded areas, flushing a large number of German tanks which were knocked out by both the air and land forces.

The weather was bad enough to keep the fighters from returning to their field near St. Dizier. They were finally forced to land at Etain, where they were met personally by General Patton, who thanked them for their courage and commended them on their flying. In all, they flew 106 sorties in 9 missions claiming 16 railroad cars, 8 motor transports, and 4 tanks and armored cars damaged or destroyed.

Twenty-eight civil affairs detachments, with a strength of 133 officers, 7 warrant officers, and 235 enlisted men were attached to the Third Army for deployment in German towns in the Saarbrücken region.

September 25
D-Day +111

Heavy artillery fire was encountered in the XV Corps area at Flin. The engineers on the bridge at Flin were forced to withdraw their equipment while the corps artillery fired a total of twenty-three counterbattery missions, causing considerable reduction in the enemy's artillery fire.

The XX Corps units continued to improve bridgeheads while Metz remained a thorn in the Third Army's side. One hundred and fifty-five rounds of 155mm shells, 100 rounds of 8-inch howitzers, and 25 rounds of 240 howitzer ammunition were fired upon Fort Jeanne D'Arc. A number of direct hits were attained, destroying two casements and an ammunition dump.

After firing a total of 107 rounds of 155mm, howitzers were fired at the concrete shelters and casements of Fort Kellerman. The only result was chipped concrete. Metz was rapidly becoming a frustration to both XX Corps and Third Army headquarters.

Adverse weather conditions precluded any activity by XIX TAC.

Out of a fleet of cargo planes, four overshot the airstrip at Etain. One of the planes was shot down by the Germans and the other three were lost. The result was that out of 20,000 blankets, 10,000 litters, and 375 oxygen cylinders, Third Army received only 2,500 blanks, 1,000 litters, and 100 oxygen cylinders.

A terrain study of central Germany was distributed to Third Army engineers and studies of the Maginot Line were obtained from the French Army.

September 26
D-Day +112

The previous rapid advances by the Third Army were reported to have disrupted the German's supply system to a great extent. During their withdrawal, they not only could not use their stocks of gasoline, oils, and greases, but they also were unable to even destroy them as they retreated toward The Fatherland.

All support from SHAEF now went to the Twenty-first Army Group. The Twelfth Army Group set itself the mission of clearing the area between its northern boundary and the Meuse River and of protecting the right flank of Twenty-first Army Group. Once again, General Montgomery was given full support by Eisenhower while the most rapidly advancing Third Army was forced to pull back when it should have been given ample supplies to attack deeply into Germany.

After Montgomery's futile attempt to take Arnhem, plans were made by the Third Army to attack Köln.

The 83rd Infantry Division, reinforced, was assigned to the Third Army. The 7th Armored Division was transferred to the First Army and moved to Longuyon.

The XX Corps planned to launch an attack on Fort Driant, while the 358th Infantry of the 90th Infantry Division was relieved of its mission by Task Force Polk, made up of the 3d Cavalry Group, the 135th Engineer Combat Battalion, and a French infantry unit (the 1st Battalion, Regiment of Paris).

Bad weather reduced the activity of XIX TAC to thirty-five

sorties, with claims of only four motor transports damaged or destroyed and three military installations attacked.

September 27
D-Day +113

The Twelfth Army Group ordered the XV Corps to be assigned to the Sixth Army Group, thus taking from the Third Army the 79th and 90th Infantry Divisions, the 2d French Armored Division, and all supporting troops.

The 11th Infantry of the 5th Infantry Division launched a probing attack on Fort Driant and met with fanatical enemy resistance which forced them to withdraw. The 83rd Infantry Division moved forward to Grevenmacher, while the XX Corps continued artillery firing on Fort Jeanne D'Arc to good effect.

With excellent flying conditions, the XIX TAC flew 517 sorties in 39 missions with excellent results. Among claims were 26 railroad lines cut; and 180 railroad cars, 45 motor transports, 38 locomotives, 5 supply dumps, 22 gun positions, 12 military installations, and 19 tanks and armored vehicles damaged or destroyed. Troop concentrations and marshalling yards were attacked with good results.

September 28
D-Day +114

An operational directive from army headquarters informed XII and XX Corps that the Sixth Army Group had continued its attack to seize the Rhine River crossings at Speyer. The First Army had the mission of clearing the area between its northern boundary and the Meuse River and to continue protecting the right flank of Twenty-first Army Group under Montgomery.

The XII Corps repulsed numerous counterattacks, maintained aggressive patrols, and continued the consolidation and improvement of positions.

The XV Corps launched its attack against the Foret de Parroy, four miles northeast of Lunéville. The XV Corps passed to control of the Seventh Army on this date.

The XIX TAC carried out 573 sorties in 39 missions claiming 72 railroad lines cut; and 371 railroad cars, 49 motor transports, 67 locomotives, 18 gun installations, and 17 military installations damaged or destroyed. Eight marshalling yards and 5 airdromes were attacked.

The town of Remich was captured.

September 29
D-Day +115

The 35th Infantry Division and the 4th Armored Division repulsed counterattacks in the area around Jallaucourt, thirteen miles northeast of Nancy.

An experiment was done with air observation posts by 4th Armored Division. The advance of each combat command was preceded by an air observation post whose radio had been set upon the command channel of the combat command. In this way the commander of each combat command had, at all times, accurate and prompt information of the situation in front of his advance. Also, the commander could, at his discretion, order the observation plane to land occasionally to take him aloft for a rapid aerial reconnaissance prior to employing his command.

The XIX TAC had a very good day, flying a total of 576 sorties in 46 missions. Their claims were 45 railroad lines cut; and 226 railroad cars, 66 motor transports, 43 locomotives, 23 military installations, 22 gun installations, 50 horse-drawn vehicles, 77 miscellaneous naval vessels, 3 highway bridges, and 3 tanks and armored vehicles damaged or destroyed. They also continued their attacks on troop concentrations and marshalling yards.

September 30
D-Day +116

The XII Corps' 35th Infantry Division attacked the Foret De Cremecy to clear the enemy, while the 6th Armored Division attacked and gained the high ground of Fresnes, Lemoncourt, and Chambéry, and the high ground to the immediate north.

Air activity was voided by bad weather conditions.

CHAPTER 3

October, 1944

During the month of October, the Third Army would concentrate on the building up of supplies, assembly and regrouping of troops, and planning for future operations. Their major preparation would deal primarily with a new major offensive designed to drive the Germans back behind the Rhine River and the entrance into Germany proper.

The complete system of supply was re-examined to conserve weapons and ammunition so that the highest possible benefits from available materials could be achieved and the required surpluses accumulated. During this period there would also be a concentrated effort to equip all Third Army troops with adequate wet and cold weather clothing for the upcoming winter months. Lastly, armored and other types of vehicles would be serviced thoroughly to bring them up to the highest standards for fighting machines.

Planning activities for the upcoming offensive included:
1. The execution of certain limited objective operations with an eye toward securing a favorable line of departure
2. Keeping the enemy from becoming too aggressive
3. Giving specialized combat experience to various units.

The XX Corps, especially, would be utilized as a training exercise area for troops in assaults on fixed fortifications while it also served to determine the tactical plan for future operations against the fortress city of Metz.

October 1
D-Day +117

After a heavy attack by the 6th Armored Division on the last day of September, Germans in the XII Corps area withdrew, and fell back to the area north of Lemoncourt, fifteen miles northeast of Nancy.

In the 80th Infantry Division, the 319th Infantry took control of the Seille River near Port-sur-Seille, eight miles east of Pont-à-Mousson.

Elements of the 83rd Infantry Division made contact with the VIII Corps of the Ninth Army on the north flank, near the outskirts of Grevenmacher, just northeast of Luxembourg.

A strict program of gasoline rationing was planned and supply company commanders were briefed on the particulars of the plan. The daily telegram requested 219,392 gallons, but only 95,840 gallons were received. Luckily, with winter approaching, winter clothing and equipment arrived in greater quantities.

Because a great number of soldiers in the Third Army were smokers, tobacco was considered a very important part of troop morale. To assure that the troops in the front lines had adequate supplies of tobacco, delivery of a ten-day requirement was speeded up on the basis of a troop strength of three hundred thousand men.

October 2
D-Day +118

Both an infantry attack and heavy aerial bombardment were launched on Fort Friant by the XX Corps and the XIX TAC. The XIX TAC, having a busy day, flew 426 sorties in 33 missions. Claims were; 29 railroad lines cut; and 243 railroad cars, 58 motor transports, 32 locomotives, 42 gun installations, and 13 miscellaneous naval vessels destroyed or damaged, with 8 marshalling yards attacked.

Psychological warfare leaflets, addressed to specific German divisions, were dropped by planes.

A new and vital link in the Third Army's communications

system, known as West Wirehead, began operations at Laxou, a suburb of Nancy. The building housing the communications complex had luckily suffered very little damage (being built of reinforced concrete and being partly underground) even though the retreating Germans attempted to destroy it.

A directive was issued specifying the hours allowable for civilian circulation in all towns in the Third Army zone. They could go about their business only from 0600 hours (6 am) until 2000 hours (8 pm).

October 3
D-Day +119

The XII Corps zone was very quiet with the exception of scattered German artillery fire.

In the XX Corps, the 5th Infantry Division met with stiff opposition when they entered Fort Driant on the west bank of the Moselle River.

A total of twenty-three field artillery battalions supported the attack on Fort Driant by firing a thirty-minute preparation, followed by supporting fires, all directed against neighboring fortresses as well as Fort Driant itself.

Guns were active against Fort Jeanne D'Arc, Fort Verdun Groupe, Batterie Moselle, and Marival. Again, only limited results were achieved due to the heavy concrete reinforced defenses. Although temporary neutralization was achieved, even the heaviest caliber weapons available to the Third Army units proved incapable of effective destruction. The forts were seemingly impregnable.

The XIX TAC was having much better luck. In 22 missions, the planes and pilots claimed 39 railroad lines cut, 78 railroad cars, 35 locomotives, 15 military installations, and four small naval vessels damaged or destroyed. Eight marshalling yards were attacked with good results.

A gasoline rationing board, with one officer and three enlisted men, was created. The allotments decided upon were five thousand gallons for the infantry divisions; twenty-five thousand gallons for the armored divisions; ten thousand gallons for the corps troops, and eighty-four thousand gallons for the Army troops. Reserve stocks currently totaled three hundred thousand gallons.

The 7th Convalescent Hospital was relieved from assignment with the Third Army.

October 4
D-Day +120

G-2 Section made an estimate of the most favorable enemy capabilities.

1. Combining delaying actions in the Third Army's zone while counterattacking with armored spearheads, and impeding the Third Army's advance with use of artillery, munitions, and aviation
2. Utilizing the ring of forts around Metz to the fullest advantage and holding the city at all costs in order to use it as a pivot to establish a general defensive line paralleling the Siegfried Line, allowing time to reorganize defenses of the Rhine River Line, and securing the tactical advantage of the upcoming wet and cold winter weather
3. Using the favorable terrain in the Third Army's zone of advance to construct one or more organized defensive positions for employment in conjunction with the inclement weather to defend and delay the Third Army's advance.

Elements of the 5th Infantry Division in the XX Corps zone continued fighting forward in Fort Driant, while units of the 10th Infantry and the 90th Infantry Divisions reinforced the attack.

The XIX TAC continued its concentration on rail transportation, cutting 22 railroad lines and damaging or destroying 248 railroad cars, 25 locomotives, 21 gun installations, and 2 railroad bridges.

Verbal orders from General Bradley, commanding general of the Twelfth Army Group, informed the Third Army that the 10th Armored Division would be assigned to the Third Army in the very near future and that the 101st Infantry of the 26th Infantry Division would be released to the Third Army without delay.

Class I supplies of meat and butter, formerly trucked from Paris, were now moved to Sommesous on a daily basis. Fifty trucks were sent by civil affairs to move three hundred tons of flour from Verdun to Nancy to avert a serious bread shortage.

The air evacuation holding unit at Toul set a record for evacuating patients by plane. Nineteen aircraft carried 494 patients to rear echelon units.

October 5
D-Day +121

Photographs from the tactical reconnaissance section revealed that German positions were being built up with new installations in the Third Army's zone of advance.

To continue the attack on Fort Driant, a special Task Force Driant was created. Its organic makeup included; a regiment of infantry, a company of engineers, and a company of tanks. Meanwhile, Task Force Polk relieved units of the 357th Infantry in the 90th Division's zone.

The XIX TAC completed 7 missions and 110 sorties. They cut 4 railroad lines and damaged or destroyed 15 motor transports, 54 military installations, 1 highway bridge, and 28 small naval vessels. Six marshalling yards were attacked. The Air Command's program of cutting railroad lines was proving highly successful. Day by day the airplane attacks were isolating the enemy from supplies and communications in the rear and preventing an effective defensive buildup.

October 6
D-Day +122

An enemy counterattack in the Fort Driant area was repulsed by XX Corps troops. The troops in the German unit were all officer candidates stationed at the officer candidate school at Metz. They were all hand-picked noncommissioned officers and fanatical Nazis, most of whom were battle-hardened veterans of the Russian Front.

Task Force Driant gained control of the northwest and southwest corners of Fort Driant, while units of the 83d Infantry Division occupied Wormeldingen and other elements of the 90th Infantry Division entered Maizieres-les-Metz in the face of strong opposition.

The XIX TAC flew close support of the Third Army and claimed 21 railroad lines cut; and 117 railroad cars, 6 motor transports, 9 locomotives, 24 gun installations, 3 highway bridges, 1 ammunition dump, and 20 tanks and armored vehicles destroyed or damaged.

October 7
D-Day +123

In an attempt to enlarge a bridgehead, the XII Corps launched an attack to the northeast. The 35th Infantry Division attacked in the direction of Fossieux and occupied that town and the high ground in the surrounding area. The 6th Armored Division advanced to Moivrons, which they occupied, and the 80th Infantry Division attacked in the direction of Lixieres.

After a forty-five minute artillery preparation, the XII Corps attacked to clear the northern half of the corps sector up to the Seille River.

The 331st Infantry of the 83rd Infantry Division completed the clearing of the Germans in Wormeldingen and elements of the 329th Infantry cleared the enemy from Echternach and Grevenmacher.

The XIX TAC flew 402 sorties, destroying or damaging 187 railroad cars, 19 gun installations, 33 military installations, and 83 miscellaneous naval vessels; and cutting 30 railroad lines.

Psychological warfare units broadcast surrender messages across the Moselle River to the enemy in Thionville. The Germans enjoyed the message, ceasing artillery firing during the broadcast.

Third Army headquarters was visited by General George C. Marshall (chief of staff of the United States Army), Lieutenant General Thomas T. Handy (deputy chief of staff of the United States Army), and Lieutenant General Omar N. Bradley (commanding general, Twelfth Army Group). The visitors were thoroughly briefed on Third Army operations.

October 8
D-Day +124

Zone observers in the XX Corps area reported the movement toward the south of a large number of enemy vehicles, including tanks.

The German defenders at Fort Driant used explosives to block XX Corps troops as they attempted to assault the fort by underground tunnels.

The XIX TAC flew 311 sorties and attacked enemy airdromes and military installations. A total of 45 German planes were destroyed or damaged on the ground, and among other claims were 40 gun installations, 39 military installations, and one ammunition dump.

The cities of Ajoncourt, Chenicourt, Jeandelaincourt, and the wooded area southwest of Letricourt were captured and occupied.

October 9
D-Day +125

Combat Command "A" of the 6th Armored Division cleared Chenicourt and reached the vicinity of Aulnois, where it was relieved by the 317th Infantry. Combat Command "A" moved into mobile reserve in the vicinity of Leyr, six miles north of Nancy, while the remainder of the division moved into corps reserve in the vicinity of Saulxures-les-Nancy, two miles east of Nancy.

Brigadier General Alva C. Warnock, commanding Task Force Warnock, replaced Task Force Driant and assembled equipment prior to continuing operations in the tunnels of Fort Driant. Meanwhile, elements of the 90th Division were clearing the Germans out of Maizieres-les-Metz in savage house-to-house fighting.

Adverse weather prevented the XIX TAC from flying.

Beginning this date and continuing for 7 days, an additional supply tonnage of 250 tons daily was requested in preparation for the arrival of an armored division. The reserve stock of gasoline totaled six hundred thousand gallons.

October 10
D-Day +126

At Maizieres-les-Metz, the 90th Infantry Division encountered stiff, fanatical resistance. Bitter hand-to-hand fighting was the order of the day and enemy troops used bazookas against buildings occupied by XX Corps.

Headquarters of III Corps, commanded by Major General John Millikin, and the 95th Infantry Division, were relieved from assignment with the Ninth Army. They were assigned to the Third Army, while the 83rd Infantry Division was transferred to the 9th Army.

Poor weather again precluded operations by the XIX TAC.

General Patton personally escorted General George C. Marshall and Lieutenant General Thomas T. Handy to the forward command posts of the XII and XX Corps.

October 11
D-Day +127

Tactical reconnaissance reported that the Germans were entrenching and constructing defense positions along the high ground east of the Seille River in the vicinity of Clemery, in the XII Corps area. This activity was exactly the type of warfare that had evolved during World War I and was just what General Patton had warned against. Had his mobile army been amply supplied, he could have kept the Germans from digging in and firming up defensive positions.

The 2d Cavalry Squadron relieved the 42d Cavalry Squadron from Parroy to Coincourt, while the 80th Infantry Division cleared the vicinity of Fossieux and the 26th Infantry Division continued to relieve the 4th Armored Division.

At Fort Driant, the Germans began using disabled tanks as outposts and placing harassing fire on the Third Army troops from self-propelled guns.

With weather improving, the XIX TAC flew 124 sorties in 10 missions. They found few targets. They did manage to cut three railroad lines and damage or destroy 33 gun installations, 6 military installations, and 6 small naval vessels.

A second visit to Third Army Headquarters was made by Lieutenant General Bradley.

October 12
D-Day +128

A G-2 estimation of enemy capabilities showed little change from the estimation made on October 4.

Tactical reconnaissance, linked with other incoming reports, indicated an organization of defensive positions in the area from Liocourt to Contril and from Dieuze to Bitche. Although counterattacks by the Germans around Nancy had decreased, entrenching activity and aggressive patrolling indicated a clear determination to contain the Third Army forces. In addition to overall defensive attitudes, the Germans began flooding areas in the zone of advance immediately in front of Third Army. Numerous troop movements, by both road and rail, plus the identification of elements of a new infantry division in the Thionville area seemed to indicate a possible enemy thrust. POWs reported the discussion by their officers of plans to attack.

The XX Corps withdrew its forces from Fort Driant and began enemy containment with newly assigned divisions. The divisions which had previously been engaged in the attack on Fort Driant were allowed to rest while they refitted and prepared for further offensive action. The training of the newly assigned divisions continued during a preparation to advance to the Rhine River to secure crossings there and to seize Wiesbaden and Frankfurt.

The XIX TAC flew 207 sorties in 18 missions. They claimed 14 railroad lines cut, and 36 railroad cars, 23 locomotives, 38 gun installations, and 13 military installations damaged or destroyed.

12th Army Group drastically reduced the field ammunition allowance until November 7, precluding any possibility of any new offensive. Immediate and strenuous restrictions were placed on the firing of field artillery ammunition, a ninety-five percent reduction being obtained. There was no ration imposed upon tanks, tank destroyers, or antiaircraft artillery ammunition, and these weapons were effectively employed in their role as secondary artillery. The imposed restrictions required extensive use of captured enemy weapons, including Russian 76.2mm guns, German 88mm, 105mm howitzers, 150mm guns, and Schneider 155mm howitzers. The ammunition for the Schneider howitzer was successfully employed in the U.S. M-1 155mm howitzer (the Long Tom).

Both Lucky Forward headquarters (front and rear echelons) and the headquarters of XIX TAC were moved to Nancy, setting up in large military casernes. This move was the first in which the three Third Army headquarters were located adjacent to one another in buildings in the same city.

October 13
D-Day +129

Considerable German troop movement was noted in the XII Corps area, and tactical reconnaissance observed a large number of troop concentrations at Moussey and Heming. Also, heavy enemy railroad and highway movements were observed in the XX Corps zone, with all types of vehicles moving to and from Metz.

Concentrating on both enemy rail and military installations, the XIX TAC flew 252 sorties in 22 missions. They attacked 10 marshalling yards and destroyed or damaged 226 railroad cars, 50 motor transports, 32 locomotives, 34 military installations, and 5 highway bridges. They cut 22 railroad lines.

In most cases, the Third Army's requirements for winter clothing and equipment were met. Sleeping bags and ground sheets began to arrive, but raincoats, mess gear, and one and two burner stoves remained in very short supply. The army's reserves of gasoline totaled eight hundred thousand gallons.

In the civilian sector, coal, lubricants, and oil were urgently needed for the mines and steel plants of the industrial valley from Briey to Thionville. As reserves diminished, the situation became more critical, threatening the employment of the majority of civilians in the area.

October 14
D-Day +130

The Germans continued to shift troops in both forward and rear areas of the XX Corps zone. Their patrols became bolder as the Third Army continued in its Twelfth Army Group-imposed defensive position.

The 90th Division continued fighting its way forward into Maizieres-les-Metz, while the 95th Infantry Division continued to close into its assembly area around Norry le Sec.

The XIX TAC carried out 230 sorties in 19 missions, clearly having more success than the Third Army. They cut 25 railroad lines and destroyed or damaged 207 railroad cars, 41 motor transports, 24 locomotives, 16 military installations, 1 fuel dump, and 9 tanks and armored cars. They attacked a total of 11 marshalling yards.

October 15
D-Day +131

The 80th Infantry Division continued its regrouping with the 328th Infantry (reinforced), closing in an area in the vicinity of Bezange-la-Grande, east of Nancy, then moving to relieve the 166th Engineer Combat Battalion (reinforced). The 137th Infantry relieved the 134th Infantry and the 134th then assembled in the vicinity of Brin-sur-Seille, northeast of Nancy. Elements of the 90th Infantry Division made only slight gains in Maizieres-les-Metz.

XIX TAC continued the pressure on German rail transportation, flying 107 sorties and damaging or destroying 28 locomotives 143 railroad cars, and 5 military installations.

Due to a serious shortage of ordnance supply, the Third Army began to make local purchases. Arrangements were made to let contracts for a number of critical items of simple construction, which would be of easy manufacture. If these were successfully produced, it was planned to contract for items more difficult to manufacture.

No gasoline was received on this date, and there was no forecast for any shipments.

October 16
D-Day +132

The 328th Infantry completed the relief of the 166th Engineer Battalion in the northern division zone, while other units in the XII Corps consolidated their positions.

Elements of the 90th Infantry Division continued house-to-house and hand-to-hand fighting in Maizieres-les-Metz.

The XIX TAC was grounded due to bad weather.

The Third Army's daily telegram to Twelfth Army Group requested 334,740 gallons of gasoline. The amount received was zero. Fifty-six thousand gallons had to be used out of the Third Army's reserve.

October 17
D-Day +133

Bad flying weather prevented the XIX TAC from flying their usual large number of sorties. Only forty sorties were flown with light claims being made.

Third Army Corps and Divisions were notified that issues of gasoline would be reduced 25 percent until further notice. The daily telegram requested 363,624 gallons, but only 13,375 gallons were received.

General Patton's headquarters were visited by General Dwight D. Eisenhower, the Supreme Commander Allied Expeditionary Force (SHAEF), and Lieutenant General Jacob L. Devers, commanding general, Sixth Army Group. The three generals reviewed plans for the upcoming resumption of the Allied offensive.

October 18
D-Day +134

Tactical reconnaissance reported that the enemy was firmly placed in defensive positions in the area from Liocourt to Bitche.

Two alternate plans were created for the upcoming resumption of the Third Army's offensive and issued on this date.

Plan A:

1. Envelop Metz defensive works from the north and south
2. Advance northeast within the zone to seize the Mainz-Frankfurt-Darmstadt area
3. Be prepared for further offensive action to the northeast.

Plan B:

1. Contain Metz on the west
2. Seize and secure all possible crossings of the Moselle River in the vicinity of Thionville, and advance on Boulay
3. Attack northeast, with two corps abreast, from the Pont à Mousson-Nancy area to seize railand road facilities in the vicinity of Falkenberg-Boulay
4. Destroy enemy forces withdrawing from the Metz area and isolate Metz defensive works
5. After Metz had been neutralized, advance northeast with two corps abreast, one corps advance on Army order, initially echeloned to the left rear.

G-2 estimates credited the Germans with the capability of making a determined defensive stand, aided by favorable terrain in the army's zone of advance which the Germans had fortified with extensive entrenchments and flooding of low areas. The capability of a limited objective enemy offensive north of Metz was also given consideration.

Thirty-four sorties were carried out by XIX TAC, but no targets were found due to adverse weather conditions.

October 19
D-Day +135

Front lines remained unchanged.

Bad weather again hampered the XIX TAC, allowing only sixty-eight sorties with very light claims.

German planes, eighty-nine in number, flew in concentration over Nancy, but no bombs were dropped.

October 20
D-Day +136

Enemy activity in the XX corps area consisted primarily of entrenching and increased of artillery and mortar fire.

Other that some very minor alterations in the XII Corps, there were no changes in the front lines.

The fighterbombers of the XIX TAC were more active. They flew 245 sorties in 20 missions. They cut 24 railroad lines, and destroyed or damaged 57 railroad cars, 70 motor transports, 12 locomotives, and 5 military installations. They attacked and destroyed a dam on the Seille River.

October 21
D-Day +137

The 26th Infantry Division launched a small attack into the XII Corps front to the east in the Bezange-la-Petite area toward Moncourt, but only gained a total of two thousand yards.

The XIX TAC flew 174 sorties, with average damage and destruction.

G-2 intelligence reported that a large railway gun, which had been shelling Nancy with its 280mm shells, was in the railroad shops at Metz for repairs. A pilot of the 10th Photo Reconnaissance Group adjusted a 155mm gun battalion upon the shops and 140 rounds were fired for effect. Sixty of these were fired under close observation. The firing was concluded with six rounds of white phosphorous shell, which caused large fires. An intelligence report indicated demolition of the gun, twenty-two cannoneer casualties, and complete wreckage of the area.

A political survey taken indicated that the region of Nancy was strongly conservative and anti-German. It was not too surprising.

Twelfth Army Group put into effect a credit system of ammunition supply. Under this system, allocations were made to the armies on the basis of overall availability and missions assigned. While ammunition was being stocked into the Advance Section Communications Zone in the Twelfth Army Group area, all shipments to the Third Army were curtailed.

Lieutenant General Carl A. Spaatz, commanding general of U.S. Strategic Tactical Air Forces, visited Third Army headquarters.

October 22
D-Day +138

The Third Army's front lines remained unchanged and enemy activity was very minor.

A Letter of Instruction from 12th Army Group indicated that "Third Army will advance in zone to the Rhine in the Mainz-Worms area and seize a bridgehead immediately if the situation permits. If it is impracticable to seize a bridgehead, Third Army will attack to the north and clear the area to the Moselle."

The XIX TAC flew 152 sorties, cutting 16 railroad lines and damaging or destroying 89 railroad cars, 53 motor transports, 18 locomotives, and 5 gun installations.

Lieutenant General Omar N. Bradley conferred with General Patton on the proposed upcoming offensive. It was decided that the date of the attack would hinge on weather conditions rather than be fixed by a specific date.

October 23
D-Day +139

The XIX TAC flew no missions due to bad weather.

Twelfth Army Group sent a letter to the Third Army headquarters indicating and stressing the necessity for strict supply discipline to conserve items in limited supply or items which, through indifference to supply discipline, might quickly reach a critical status. Reserves were to be built up only within prescribed levels.

The adverse weather conditions that the Third Army was experiencing gave rise to a new invention for the medium tank. Called duck feet, these extended end connectors were attached to the tracks of the tanks to give the tank more secure flotation and to allow them to make better progress in the mud. About twenty-five thousand of these items were received on a priority basis and installed on tanks of the XII Corps. Contracts were placed with civilian manufacturers in Nancy for an additional two hundred thousand connectors.

October 24
D-Day +140

The 134th Infantry relieved the 320th Infantry, making the only change in the XII Corps lines.

Three shells of 280mm artillery were fired at Third Army headquarters, narrowly missing General Patton's quarters. One shell landed between the two wings of the 12th Evacuation Hospital in Nancy. It dug a thirty-six foot-long trench into the ground and came to rest twenty feet deep. It was, of course, a dud.

No flying for the XIX TAC due to bad weather.

General Patton informed SHAEF that since October 1, he had received 2.1 million gallons of gasoline less than what he had requested in the daily telegrams. He also indicated that this deficiency steadily decreased army reserves, although units were strictly rationed. Only enough gasoline remained for less than two operational days. A new daily allocation of gasoline to units was approved by the chief of staff, allotting 12,500 gallons to armored units instead of 25,000 and 6,500 gallons to infantry divisions instead of 5,000; there also was an increase in the allocation to corps for corps troops.

The Third Army's supply of "B" rations was critical.

October 25
D-Day +141

G-2 now estimated that the Germans no longer had the capability to launch a limited objective offensive north of Metz.

To keep them from being inactive and becoming apathetic, intensive training of troops by the 5th Infantry Division was started in the XX Corps zone, while the 90th Infantry Division completed its regrouping.

Bad weather again limited the XIX TAC to only forty-four sorties, but they did manage to cut nine railroad lines and to damage or destroy twenty-eight railroad cars and twelve gun installations.

Due to the increasing shortages of critical supplies, many

items of captured German ordnance were modified for use by the Third Army. About fourteen thousand German spark plugs were renovated for use in the M-4 Sherman tank engines, and many German motorcycles were rebuilt with captured spare parts and issued to U.S. troops.

General Patton was visited by Lieutenant General John C.H. Lee, commanding general of the Communications Zone, European Theater of Operations (COMZ-ETO).

October 26
D-Day +142

The XIX TAC flew nine missions totalling 226 sorties. In addition to the 27 railroad lines cut, there were 15 locomotives, 9 military installations, 3 highway bridges, and 2 miscellaneous naval vessels damaged or destroyed.

While additional units were being moved into the Third Army zone, positions were maintained and the front lines remained unchanged.

Twelfth Army Group was informed that even with rigid rationing of gasoline, unit reserves were being lowered. Also noted was the increasing shortage of tires, inner tubes, and patches; all reaching a danger stage.

October 27
D-Day +143

Front line positions remained unchanged in the XII Corps area, with aggressive patrolling being carried out. The 10th Armored Division continued to move toward the XX Corps assembly area.

The XIX TAC was grounded due to unfavorable weather.

General Bradley issued verbal orders to the effect that the Third Army could begin reorganizing the tank destroyer battalions (self-propelled).

Special trainloads of "B" rations arrived.

October 28
D-Day +144

An increase in the German's flare activity indicated the probability of night movements of units.

Elements of the 90th Infantry Division resumed the attack on Maizieres-les-Metz, with satisfactory progress made. In another part of the XX Corps area, an antiaircraft gun battalion shelled an enemy troop concentration near the Verdun forts at Metz causing heavy losses to the enemy.

The XIX TAC claimed the damaging or destroying of 219 railroad cars, 65 motor transports, 33 locomotives, 31 military installations, and 5 highway bridges in addition to the cutting of 25 railroad lines in 241 sorties in 11 missions.

October 29
D-Day +145

Elements of the 90th Infantry Division finally seized the town of Maizieres-les-Metz, the only exception being the town hall, where the Germans were barricaded and resisting stiffly. The final attack on Maizieres-les-Metz was preceded by a full thirty minutes of preparation fire by the XX Corps artillery, with emphasis placed on counterbattery firings. Initially, the Germans reacted strongly, but with these positions promptly attacked with counterbattery fire, early ascendancy was achieved over the enemy artillery and it was maintained throughout the attack.

Units of the 10th Armored Division arrived in the corps area around Mars-la-Tour, west of Metz. Otherwise, no changes occurred in the corps area.

The fighterbomber combat planes of the XIX TAC had one of their best days yet. In 17 missions, totaling 419 sorties, they attacked enemy aircraft, marshalling yards, railroads, and gun positions. Four hundred and seven tons of bombs were dropped and 100 German fighters were engaged in the air. Twenty-four of the Germans were shot out of the sky while the XIX TAC lost only six planes. Before the end of the missions, 5 bridges, 59 locomotives, 156 railroad cars, and 13 motor cars were destroyed as well as 9 marshalling yards and 22 military buildings bombed.

On this date, one fighter group was taken from the XIX TAC to be reassigned to the First Army to the north.

The principle operation achievement for the day was the clearing of Maizieres les Metz.

October 30
D-Day +146

While positions remained unchanged in the XII Corps area, the Germans employed only harassing mortar and artillery fire along the front.

All organized resistance by the Germans ended at 1400 hours in Maizieres-les-Metz when the town hall was over-taken by the 90th Infantry Division.

The XIX TAC flew fifty-three sorties, but no claims were made.

The Twelfth Army Group was requested to ship available gasoline to the Third Army over and above the requirements of other armies. The reasons being were to build up of re-serves and because the supply situation made the Third Army incapable of sustaining any immediately launched offensive.

October 31
D-Day +147

In the XX Corps zone, the 2d Infantry and units of the 10th Infantry relieved units of the 95th Infantry Division in the Moselle River bridgehead. Elements of the 10th Armored Division relieved the 358th Infantry, which then moved to an area west of Audun, northwest of Metz. There remained no change in the front lines.

The XIX TAC, still hampered by bad weather, managed to fly eighty sorties, cutting only one railroad line and damaging seventeen military installations.

The major result of the day's operations was the continued practice of rotating and regrouping the Third Army units in contact with the Germans. The idea was to give maximum rest to troops who had been in combat for a considerable amount of time and keep the enemy guessing as to the actual plans of the Third Army.

Advance Section Communications Zone was asked for an emergency shipment of thrity-thousand gallons of diesel fuel. They were also informed that the daily telegram requests were not being met. After being told that there was no diesel fuel available, Third Army then contacted Seventh Army. They made a deal to exchange ten thousand gallons of No. 10 motor oil for ten thousand gallons of diesel fuel. The exchange to be made on November 1.

CHAPTER 4

November, 1944

Developments during the month of November saw the Third Army return to the offensive. Due to the acute, critical supply situation that hampered the Third Army since September 25, the Third Army had been forced to resign their role in the ETO to that of a defensive army. Because General Patton despised the term defensive, he began what he termed an aggressive patrol, doing what he could with the meager supplies that he received. The outstanding achievement that would occur during November was the capture of the city of Metz. It would be the first time since 451 A.D. that the city would be taken by assault.

Trench foot would become a great problem for Third Army troops, incapacitating more soldiers than injuries. Confronted with problems ranging from extreme weather conditions to flooded streams and terrain, the Third Army would still drive the Germans into their homeland, behind the Siegfried Line.

November 1
D-Day +148

To start the Third Army's new offensive, G-2 initiated a report giving the favored enemy capabilities.
1. Defense and delaying tactics in the zone of advance, counterattacking locally with infantry and armor in an attempt to

block and contain the army's eastward movement, and a fortress stand at Metz

2. The Germans could pivot on Metz to establish a general defensive line paralleling the Siegfried Line and take advantage of favorable terrain in the Third Army zone of advance to construct new organized defensive positions.

A letter directive from Twelfth Army Group stated that the 83d Infantry Division would be at the disposal of the Third Army in forthcoming operations with certain restrictions. The restrictions were that the division was not to be used for an assault crossing of the Moselle River (but could be used to cross established bridgeheads) and was not to be used beyond the Saar River.

Elements of the 80th Infantry Division occupied and cleared the Germans out of Abaucourt and Letricourt.

The XIX TAC flew 12 missions with 247 sorties and dropped a total of 125 tons of bombs, destroying 3 enemy planes on the ground and losing 2 aircraft.

The area west of the Seille River was cleared of Germans in the 80th Infantry Division's zone, while relief of the 95th Infantry Division was completed and relief of the 90th Infantry Division continued.

In general, the supply situation was improving. Although items such as blankets, sweaters, field jackets, raincoats, overcoats, one- and two-burner stoves, and tents were inadequate, the gasoline receipts improved rapidly. There were 1,174,315 gallons of V-80 gasoline (an 80-octane fuel standard for all vehicles), but there was a shortage of diesel fuel.

November 2
D-Day +149

Relief of the 90th Infantry Division was completed.

The XX Corps employed thirty-nine captured artillery pieces (including some the Germans had taken from the French and Russians) in order to minimize the effects of stringent ammunition restrictions. To date, the XX Corps had fired a total of 30,920 rounds of ammunition, valued at $702,391 out of taxpayers' pockets.

Bad weather kept the XIX TAC out of the skies.

Tank cars with bulk gasoline arrived at Domgermain, four miles southwest of Toul, the principal decanting point within the Third Army zone.

November 3
D-Day +150

An operational directive from Twelfth Army Group headquarters finally gave the green light. Patton and his Third Army were verbally ordered to

1. Envelop the Metz defensive works from the north and south and to destroy any enemy forces withdrawing from the Metz area.
2. Advance northeast within the army zone to seize the Mainz-Frankfurt-Darmstadt area.
3. Be prepared for further offensive action to the northeast.

The time of the attack was to be announced later. XIX TAC was again to provide air support based on target priorities submitted by the XII and XX Corps.

General Patton immediately ordered the XII Corps to advance northeast from Pont-à-Mousson to Falkenberg and destroy the forces withdrawing from Metz. They were also to advance as rapidly as possible to the northeast to establish a bridgehead east of the Rhine River, seize the Darmstadt area, and be prepared for further advance.

The XX Corps was to stay at Metz and contain the fortress city with part of its troops; while with the 80th Infantry Division and the 83rd Infantry Division it was to advance east of the Rhine River, seize the Mainz-Frankfurt area, and be prepared for further advance.

Poor weather conditions again limited the operations of the XIX TAC. They flew only fifty-one sorties in four missions escorting medium bombers through clouded skies. The bombers then dropped their bombs and left with unobserved results. Also, six tactical reconnaissance and four photo missions were flown.

A memorandum was sent to Advance Section Communications Zone stressing the critical need for tires, tire patches, and antifreeze mixture. Diesel fuel remained in critically short supply.

A supply of ten thousand pairs of shoes, ten thousand sets of underwear, and five hundred pounds of soap was procured for displaced persons and refugees in the Metz area.

The Right Reverend Henry W. Hobson, representing the General Commission on Army and Navy Chaplains, and Major General William R. Arnold, the chief of chaplains, called on General Patton and conferred with the Third Army Chaplain, Colonel O'Neill.

November 4
D-Day +151

Units were rotated periodically in the XII Corps area, though the front lines changed very little. Elements of Task Force Polk attacked and recaptured Berg, northeast of Thionville, and then occupied the town.

New railheads were established at Nancy, Chambley, Belleville, Dieulouard, Baroncourt, Trieux, and Audun-le-Roman. These were used chiefly for supply of the Third Army.

An engineer combat group designed splash shields to prevent water from splashing over the bows of storm and assault boats.

A request was approved for five L-1 litter planes and for pilots and crew chiefs for the aircraft.

The XIX TAC flew eighty sorties in four missions. One plane was lost escorting heavy bombers.

November 5
D-Day 152

"Target Data" (a top-secret letter) was issued to corps commanders. The letter covered air support and target data for the upcoming attack.

The XIX TAC flew 15 missions of 252 sorties and dropped 83 tons of bombs. In addition to flying 24 tactical reconnaissance and 12 photo missions, they succeeded in destroying 28 of the newest type of German airplanes—Messerschmitt jet-propelled models which never had the chance to leave the ground.

In preparation for the new offensive, at least gasoline supplies were adequate. Strategic sites east of the Moselle River were decided upon for reserves of rations. ComZ advised the Third Army that they would receive a daily maximum of one thousand tons (about 320 thousand gallons) in bulk to supplement shipments in cans. ComZ had been instructed to bring all U.S. armies up to a five-day supply, which was figured on a basis of 15.47 pounds of gasoline, lubricants, and grease per man per day.

November 6
D-Day +153

German artillery fire increased with heavy concentrations in Gremecey and Bioncourt in the XII Corps area. German squads were sent out on night patrols in an attempt to capture American prisoners.

The Twelfth Army Group sent out Amendment No. 3 to Letter of Instruction No. 10, revising target dates for all three armies in the group. It was as General Patton had once said of the pre-D-Day planning, "...the masterminds at SHAEF are changing their minds more than we change our underwear."

The Twelfth Army Group was to regroup and prepare for an advance to the Rhine River. The target date for the Third Army was November 5, while the target date for First Army and Ninth Army was November 10. Also included in the instructions were alterations in the missions of the Twenty-first Army Group (Montgomery) and Sixth Army Group. After the First Army had reached the Rhine River, the Ninth Army was to attack northward between the Rhine and Meuse Rivers in conjunction with the Second British Army. The Ninth Army was to then take over the area west of the Rhine River to the city of Rees. A new intergroup boundary was to be announced later. (No mention was made of the fact that the Third Army's role in the plan was to begin on November 5 and the date on the order was November 6).

Due to bad weather, the XIX TAC remained on the ground.

Diesel fuel finally arrived in sufficient quantity to remove it from the critical list of supplies.

Engineers completed a new design for a special type of bridge to be built when crossing the Rhine River.

November 7
D-Day +154

The Third Army was finally allowed to pass through the green light which had been flashed by Twelfth Army Group four days previous, on the November 3.

At 0600 hours on November 7, with General Patton in the vanguard, the Third Army opened the Battle of Germany which destroyed the Germans frail hopes for a winter breathing spell. The Germans would not be allowed to rest, refit, or reorganize their battered, exhausted divisions.

Without the benefit of preliminary aerial bombardment, in rain and with unprecedented flood conditions prevailing, Patton's attack achieved a complete tactical surprise. German prisoners would later admit that they and their higher echelons considered it utterly impossible for the Third Army to launch such an offensive under such unfavorable weather and terrain conditions. It would prove to be a typically impossible mission done easily by the Third Army. The staff of the Third Army, called "mediocre" by General Bradley, would prove to be the most consistant, loyal, and able staff in the ETO.

The attack was launched by the XII Corps (26th, 35th, and 80th Infantry Divisions). The 328th Infantry of the 26th Infantry Division, drove from west of Moncourt through Moncourt and Bezange-la-Petite. The 101st Infantry of the 26th Infantry Division crossed the canal northeast of Moyenvic, while elements of the 104th Infantry drove into Vic-sur-Seille. In the 35th Infantry Division's zone, the 320th Infantry went through Fresnes-en-Saulnois while units of the 137th Infantry occupied Malaucourt-sur-Seille and Jallaucourt. Concurrently, the 80th Infantry Division was advancing with the 319th Infantry going through Aulnois-sur-Seille, the 318th Infantry in Mailly-sur-Seille, and the 317th Infantry east of

Clemery. The corps had the 26th Infantry Division in the south, the 35th Infantry Division in the center, and the 80th Infantry Division in the north.

To support the XII Corps attack, corps artillery and tank destroyer units fired from H-60 until H-147. After the first half hour, divisional artillery was released for on call missions and targets of opportunity in close support of the divisions were allowed. Ninety concentrations were fired on towns, 13 on defiles, 190 on enemy artillery locations, 40 on enemy command posts, 31 on enemy antiaircraft artillery locations, 14 on assembly areas, 1 on a strongpoint, and 1 on a farm building. Upon completion, their fire was continued until 1200 hours to maintain intense neutralization. After 1200 hours, fires were delivered on call. This heavy support not only prevented any aggressive artillery reaction, but it also caused serious disruption of the enemy's communications.

Bad weather and poor flying conditions kept activity of the XIX TAC to a minimum, allowing only night photography missions.

Jallaucourt, Malaucourt, and Rouves were captured.

A fire at the gasoline decanting point at Domerman was started by hot coals from a switch engine. It destroyed a total of 6,000 gallons of gasoline and 9,178 gasoline cans. Shipments of tire patching material were reported to be on their way, while antifreeze mixture was being flown directly from the United Kingdom.

Seven tons of potatoes from German-planted fields at Etain were turned over to the mayor of that city to relieve the town's shortage of food.

Experiments were made with a new anti-concussion earplug device for artillerymen. Made of acrylic (a new type of plastic), it was molded to fit the individual ear and afforded considerable relief from the concussion of artillery fire, according to the test results made under fire.

November 8
D-Day +155

While the XII Corps was racing toward the Rhine River, the

XX Corps was launching a full-strength drive against the strongly fortified city of Metz, handicapped by the flood conditions of the Moselle River.

The 5th Infantry Division jumped off the starting line first with a strong attack, followed by coordinated drives of the other divisions of the corps.

The 6th Armored Division crossed the Seille River at Port-sur-Seille, preparing for further advance. They were protected by a heavy smoke-screen operation during the crossing, even though hampered by flood conditions.

The 5th Infantry Division went through Cheminot, south of Metz, while the 90th Infantry Division established bridgeheads across the Moselle River near Thionville, using DUKW's (standard two-and-one-half ton amphibious vehicles) on an experimental basis which proved to be completely successful.

The 10th Armored Division assembled, preparing to use the established bridgeheads, while other bridgeheads around Uckange were captured by the 95th Infantry Division.

On the extreme northern flank of the corps zone, operational control of the 83rd Infantry Division reverted to XX Corps from the First Army.

Weather conditions improved, and the XIX TAC flew 471 sorties in 29 missions. The fighters and bombers dropped 134 tons of bombs, including tanks of napalm dropped on foxholes and along trenches with good results. Two German planes were destroyed on the ground and six were shot out of the air.

Bridging requirements were taxed heavily because of the German's good use of demolitions. They took full advantage of the rain and blew craters at low spots on the river banks which made bridging necessary not only for the river but also for these manmade gaps as well. In XII Corps alone thirty-five hundred feet of Bailey bridges were expended for this type of river crossing.

The continuing rains caused other rivers to raise to flood heights, covering the entire plain across the Moselle valley and washing out all bridges except the one high level structure at Pont-à-Mousson.

November 9
D-Day +156

The Germans continued to offer only sporadic and loosely organized resistance. In some instances entire companies surrendered collectively. Thick mine fields and flood conditions continued to delay XX Corps advance.

Good progress was made by the XII Corps. The 26th Infantry Division went forward to Hampont while the 35th Infantry continued to advance with its 134th Infantry occupying Coutures. The 137th Infantry seized high ground east of Laneveville-en-Saulnois, capturing Delme. To the north the 80th Infantry Division advanced to an area eight miles northeast of Pont-à-Mousson, followed closely by the 6th Armored Division.

The Eighth Air Force sent 1,476 heavy bombers to deliver a saturation attack on all fortified towns east of the bridgehead area in support of the XX Corps attack to capture the city of Metz. With communications being cut, German units were temporarily left as separate fighting forces. The principle targets of the bombers were the towns of Metz, Verny, Orny, Pommerieux, and Saarbrücken. During the attack there were 2,305 tons of bombs dropped on the city of Metz alone.

The XIX TAC flew in support of the heavy bombers in addition to their own attacks, which totaled 312 sorties in 21 missions. They dropped 61 tons of high explosives and 41 tons of napalm tanks, losing four planes during the operations.

To prevent the bombers from making a mistake and bombing their own forces, antiaircraft units provided two flak lines to guide the planes. An example of a mistake would be the short bombing which took place in Normandy, when many Americans were bombed by their own planes, one of the casualties being General Leslie McNair. The flak lines were each two miles long and consisted of bursts from eight guns sited in at 500 yards apart. They fired their shells to appear at an altitude of seventeen thousand feet, which was three thousand feet below the attack flight.

General Patton was visited by Lieutenant General Carl A. Spaatz, commanding general of the U.S. Strategic Tactical Air Force, and Lieutenant General James H. Doolittle, commanding general of the Eighth Air Force.

November 10
D-Day +157

Although the Germans managed to stiffen their opposition against the Third Army's advance, they could not stop them completely. In a matter of two days, Third Army soldiers had captured the towns of Nomeny, Rouves, Eply, Raucourt, St. Jure, Vigny, Buchy, Beux, Secourt, Achatel, Sailly, Moncheux, Juville, Foville, Thezey-St. Martin, Lemoncourt, Oriocourt, Delme, Viviers, Fresnes-en-Saulnois, Amelecourt, Fonteny, Chateau-Salins, Salonnes, Vic-sur-Seille, Morville, Hampont, Obreck, Moyenvic, and Bezange-la-Petite.

The 10th Armored Division moved up to join the action along with the 5th, 90th, and 95th Infantry Divisions in the XX Corps area.

Poor weather stopped the flying by XIX TAC, with the exception of ninety-one sorties.

Engineers started building the longest Bailey bridge to date. It was a two-hundred-foot structure at Thionville, spanning a gap on a destroyed highway bridge. The bridge was completed before two other bridges were finished at Malling, in spite of thirty-six hours of German mortar, machine gun, and artillery harassment fire. It was used immediately by part of the 10th Armored Division.

November 11
D-Day +158

The Germans began to withdraw all along the Third Army's front line, fighting only delaying actions in some places, mostly forests and towns with favorable defenses.

The 83d Infantry Division reverted to control of the First Army by verbal order of General Bradley. General Patton would later record in his personal diary that this action by Bradley was probably one of the major errors of the entire war effort in the ETO. He wrote, "If Bradley had not welshed on his agreement, we would have taken Saarburg within forty-eight hours after we got Konigsmacker. Once we had [Konigsmacker], they couldn't have stopped us from taking Trier, and if we'd had Trier it would have been impossible for the Germans to have launched their Ardennes Offensive. It seems to be a case of 'For want of a nail, a shoe was lost; for want of a shoe, a horse was lost,' etc. I'm firmly convinced that Bradley's refusal to allow me to use the 83rd, as he had promised, was one of the underlying causes of the Battle of the Bulge."

The 26th Infantry Division drove to the northeast in the XII Corps area, and made substantial gains while the 35th Infantry Division, also going northeast, took the town of Vaxy. The 80th Infantry Division went due north and liberated an area which included the towns of Bacourt and Prevocourt. The 4th Armored Division's Combat Command "A" captured Conthil while Combat Command "B" captured Baudrecourt and began plans to attack Metz from the rear.

The 5th, 90th, and 95th Infantry Divisions of the XX Corps continued their attack, enlarging their bridgeheads across the Moselle River, with the 10th Armored Division moving up to assume a major role in the upcoming action. The 95th Infantry Division continued its crossings of the river around Thionville and Uckange, while to the south, the 5th Infantry Division made only moderate advances to the east.

The XIX TAC flew 10 missions with 162 sorties, dropping 31 tons of bombs and 32 tanks of napalm, and firing 18 rockets.

Towns liberated on this date were Fort Koenigsmacker, Gerbecourt, Tincry, Prevocourt, Bacourt, Morville-sur-Nied, Tragny, Thiomonville, Buchy, Nocourt, Solonnes, and Fonteny.

There were new Third Army railheads established at Chambrey, Moncel, Brin, Bettembourg, and Dudelange.

A need for more labor troops in hospital units became apparent. The current practice of using POWs was being curtailed because the Third Army was nearing the German border and the possibility of their escaping increased.

Due to the cold, wet weather, many cases of trench foot were reported in hospital units. General Patton immediately gave verbal orders that each commander was to see to it personally that every man in every squad not only had a fresh, clean pair of socks each day, but that he used them. Also, a directive was issued that company commanders were to make certain that soldiers dried their boots and feet after a river crossing or a rainy spell.

General Patton became fifty-nine years old.

November 12
D-Day +159

The XII Corps was meeting stubborn resistance in Bazoncourt and along the road from Han-sur-Nied to Herny. The 26th Infantry Division captured Chateau-Voue and Wuisse, while the 101st and 328th Infantry Regiments fought through the woods north of Dieuze and consolidated their positions.

In the 35th Infantry Division's area, the 134th Infantry captured Dalhain and Belange, while the 137th Infantry and the 320th Infantry captured Chateau-Brehain. While the 318th Infantry was capturing Herny, the 6th Armored Division captured Vatimont and supported the 80th Infantry Division from Herny to Han-sur-Nied.

The 90th Infantry was enlarging its bridgehead while the 95th Infantry Division's 378th Infantry continued to cross the Moselle River. South of Metz, the 5th Infantry Division cleared Corny, Pommerieux, Liehon, Sanry-sur-Nied, and Ancerville on their way to the north.

The XIX TAC flew only a few night sorties, attacking two trains and strafing a convoy on a road.

Reinforcements were now coming into the Third Army at a rate of about 1,800 per day and would continue to do so for another week.

Again, orders were issued to all company commanders and troops concerning the problem of trench foot. Troops were instructed to massage their feet and to keep them dry by changing to clean socks, which were issued daily with their other rations. General Patton had spoken with one of his younger staff officers, explaining that, "...it is more important in war to keep your feet in good condition than it is to brush your teeth."

November 13
D-Day +160

The Germans continued their attempts at delaying tactics, using counterattacks, extensive mine fields, roadblocks, obstacles, and increased artillery fire. The mine fields were proving to be formidable barriers for troops in the XX Corps.

Written orders from General Bradley on this date confirmed the transfer of the 83d Infantry Division to the First Army.

There was no activity by the XIX TAC due to inclement weather.

In their continued advance to the east and northeast, the XX Corps and the XII Corps units captured the towns of L'Aisne, L'Yser, Orny, Coin-les-Cuvry, Pouilly, Cuvry, Kerling, Freching, Kuntzig, Inglange, Masse-Yutz, Ponttoy, and Immeldange. The towns being captured were sounding more and more like German names.

November 14
D-Day +161

In the XII Corps area, the 26th Infantry Division's elements occupied Harracourt and Marsal, with elements of the 328th Infantry driving south, toward Dieuze. The 4th Armored Division was working in close proximity with the 26th Infantry Division, capturing Guebling and Zarbeling. Just to the north, the 6th Armored Division seized Landrof.

The 95th Infantry Division, in the XX Corps area, captured Ouvr St. Hubert, Feves, and Fort D'Illange while the 10th Armored Division began crossing the Moselle River near Thionville and Malling aided by smoke-screen cover. To the south of the 10th Armored Division, the 5th Infantry Division captured Mecleuves in its flanking drive toward Metz.

Again, bad weather prevented any activity by XIX TAC.

November 15
D-Day +162

A new study issued by G-2 indicated that the Germans would most probably continue their fortress stand at Metz and attempt to impede the Third Army's advance by means of a diversion of troops, artillery, and aviation attacks. The Germans could withdraw and supplement defensive positions while bringing up reinforcements from other sectors and manning the fortifications of the Siegfried Line.

Enemy delaying actions strengthened perceptibly in the XII Corps area, where strong counterattacks were launched and artillery fire was extremely heavy.

The XX Corps continued its attacks on Metz.

The XIX TAC flew two missions of thirty sorties and dropped thirty-five tons of bombs, also strafing an enemy convoy and attacking marshalling yards near Metz.

The Third Army was visited by the Supreme Commander of Allied Expeditionary Forces, General Dwight D. Eisenhower.

November 16
D-Day +163

The XII Corps regrouped, planning for further advances to the east. Only minor advances were realized along the front line.

In the XX Corps area, the 5th Infantry Division captured Peltre, Sorbey, and a fort at Chesney. The 95th Infantry Division captured Vigneulles, Saulny, Lorry-les-Metz, Plesnois, and Norry-le-Venour. Elements of the 90th Infantry Division took the towns of Metzervisse, Buding, and Renange, while the 10th Infantry Division cleared Nonneren, St. Marguerite, and St. Francois-Lacroix.

In conjunction with attacks by the XX and XII Corps, the XIX TAC fired rockets in 112 sorties, dropped almost 33 tons of bombs, one half-ton of napalm, and fragmentation bombs.

Approximately thirty-five thousand gallons of gasoline were destroyed when a fire, caused by the backfire of a thirty-gallon dispenser, erupted at a supply point at Nancy.

November 17
D-Day +164

The Germans held to their defensive attitude in the XII Corps area, but in the XX Corps area their delaying actions were disorganized and a large number of prisoners were being captured. In the Metz area, enemy resistance was sporadic, although the strongest opposition remained along the Fort Driant-Fort Jeanne D'Arc line of forts.

The XX Corps continued advancing, with the 5th, 95th, and 90th Infantry Divisions capturing a number of small towns. The advancing Third Army's XX Corps now resembled a horseshoe in its attack formation, and the Germans were withdrawing at an accelerated pace.

Finally, a break occurred in the weather conditions, allowing the XIX TAC to resume large operations. In support of the corps, 20 missions were flown, totaling 317 sorties. Dropped on the Germans were fragmentation bombs, napalm, 78 tons of high explosive bombs, and leaflet bombs, in addition to rockets fired. Also attacked were enemy airdromes.

The forces encircling Metz were now only four miles apart.

Supply requests indicated that there was a shortage of coal, wire W-130 (for telephones), mess kits, canteen cups, knives, forks and spoons, tires, tire patches, tubes, and antifreeze. The number of troops drawing from supply in the Third Army totaled 311,963.

In a three-week period, the Third Army authorized subsistence trains to carry 340 tons of potatoes, 580 tons of flour, and 32 head of cattle to the city of Nancy for use by civilians.

November 18
D-Day +165

The breaching of the approaches of defense to Metz eliminated the capability of the Germans to wage a fortress stand. Gone was the German's controlling pivot of their defenses and dispositions west of the Siegfried Line. Enemy resistance weakened visibly in the XX Corps area and a general withdrawal along the entire corps' front was indicated. Resistance continued in the forts at Metz, but only eight major structures remained to be captured.

The encirclement of Metz was complete when the 5th Infantry Division made contact with Task Force Bacon. The contact was made due east of the city. A chemical mortar unit with the 5th Infantry Division hit an ammunition dump, resulting in an explosion which knocked out several pieces of enemy heavy artillery. Two more forts fell to the 95th Infantry Division, with the 90th Infantry Division mopping up in the rear of advances made by the 10th Armored Division.

Enemy air activity increased, with 31 aircraft attacking the advancing the Third Army units. Antiaircraft units shot down 7 of the planes and claimed 8 as probably destroyed. In opposition, the XIX TAC flew 25 missions with 347 sorties.

Arrangements were made to bring a group of former civilian managers and operators of local coal mines into the Third Army's area. They were to enter mines immediately after their capture to insure that they were not flooded due to seepage.

November 19
D-Day +166

An estimate from G-2 indicated that despite reinforcements, the Germans in the advance route of the Third Army were the equivalent of only seven divisions due to the severe, heavy losses of the previous week's operations.

Street fighting was in progress in Metz, and the major forts in the city held out, surrounded by Americans.

Combat Command "A" of the 4th Armored Division captured Virming, and then the 4th Armored Division joined the 26th Infantry Division in an attack on the town of Dieuze, considered tactically important. Meanwhile, the 6th Armored Division and the 35th Infantry Division attacked eastward, immediately north of the 26th Infantry Division.

The 5th and 95th Infantry Divisions entered Metz.

The XIX TAC was having a field day with the withdrawing Germans. They flew 403 sorties of armed reconnaissance, corps support, and bomber escort. Although 13 aircraft and 8 pilots were lost, they destroyed or damaged 387 motor transports, 18 tanks and armored vehicles, 57 locomotives, 429 railroad cars, 48 gun positions, and 37 factories and buildings. Ten railroad lines were cut. Twelve attacks were made on marshalling yards and the same number on towns.

November 20
D-Day +167

The German withdrawal of the bulk of their forces left only a skeleton force along the XII Corps front. During their retreat, they still managed to build numerous roadblocks, blow up bridges, lay mine fields, and offer sporadic artillery fire, all of which impeded both the XX and the XII Corps' advances.

Finally, after two months of bitter bloodletting and frustration, Metz was reported to be cleared. Elements of the 5th and 95th Infantry Divisions surrounded the forts on the south and east of Metz and captured Fort Queuleu, while a chemical company of the 5th Infantry Division crossed the Seille River under the cover of a smoke screen.

November 21
D-Day +168

In the XII Corps area, the 26th Infantry Division captured Albesdorf, Torcheville, and Insweiler, while the 4th Armored Division captured Loudrefing, Rening, Rodalbe, and Cutting. The 4th Armored Division advanced to the west bank of the Rhine-Marne canal at Mittersheim.

To the north, the 35th Infantry and 6th Armored Divisions continued a coordinated attack to the east, capturing Helimer, Fremesdorf, and Fletrange. The 80th Infantry Division was advancing slowly but inexorably along the northern flank of the XII Corps area.

In Metz, the 5th and 95th Infantry Divisions of the XX Corps continued attacking, mopping up the last remains of the tenacious Germans. The 95th Infantry Division captured Ile-Chambiere and mopped up Ill-du-Saulcy, while the 10th and 11th Infantry Regiments (5th Infantry Division) assisted the

377th and 378th Infantry Regiments (95th Infantry Division) and Task Force Bacon in the final reduction of the fortress city.

Four hundred eleven planes of the XIX TAC flew almost entirely as escorts to the IX Bomber Command and the Eighth Air Force.

The Third Army's estimation of the requirements for ammunition for a six-month period, made on the basis of rounds per gun per day, was fifty for 105mm howitzers (high explosive only); thirty-five for 155 howitzers; twenty-five for 155mm guns; and twenty-five for eight-inch howitzers.

November 22
D-Day +169

On this date, at 1435 hours, all resistance at Metz ceased. The city called The Bastion of the East was captured by assault by General Patton's Third United States Army.

In the year 451 A.D., the city was stormed and devastated by the Huns, who then occupied it for sixty years. In 1870, the city was surrendered by a French garrison during the Franco-Prussian War after the city had run out of food. The city then remained in German hands until the end of the First World War, at which time the French recaptured and held it until the Third Reich's blitzkrieg of 1940 forced the French to surrender. The Germans then occupied it again.

With the fall of Metz to the XX Corps, after a two months' siege, handicapped by the worst flood conditions in twenty years and by weather preventing maximum air support, a new route to the German frontier was opened and the last important obstacle in front of the Siegfried Line was removed.

An Amendment No. 5 to Letter of Instruction No. 10 from the Twelfth Army Group was received, dated November 21. It adjusted the boundary between the First and Third Armies.

All XIX TAC missions were cancelled due to bad weather.

The civilian food train from Paris to Nancy was altered from twice weekly to a daily operation, except for Sunday.

The Third Army's line of advance for the day was to the east and northeast. Captured cities were St. Jean Rohrback,

Diefenbach, Petite-Tenquin, Greningen, Munster, and Miter-sheim.

The crowning achievement for the day and for the month was the total subjugation of Metz.

November 23
D-Day +170

Using the usual delaying tactics, the Germans defended towns and strongpoints with both infantry and tanks. The 26th Infantry Division met heavy resistance in Foret Dom D'Albesdorf, north of Munster, and the 4th Armored Division pushed some elements across the Saar River at both Rommelf-ingen and Gosselmingen, with leading units reaching as far as Postdorf and Kirberg.

The 35th Infantry Division kept driving and attacking, reaching Rening and Insming, while the 6th Armored Division regrouped in preparation for an upcoming attack.

The 95th Infantry Division was relieved by the 5th Infantry Division around Colligny, east of Metz, while the 90th Infantry Division relieved the 10th Armored Division in the task of mopping up.

The XIX TAC was grounded by bad weather.

November 24
D-Day +171

The 26th Infantry Division captured and cleared Bois-De-Vibers-Villers, Bois-de-Gevricourt, Bois-de-Hammessiel, and Foret-Dom D'Albesdorf. The 4th Armored Division took Postdorf and Barendorf, and then crossed the Saar River at both Gosselmingen and Rommelfingen. The 35th Infantry Division captured Uberkinger, Kappelkinger, and Rening and then regrouped its forces. The 6th Armored Division captured Vallatte in its push toward Puttelange, and the 80th Infantry Division in the north launched an eastward drive taking Faulquemont and Mainvillers, finally reaching Laudrefang.

In the XX Corps, the 95th Infantry Division captured Brecklange, Boulay-Moselle, Halling, and Narbefontain. The 90th

Infantry Division, fighting along the German border near Luxembourg, captured Biringen, Neunkirchen-les-Bouzonville, and Remeldorff. The 10th Armored Division, meeting with stiff resistance inside Germany, captured Tettingen, Butzdorf, and Oberlueken.

The XIX TAC was kept from flying by bad weather conditions.

A request was sent to the Twelfth Army Group for winter supplies. The list included 30,000 overshoes, 97,000 ground sheets, 225,921 mufflers, 260,000 trousers, 260,000 jackets, 182,789 sleeping bags, 226,000 sweaters, and 175,358 pairs of combat boots.

A mobile water purification unit was sent to Metz to alleviate the water supply problem suffered there.

General Eisenhower visited the Third Army headquarters.

November 25
D-Day +172

The XII Corps captured Wittersburg, Hilsprich, Morsebrown, Remering, and Hirbach, crossing the Saar River and driving into the Maginot Line at Zimmingen.

The XX Corps' 5th Infantry Division accepted surrender of Forts Verdun, St. Blaise, Marival, and St. Sommy. The 95th Infantry Division attacked and occupied Boulay, Momerstroff, Narbefontaine, and Ricrange, making contact with the 80th Infantry Division.

In the northern sector, the 90th Infantry Division captured Oberesch and Schwerdorff. The 10th Armored Division crossed the German border to capture Bethingen.

With good flying conditions, the XIX TAC flew 220 fighter-bomber sorties in corps support and armed reconnaissance. They accounted for the destruction and damaging of 183 railroad cars, 67 motor transports, 18 locomotives, 4 gun positions, and various miscellaneous targets.

Third Army reinforcements were arriving at a rate of five hundred to six hundred per day as new railheads were cleared for service at Florange, Hampont-Hudigen, Habundange, and Conthil.

November 26
D-Day +173

Tactical reconnaissance reported to Third Army headquarters that there were heavy rail movements into the Third Army zone of advance. The size was indicative of several divisions. Considering previous losses sustained by the Germans, it was believed that they were making a frantic effort to reinforce their front lines. This knowledge did not alter the previously outlined capabilities of the Germans.

XII Corps continued to attack along all of its fronts, while the XX Corps continued to contain the forts around Metz.

The XIX TAC flew 217 sorties in corps support and escort missions, losing 2 planes during the operations. They claimed destruction or damage to 99 railroad cars, 27 locomotives, and many other miscellaneous targets. In all, 14 towns were attacked and bombed.

In an attempt to relieve the shortages being suffered by the civilian population of Metz, twenty-two tons of emergency supplies were sent to the city along with a thirty-day supply of flour.

November 27
D-Day +174

Reports of enemy resistance varied from strong to scattered as the Germans withdrew toward their Siegfried Line in the midst of the attacks of the XX Corps and the XII Corps.

The 4th Armored and 26th Infantry Divisions captured Altweiler, Hunkirich, Kappelkinger, and Neuweyershot. Combat Command "A" of the 4th Armored Division attacked and captured Durstel, Gungweiler, and Assweiler. Combat Command "B" attacked and captured Wolfskirchen.

Farther to the north, the 35th Infantry Division completed its regrouping and prepared for attack. The 6th Armored Division captured Lixingen-les-St. Avold, Lanningen, Vahl-Ebersing, Masstadt, Cappel, and Barst-Marienthal. They also coordinated with the 80th Infantry Division in the capture of St. Avold. The 80th Infantry Division, operating on the corps' northern flank, captured Macheren, Hombourg-Haut, Seng-busch, Farebersviller, and Lachambre.

The 5th Infantry Division assumed control of part of the XX Corps' southern flank where it relieved elements of the 80th Infantry Division while also continuing the reduction of the remaining forts at Metz. The 95th Infantry Division advanced rapidly, occupying more than twenty-five small towns and reaching positions on the German border. Also reaching the frontiers of Germany was the 90th Infantry Division, which captured the town of Niedaltorf.

The XIX TAC flew no missions due to bad weather.

Third Army headquarters was visited by W. Averell Harriman, the U.S. ambassador to Russia.

November 28
D-Day +175

In the XII Corps area, the 26th Infantry Division advanced to Hinzingen as the 4th Armored Division went northward, capturing Durstel, Berg, Burbach, Harskirchen, Zollingen, and Pisdorf. The 6th Armored Division captured Diffenbach, Cappel, Barst, Biding, and Marienthal while the 35th Infantry Division was assembling in the corps reserve area. Also re-grouping was the 80th Infantry Division.

The 5th Infantry Division continued its harassment of the enemy-held forts around Metz. The 95th Infantry Division captured Rammelfangen and Duren, the 90th Infantry Division cleared the Germans west of the Saar River, and the 10th Armored Division was relieved by the 3d Cavalry Group.

Bad weather canceled flying by XIX TAC.

One hundred and fifty tons of frozen beef, twenty tons of frozen pork, fifty carloads of flour, one hundred and fifty tons of flour in storage, and a large quantity of canned goods were among captured German foodstuffs distributed among the civilian population of Metz.

Captured quantities of coal were issued to all troops on a basis of two pounds per man per day.

Lieutenant General Lucien K. Truscott, commanding general, Fifth U.S. Army, and Lieutenant General Walter B. (Bedell) Smith visited the Third Army headquarters.

November 29
D-Day +176

An estimate of the current enemy strength in the Third Army zone of advance was reported to be the equivalent of 5 divisions, consisting of 39,000 troops and 140 tanks or assault guns. Available as immediate reserves were an estimated 36,000 infantry troops and 15,100 Panzer troops with 195 tanks or assault guns. There was no change in the estimated enemy capabilities, the most favored being that he could defend and delay in successive prepared positions.

In preparation for its continued eastward attack, the XII Corps regrouped the majority of its forces.

The 4th Armored Division attacked and captured Thal.

Fort-St. Privat, a strongpoint in the vicinity of Metz, was subdued by the 5th Infantry Division. Because part of the division was not needed at Metz, it was attached to the 95th Infantry Division, assisting in the capture of Kerprich, Hemmersdorf, and Olsingen.

The 90th Infantry Division consolidated its gains and began patrols to the Saar River, while the 10th Armored Division pushed its attack to the east on the XX Corps' northern flank inside Germany. At the end of the day, Combat Command "B" of the 10th Armored Division was in the vicinity of Silwingen.

The XIX TAC did not fly.

Engineer supplies were greatly backlogged and there was a severe shortage of field jackets.

November 30
D-Day +177

German activity was at a minimum, consisting primarily of artillery and mortar fire and active patrolling.

General Patton issued orders that the 6th Cavalry Group (reinforced) would be formed. The unit was to be made up of a headquarters and headquarters troop; the 6th Cavalry Reconnaissance Squadron; the 5th Ranger Battalion; Company "C" of the 602d Tank Destroyer Battalion; Company "B" of the 293d Engineer Combat Battalion; and Troop "E" of the 28th Cavalry Reconnaissance Squadron. The group was formed and attached temporarily to the XX Corps.

The XII Corps continued with its regrouping of the majority of its units while the 4th Armored Division's Combat Command "A" occupied the high ground northeast of Thal and Combat Command "B" moved to the high ground southwest of Mackweiler. The 6th Armored Division maintained its patrols and its contact with the northern flank of XX Corps.

In the XX Corps area, the 5th Infantry Division continued to exert pressure on the forts around the city of Metz. The 10th Infantry Regiment was attached to the 95th Infantry Division and advanced to Niedervisse. The 95th Infantry Division occupied Teterchen, Oberlinberg, Itzbach, and Felsberg. Elements of the 90th Infantry Division were now well within German borders, fighting in Buren, northeast of Saarlautern. They captured Fremersdorf, while the 10th Armored Division (also within German borders) captured Fitten and Ballern.

Herbert H. Lehman, director of the United Nations Relief and Rehabilitation Administration, visited Third Army headquarters.

CHAPTER 5

December, 1944

The Third Army's operations during December would be divided into two phases. In the beginning of the month, the Third Army was advancing toward the Siegfried Line. Later, the Third Army would be called upon to perform a veritable miracle of maneuver, turning ninety degrees to the north and smashing into the southern flank of the German's Ardennes salient. This would be done with such success that it would be the deciding factor in the German's ability to wage an effective defense against Allied forces in Europe.

December 1
D-Day +178

The Third Army's G-2 Section, under direction of Colonel Oscar Koch, estimated that the favored enemy capability at this time would be to defend and delay in successive prepared positions in an effort to block the army's advances and attacks on the Siegfried Line. Less favored was the thought that the Germans would implement counterattacking tactics locally with infantry and armor. However, it was determined that the Germans could still reinforce against any section of the army's zone within a twenty-four-hour period.

The III Corps remained nonoperational at Etain.

The 26th Infantry and 4th Armored Divisions were operating jointly on the XII Corps' southern flank. The 35th Infantry Division maintained contact with the 6th Armored Division on its northern flank and the 26th Infantry Division on its southern flank.

The XX Corps had the 5th Infantry Division in contact with the 80th, 95th, and 90th Infantry Divisions along the Corps' front lines and the 10th Armored Division on the Corps' northern flank.

The XIX TAC flew 126 sorties, both in corps support and escort missions. Their best claims for the day came from motor vehicles with 41 destroyed. They also accounted for the destruction of 32 railroad cars and 27 horse-drawn vehicles.

With the exception of tires, tubes, and tire patching kits, the supply situation was adequate.

Photo reconnaissance of the routes of approach to the Siegfried Line was completed.

December 2
D-Day +179

Analysis of German railway movements indicated that the major portion of rail traffic during the period from November 17 to December 2, was toward the Saarbrücken and Eifel areas. A total of three hundred trains were observed on November 17, with marshalling yards very active. A large number of trains were moving into the First Army area north of the Third Army's zone of advance. Colonel Koch indicated a definite buildup of both troops and supplies.

Several counterattacks were broken up one mile south of Mackwiller in the XII Corps area. The German's resistance was broken in Sarre-Union by the use of tanks in support of infantry strongpoints.

Task Force Fickett (6th Cavalry Group, reinforced) occupied positions along the XX Corps southern flank after relieving units of the 10th Infantry near Carling, four miles north of St. Avold. The 95th Infantry, preceded by aerial bombardment and artillery preparation, captured Niederlimberg.

The XIX TAC suffered losses of 9 planes flying in Corps support, but still managed to inflict damage on the Germans. They either damaged or destroyed 329 railroad cars, 46 motor vehicles, and 35 locomotives; they also cut 35 railroad lines and attacked other military targets. In addition, they claimed 7 enemy aircraft shot down and 2 disabled.

During the day, the Third Army advanced to the northeast, capturing Bisten, Neuforweiler, Pikard, Itzbach, Niederlimberg, and Beaumaris. Mopping up operations took place in Sarre-Union and Saarlautern.

A request of supplies from Twelfth Army Group totaled 5,165 tons of materials daily in addition to 116 tons for daily reserve.

December 3
D-Day +180

In a determined counterattack to regain Sarre-Union, the Germans used tanks and infantry in some vicious house-to-house fighting. They also counterattacked in an attempt to regain positions lost at Lauterbach.

Elements of the 26th Infantry Division cleared woods two miles southwest of Sarralbe, while the 35th Infantry Division cleared Bettring, Holving, and Puttelange. There were no changes in the positions of 6th Armored and 80th Infantry Divisions.

Due to inclement weather, only eight sorties were flown by XIX TAC; one town being attacked with unobserved results.

The Third Army supply section requested 2,250 parka-type overcoats on the basis of 30 per battalion.

Former Governor Herbert H. Lehman, of the United Nations Relief and Rehabilitation Administration, inspected some forward areas of the Third Army, studying the problem of refugees and displaced persons.

A major change occurred in two command situations. Major General Hugh J. Gaffey, chief of staff of the Third U.S. Army, left the Third Army headquarters to assume command of the 4th Armored Division after Major General John "P" (Professor) Woods was relieved of that command. Brigadier General Hobart R. Gay was appointed chief of staff.

December 4
D-Day +181

The town of Sarre-Union was officially cleared as of 1730 hours. Only scattered resistance was met in the northern portion of the XII Corps zone until troops reached Ebering. German resistance in the southern portion remained very stubborn.

An operational directive instructed the III Corps to begin relief of the 5th Infantry Division in the Metz area. The 87th Infantry Division of the III Corps was to contain the forts still resisting by exerting pressure but not directly assaulting them.

Elements of Combat Command "B" of the 4th Armored Division continued advancing to the north in XII Corps zone, seizing a bridge intact across the Eichel River at Vollerdingen and setting up a small bridgehead.

The 6th Armored Division reopened its attack, capturing Cadenbrown, Metzingen, Tenteling, Diegling, and Ebering.

The 5th Infantry Division drove into the vicinity of Differten, while the 95th Infantry Division encountered heavy street fighting at Saarlautern but managed to establish a bridgehead at Lisdorf.

In only five missions totaling fifty-seven sorties flown by XIX TAC, they damaged or destroyed forty-nine railroad cars and twenty-two motor vehicles.

December 5
D-Day +182

G-2 estimates indicated that there was definitely an enemy withdrawal in progress into and behind the Siegfried Line.

Elements of the 87th Infantry Division closed in the vicinity of Metz. Although the normal organization of a corps featured two divisions under its command, the 87th was the only tactically operational unit then under command of the III Corps.

While the 4th Armored Division's Combat Command "B" crossed the Eichel River with their bridgehead at Vollerdingen, Combat Command "A" crossed the river one mile to the south at Domfessel, making a rapid seven-mile advance to the northeast with leading units at Bining, Schmittville, and Kulhausen. The 6th Armored Division captured Houhling and Ippling, west of Sarreguemines, while the 80th Infantry Division took the high ground and improved its positions to the north.

In the XX Corps zone, the 5th Infantry Division advanced from two to five miles, capturing Karlsbrunn and Merlebach southwest of Saarbrucken. Elements of the 95th Infantry Division enlarged its bridgehead at Lisdorf. The 90th Infantry Division made four separate assault crossings of the Saar River between two and five miles north of Saarlautern, capturing Pachten. To insure the element of surprise, no artillery preparation was fired, but an intensive schedule of counterbattery fire was launched from H-Hour to H+45 consisting of about eight thousand rounds on a total of thirty-nine enemy artillery locations. The 10th Armored Division continued its aggressive patrolling on the northern flank of the corps.

The XIX TAC flew 168 day and 7 night sorties. They dropped 46 tons of bombs and knocked out 30 locomotives and 108 railroad cars. One plane was lost.

December 6
D-Day +183

The consideration of G-2 was currently that the Germans were primarily concerned with the defense of the Ruhr, although it was believed that the Third Army's possible breakthrough of the Siegfried Line might force a shift of that view, requiring more of the Westphalia Panzer's reserves to be shifted to the south. Enemy reinforcements were considered urgent and certain to appear due to German losses so great that their estimated strength on the Third Army's front had decreased to an equivalent of four-and-one-half divisions, consisting of 35,000 combat troops and 135 tanks or assault guns.

The III Corps moved from its concentration area at Etain to Metz, opening a new command post there.

The 4th Armored Division occupied Singling with its Combat Command "B" while the troops of Combat Command "A" made small advances in the vicinity of Bining. The 104th Infantry of the 26th Infantry Division reached the outskirts of Etting, while the 328th Infantry cleared Sarralbe and the 101st Infantry reached Kulhausen. The 6th Armored Division took Welferding and the 2d Cavalry Group pushed patrols forward to Forbach, Geting, and Emmersweiler.

The Roselle River was crossed at Petite-Roselle by elements of the 11th Infantry (5th Infantry Division), while the 10th Infantry reached Wehrden on the Saar River. In the rear, Fort St. Quentin surrendered to elements of the 5th Infantry Division. The 379th and 378th Infantries (95th Infantry Division) met with savage house-to-house fighting in the town of Saarlautern.

The XIX TAC cut 26 railroad lines and damaged or destroyed 10 locomotives and 126 railroad cars by dropping 535 tons of bombs in 29 sorties. There continued a critical shortage of personal G.I. equipment. Badly need were overshoes, blankets, field jackets, raincoats, sleeping bags, shelter halves, mufflers, meat cans, and canteen cups.

December 7
D-Day +184

Annotated photographs showing the defenses of the Siegfried Line were distributed.

There was no change in the III Corps situation, the 87th Infantry Division not yet being committed in its mission of containing the remaining forts at Metz.

While Combat Command "A" continued fighting at Bining, other elements of the 4th Armored Division were inactive because they were being relieved by the 12th Armored Division of the XV Corps, Seventh Army.

Fort Plappeville, west of Metz, surrendered to the 5th Infantry Division. The 5th Infantry Division also cleared the small towns of Wadgassen, Hostenbach, Wehrden, and Furstenhausen. Small advances were realized by the 379th Infantry of the 95th Division. The 358th Infantry of the 90th Infantry

Division repulsed a heavy counterattack on its bridgehead at Pachten.

Poor weather prevented the XIX TAC from flying.

December 8
D-Day +185

The 87th Infantry Division of III Corps completely relieved the 5th Infantry Division's remaining elements following the surrender of Fort Driant.

On the southern flank of III Corps, the 4th Armored Division continued to be relieved by the 12th Armored Division during the readjustment of the inter-army boundaries.

After a heavy air bombardment used to soften up the Germans, the 26th Infantry Division attacked to the northeast, capturing Achen and entering Wiesviller. The 35th Infantry Division resumed its attack (with the aid of tank destroyers), crossing the Saar River at four different places—one at Sarreguemines and three to the southeast at Remelfing, Zetting, and Dieding.

Task Force Fickett relieved elements of the 5th Infantry Division.

At this point there remained only one holdout at Metz—Fort Jeanne D'Arc continued to resist.

The XIX TAC dropped 73 tons of bombs and 134 tanks of napalm on various military installations during 271 sorties.

December 9
D-Day +186

An additional G-2 survey of enemy rail movements for the period from December 3 to December 9 estimated that the Germans were definitely building up at least six-and-one-half divisions in the Eifel area. In spite of being hampered by inclement weather, air reconnaissance was continued. It appeared that the number of enemy train sections in marshalling yards varied, also indicating much railroad activity.

A report sent from the Third Army G-2 section to SHAEF indicated the probability of the upcoming Ardennes Offensive. The report was ignored. Later, Colonel Oscar Koch would write, "...the situation north of the Moselle demanded special attention," but no special attention would be given until the situation became acute.

Street fighting continued in the Sarreguemines area in the XII Corps zone. German troops hidden in fortified houses and pill-boxes contested the continued advance of the 95th Infantry Division in the Saarlautern bridgehead. Farther north, the 90th Infantry Division met with stiff resistance in the XX Corps area.

The 6th Cavalry Group maintained positions on the southern flank of the XX Corps after relieving the 5th Infantry Division. The 5th then retired to an assembling area just north of St. Avold.

Continuing bad weather did not keep the XIX TAC completely out of the air. They flew fifty-six tactical sorties and five reconnaissance sorties. Limited bombings and strafings of gun positions and a marshalling yard were completed.

A demonstration was conducted to acquaint the XII Corps artillery with the use and characteristics of a new device called the Pozit Fuse. The new Top Secret fuse was a special, automatic device which exploded automatically by magnetic attraction when it came within approximately thirty feet of either the ground or any metal objects. A similar demonstration was carried out for the XX Corps the following day. General Patton mentioned the new device in his private diary referring to it as, "...that funny fuse." Luckily, it would be put into use at the time that it could help the most, assisting greatly in the counterattack against the Germans in their Ardennes Offensive.

New railheads surveyed and cleared for the Third Army use were opened at Lening, Esch, Sarralbe, Mars-la-Tour, Uckange, Audun-le-Tiche, Chambrey, and Morhange.

Two groups of Allied military personnel were discovered in German POW camps. Of 1,138 Russians at Denting, 300 were suffering from tuberculosis and 219 were in dire need of medical and surgical care. At Creutzwald, 110 of 798 prisoners were bed-ridden and 85 percent had nutritional deficiencies. It was much different from the treatment of German soldiers who were in American POW camps. During one inspection, it was discovered by General Patton that the German POWs were being fed almost twice the daily rations that were given to American soldiers. Patton ordered the commanding officer to personally weigh each portion and not to give as much as a fraction of an ounce more to the Germans than was prescribed by the Rules of the Geneva Convention.

December 10
D-Day +187

The III Corps continued to contain Fort Jeanne D'Arc, the last resisting fort at Metz.

In the 26th Infantry Division's area, the 104th Infantry captured Gros Rederching and the 328th Infantry advanced to the north, taking the high ground northeast of Woelfling.

In the 87th Infantry Division, the 346th Infantry was attached to the 26th Infantry Division and the 101st Infantry retired to Metz to conduct an infantry replacement training program.

The 4th Armored, 6th Armored, and 80th Infantry Divisions maintained their positions.

The XIX TAC flew thirty-two sorties. To get to and attack four marshalling yards and twenty locomotives, the pilots had to engage in dogfights which culminated in five confirmed, one probable, and four damaged German aircraft.

The production of extended end connectors (duck feet) reached a peak of about thirty-five hundred daily and many additional tanks appeared on the lines equipped with them.

The Twelfth Army Group advised that the German were camouflaging high-explosive bombs to look like coal. Troops were cautioned to be aware of the situation.

On orders of the Office of Chief Quartermaster, ETO, the number of fresh meat meals for troops was increased from seven to ten per week.

The townspeople of Eft-Hellendorf assembled outside of the military government office during a flag raising ceremony, where they had proclamations read to them concerning their obligations.

December 11
D-Day +188

An operational directive sent to the commanding generals of the III, XII, and XX Corps stated that the Third Army would continue its present mission of advancing northeast within its zone to seize the Mainz-Frankfurt-Darmstadt area and be prepared for further offensive action to the northeast.

The III Corps (now the 26th Infantry Division and supporting troops) was to assume command of the 6th Armored Division, temporary control of the 6th Cavalry Group (mechanized and reinforced), and assume command of the 42nd Infantry Division upon its arrival. The corps was to maintain its current mission of keeping in contact with XII Corps on the south and the XX Corps on the north, and keeping maximum pressure on the Germans within its zone of advance. Upon completion of the refitting of the 26th Infantry Division, the corps was to drive the enemy east of the Saar River and seize and secure a bridgehead across the Saar River.

The XII Corps (35th, 80th, and 87th Infantry Divisions and 4th and 6th Armored Divisions and supporting troops) was directed to pass control of the 6th Armored Division to the III Corps at once and to continue its current mission.

The XX Corps (5th, 90th, and 95th Infantry Divisions, and the 10th Armored Division and supporting troops) was to pass control of the 6th Cavalry Group to the III Corps and continue its current mission.

Bad weather prohibited flying by the XIX TAC.

Under new arrangements, bulk shipments of one thousand tons of supplies were placed on an automatic basis to be shipped to the Third Army directly from the ComZ. No telegram or other type of request was required. Requests for additional gasoline and/or Allied products were placed on a daily telegram basis to be submitted directly to the Verdun depot. Additional gasoline was now received in packaged forms.

December 12
D-Day +189

A report was sent by the Third Army G-2 to SHAEF, repeating the warning of the very great probability of the Germans buildup to the east of the First Army. More than abundant information was contained in the report to support Colonel Koch's views concerning preparation for a major offensive in the Ardennes area.

Fort Jeanne D'Arc, the last remaining strongpoint of the Metz fortresses, surrendered to the 101st Infantry Regiment of the 26th Infantry Division. Effective this date, the 26th Infantry Division was assigned to III Corps.

Elsewhere in the 26th Infantry Division's zone of operations, the 328th Infantry captured the high ground southeast of Obergailbach.

The XIX TAC flew 256 sorties, dropping 88 tons of bombs. Fifteen German planes were shot down and the XIX TAC suffered a loss of 8 planes. Claims included oil storage tanks, ammunition dumps, locomotives, and railroad cars.

Bridgeheads were expanded over the Saar River at Saarlautern and Ensdorf, with crossings accomplished at the Blies River in the Sarreguemines area.

December 13
D-Day +190

Indications from estimates by G-2 were that an operation was in the planning stages that would employ the four divisions of the Germans Sixth Panzer Army as a spearhead in a counteroffensive. The four reconstructed divisions of the Sixth Panzer Army remained west of the Rhine River in the vicinity of Cologne despite the growing threat of the Third Army breakthrough of the Siegfried Line. Another Panzer division was also reported in the vicinity of Cologne in reserve with forces concentrated north of the Moselle River, close to the boundary of the First and Third Armies. It was concluded that the hoarding of the Sixth Panzer Army was an effort to employ this armor in a coordinated effort, making every attempt not to engage them in a piecemeal attack.

A report was sent to SHAEF warning of the continuing buildup of German forces east of 1st Army's VIII Corps area.

At Fort Jeanne D'Arc, the III Corps took a total of 514 prisoners.

In the north, the 35th Infantry Division made another crossing of the Blies River near Bliesbruck, four miles east of Sarreguemines and encountered heavy artillery fire during the operation.

The 4th and 6th Armored Divisions remained inactive.

The 95th Infantry Division made only small gains to the north and east with the 377th and 379th Infantry regiments.

Out of three missions flown by XIX TAC, two were in escort of the IX Bomber Command, and the third was a mission in which a train was attacked, damaging the locomotive, twenty boxcars and cutting the rail line.

Commanding generals of the Ninth U.S. Air Force, the XIX and XII Tactical Air Commands conferred with General Patton and representatives of the Seventh U.S. Army in an effort to coordinate the proposed aerial bombardment of the Siegfried Line, which was in connection with an upcoming attack tentatively planned for December 19. In all, the air attack was to include 500 to 600 medium bombers, 1,200 to 1,500 heavy bombers (supported by fighters), and 600 to 1,000 Royal Air Force bombers. The plan was to be repeated three or four days in succession.

December 14
D-Day +191

Resistance varied from strong to sporadic in the III Corps. Part of the Third Army's zone between XII and XX Corps were assumed by III Corps when it took control of the 26th Infantry, 6th Armored, and 42nd (upon arrival) Infantry Divisions, and Task Force Fickett.

Readjustment between corps boundaries left the XII Corps with the 35th, 80th, and 87th Infantry Divisions and the 4th Armored Division.

The 4th Armored Division was involved with a training and rehabilitation program.

In the 87th Division's zone, the 346th Infantry reached the German border east of Sarreguemines and took Rimling, while the 347th Infantry cleared Obergailbach. In the 35th Infantry Division, the 137th Infantry resisted two counterattacks, advancing a half-mile into the woods north of Habkirchen, while the 134th Infantry gained one mile in the vicinity of Relcheim. On the right flank, the 320th Infantry cleared the town of Nideer-Gailback during a one-mile advance. There were no changes in the 80th Infantry Division's zone.

The Third Army's Psychological Warfare unit broadcast a message to German troops in Blies-Brucken, whereupon twenty-eight German soldiers surrendered.

In the XX Corps area, the 5th, 90th, and 95th Infantry Divisions and the 10th Armored Division (and Task Force Polk) became part of that corps' zone.

The XIX TAC dropped 35 tons of bombs, damaging or destroying 28 motor vehicles, 6 locomotives, and 55 railroad cars. In all, 131 sorties were flown.

Prior to this date, the new Pozit Fuse was used only in bombs dropped by aircraft. The idea was that it was a new device, and as such, all attempts must be made to keep it top secret. It had not been used on artillery shells for fear that an Allied area might be attacked and captured. If that happened, the new device could be stolen by the Germans to be analyzed and copied. Clearance was obtained on this date to release the new fuse in the inner zone of Allied antiaircraft artillery at Saarlautern.

December 15
D-Day +192

Three local counterattacks by the Germans were encountered in the XII Corps area.

XIX TAC flew 144 sorties in mushy weather, attacking an ammunition dump and two supply dumps. Observed from the aircraft were some large explosions, but other than that, the poor visibility disallowed any knowledge of true damage. Also destroyed or damaged were seven locomotives and 52 railroad cars.

By order of General Patton, an additional five percent surcharge of all Army and Corps troops (other than medical and colored personnel) were to be transferred to the III Corps Training Center. The move was designed to provide riflemen reinforcements for infantry divisions. Previously, five percent had been obtained in a similar manner for the 48th Replacement Battalion of III Corps.

A total of 981 Allied POW's were liberated at a camp located near Sarreguemines.

Overshoes remained on the critical supply list, a total of 82,500 pairs in sizes ten and above being needed for initial issue.

Escape hatches for medium tanks became critical and contracts for their manufacture were placed with French firms.

December 16
D-Day +193

The repeated warnings to SHAEF by Patton's G-2 officer, Colonel Koch, were finally borne out. Spearheads of the hoarded Sixth SS Panzer Army opened the Ardennes Offensive in the VIII Corps and VII Corps zones of the First Army.

On the Third Army front, the Germans remained completely defensive in the III Corps area but fought some strong delaying actions in the XII Corps area. The Germans slackened their resistance in the Dillingen bridgehead in the XX Corps zone but continued stiff resistance in the Fraulautern-Ensdorf bridgehead area.

When the Third Army was officially informed of the German offensive against the First Army, Patton fully understood the implications. He had, two days previously, instructed his staff to make a study of the situation and be ready with at least two wholly different plans of operation that could be implemented quickly to alleviate the danger of the Germans push westward. Knowing that he would be asked to assist, he wanted to be ready for the upcoming operation. Only a few days earlier, Patton had noted in his personal diary that, "...the 1st Army is making a terrible mistake in leaving the VIII Corps static, as it is highly probable that the Germans are building up east of them....had the V and VIII Corps been more aggressive, the Germans could not have prepared this attack. One must never sit still."

Air claims by the XIX TAC for the day were 143 motor vehicles, 40 locomotives, and 608 railroad cars damaged or destroyed. They flew 237 sorties in 21 missions.

The Third Army continued to improve its bridgeheads at Saarlautern and Ensdorf while slowly advancing toward the northeast.

December 17
D-Day +194

An analysis prepared for the period of December 15-17 showed that the scale of enemy rail movements remained on the same high level of activity as those covered in previous reports. Tactical reconnaissance reported that a total of 49 trains moved south and west from marshalling yards located directly in the pathway of the First and Third Armies. It was obvious that they were bringing in reinforcements for the enemy thrust in the Ardennes-Eifel area.

It appeared that the counteroffensive was launched against the First Army in an attempt to disrupt the Allied winter drive. Although the Germans had seemingly committed the bulk of their Panzer divisions and infantry reserves to this attack, there remained available to them a group of divisions waiting to exploit any gains made in the Eifel front. Even though the attack against First Army made them vulnerable to southern attack by both the Third Army and Seventh Army, it was a gamble that they were evidently willing to take. They undoubtedbly did not believe that the Third Army could react with the speed that it did.

Attacking to the northeast, the 6th Armored Division in the III Corps area reached the area just south of Lixing. The 26th Infantry Division continued with their regrouping and training in the Metz area.

The XIX TAC flew 356 sorties in 29 missions. They dropped more than 93 tons of bombs on the Germans even though there were numerous dog-fights with the fighterbombers claiming 17 confirmed, 3 probables, and 1 damaged plane. Americans losses were only 9 planes. Among the claims for the day were 207 railroad cars, 12 locomotives, 51 motor vehicles, and 52 gun installations either damaged or destroyed. Nine marshalling yards and 11 towns were attacked.

Experiments were begun using a truck-mounted magnet for the purpose of sweeping shrapnel from highways. In one 5 mile stretch, a total of 125 pounds of shrapnel was removed from a road.

December 18
D-Day +195

To the north of the Third Army, things were becoming critical. The German Ardennes Offensive (which General Bradley thought to be only a spoiling attack) was reaching an acute stage against the First Army's VIII and V Corps. The attack was made by a strong force of German units, initially consisting of about fifteen divisions, in addition to those previously identified in the sector. Generating that attack was the Sixth SS Panzer Army, commanded by General Von Rundstedt, commander of all enemy forces on the Western Front. Penetrations had been made into the zone of VIII Corps and into the 99th Infantry Division's area within V Corps. This penetration had reached about forty miles in depth and thirty miles in width. It ranged from St. Vith to St. Hubert, with flanks anchored in the south at Echternach, Diekirch, and Ettelbrück, and in the north at Monschau, Malmédy, Stavelot, and Marche. From the scant tactical information being received from VIII Corps, the situation was assessed as being very fluid. The combat efficiency of the VIII Corps was an unknown factor.

Patton's plan was that the Germans were to be allowed to advance a distance of about 40-to-50 miles into the Ardennes salient so that the Third Army could advance to the northeast and "...chop them off at the neck." This plan would have allowed the Allies to then encircle the Germans and destroy them entirely. His plan would be negated at the staff meeting to be held on the next day. Eisenhower opted for a safer plan which would simply stop the German's advance and then push them back into their original area of the Moselle without destroying the bulk of their forces. Eisenhower issued orders (through the Twelfth Army Group) that General Patton was to assume command of the VIII Corps south of the enemy breakthrough. He was to attack to the north to halt the German penetration into First Army's zone.

General Patton immediately issued verbal orders that

1. The XII Corps was to relinquish control of its assigned zone to the Seventh Army
2. Control of the 80th Infantry and 4th Armored Divisions (and attached troops) were to go to the III Corps and the 87th Infantry Division was to go to the Seventh Army
3. The III Corps was to relinquish responsibility for their zone to the XX Corps, passing control of the 6th Armored Division and 6th Cavalry Group (reinforced) to XX Corps. They would move the 26th Infantry Division to Arlon and assume control of the 4th Armored Division and the 80th Infantry Division;
4. The XX Corps was ordered to take over the III zone and assume control of the 6th Armored Division and the 6th Cavalry Group (reinforced). The XX Corps was to relieve the 5th Infantry Division and move it to Luxembourg.

The XIX TAC flew only 66 sorties, with several dogfights. In the First Army area the IX TAC and XXIX TAC together shot down thirty-four German aircraft.

Both Military Police and Transportation Sections were confronted with massive, complex troop movement problems. Special officer couriers were dispatched to each M.P. battalion with four troop movement routes. All possible personnel were concentrated on traffic duty. There was a constant flow of traffic during the period of movement, with more than 11,800 vehicles passing over the four routes. The Third Army was able to get through and make its attack as scheduled even though vehicles encountered a landslide, a weakened bridge, enemy bombing and strafing, and several wrecks which caused a number of detours.

In support of the attack, engineers were confronted with an emergency map printing problem. Maps had to be supplied to three corps and thriteen divisions for an area previously north of the Third Army boundary. Units supplied were III, VIII, and XII Corps; 4th, 5th, 26th, 28th, 35th, 80th, and 87th Infantry Divisions; 4th, 6th, 10th, and 11th Armored Divisions; and the 17th and 101st Airborne Divisions. The total amount of maps issued to the Third Army and its Corps during the month weighed fifty-seven tons.

Supply plans had to be revised to support the new tactical operation. Adding to the burden, the VIII Corps was now under the Third Army control and had to be supplied. A complete revamping of ammunition shipments was required, due in part to the responsibility for the supply of VIII Corps. All possible shipments were diverted to the northern flank of the army and every conceivable means of transportation was used to rebuild stocks in the depot nearest the northern front.

A radical revision was necessary for the Third Army's communications system. It involved the removal of a complete network and command post system installed at St. Avold and the moving and reinstallation of that system to headquarters located in Luxembourg. Some circuits were quickly furnished by the initial use of existing facilities of the Twelfth Army Group and the Postes Telephones Telegraphes system.

December 19
D-Day +196

The Germans continued to make progress, penetrating as deeply as Wiltz and completely encircling the town.

In the Third Army, the III Corps began to move the 26th Infantry Division from Metz to an area northeast of Arlon, while the 4th Armored Division and the 80th Infantry Division continued to move to the vicinities around Arlon and Luxembourg respectively.

The XII Corps took over temporary control of the III Corps'

zone in addition to its own. The 87th Infantry Division consolidated its front lines.

Artillery was extensively regrouped to support offensive operations on the northern front. Attached to the III Corps were one field artillery group (two light, three medium, and one heavy battalion) detached from XII Corps and two field artillery groups (one light and one medium battalion) detached from XX Corps. Additionally, one field artillery observation battalion (newly arrived in Europe) was attached to III Corps. On the night of December 19-20, all of them began to move to the assembly area near Villers.

Bad weather grounded the XIX TAC until 1400 hours. When the skies cleared they flew 102 sorties, shot down 10 planes confirmed and 1 probable, and lost 3 of their own planes. They escorted Lancaster bombers over the First Army zone.

December 20
D-Day +197

The Germans launched two counterattacks in the XII Corps area, against the 35th Infantry Division.

Tactical reconnaissance observation indicated heavy vehicular traffic on the XX Corps' northern flank. The Germans resisted in the bridgehead areas with small arms, machine gun, and artillery fire. An average of six hundred artillery rounds an hour fell in the Ensdorf bridgehead.

General Patton formalized his previous verbal orders with a new written directive giving new missions to his corps commanders. In part the directive read

1. First U.S. Army will attack south and restore the front in the Malmédy area and destroy the enemy in zone.
2. Third U.S. Army will change direction and will attack to the north from the area of Luxembourg to Arlon to destroy the enemy on its front and be prepared to change direction to the northeast and seize crossings of the Rhine River.
3. The III Corps will attack north in zone on Army order in the direction of St. Vith and destroy the enemy on its front; and maintain contact with XII Corps on the east and with VIII Corps on the west.

4. The XII Corps will hold the west bank of the Moselle River in zone and on Army order will attack initially north on the right of III Corps and destroy the enemy in zone; will push aggressive patrols to the east and northeast to determine location of crossings of the Sauer River and Our River and the strength of the enemy in Echternach area; will be prepared on army order to change direction of attack to the northeast to force crossings and penetrate the Siegfried Line in zone and to advance in the direction of Bitburg; will maintain contact with XX Corps on the south and the III Corps on the west; will protect the right (east) flank of the Third Army.
5. The VIII Corps will continue defense of zone regroup forces in zone prepared to attack north on army order to destroy enemy in zone and maintain contact with III Corps on the east.
6. The XX Corps will defend Saarlautern bridgehead; hold and defend present front lines; pass to the Seventh Army control of zones now held by 6th Armored Division and 6th Cavalry Group; on relief of 6th Armored Division and 6th Cavalry Group, assemble 6th Armored Division in the area from which it will be prepared to counterattack in any direction in the Third or Seventh Army zones; be prepared to pass control of 6th Cavalry Group to III Corps; maintain contact with XII Corps and the Seventh Army; protect southeast flank of the Third Army.
7. In the attack, all corps will advance in multiple columns; all columns to be composed of tanks and infantry.
8. The III Corps will attack on December 21, XII Corps and VIII Corps will attack on army order.
9. The following air support will be provided for this operation:
A. heavy bombers by Eighth Air Force;
B. medium bombers by Ninth Air Force;
C. seven fighterbomber groups, one tactical reconnaissance group, and one night fighter squadron by XIX Tactical Air Command.

By this date, six new supply points had been set up around Longwy with 235 thousand operational type rations and three hundred thousand gallons of gasoline on hand. Because of the altered tactical situation, the daily receipt and decanting of 1,000 tons of bulk gasoline became too great a problem for the Third Army. Bulk gasoline was shipped to them in quantities of only five hundred tons daily.

A conference was held with Royal Air Force officers concerning improvement of communications. This was necessary to insure that sufficient warning of approaching heavy bomber formations would be given to Allied antiaircraft locations.

Engineers began a study of major roads and bridges in Belgium, Luxembourg, and Germany.

Bad weather prohibited all aerial activity.

In the surrounded city of Bastogne, American soldiers of all ranks were making humorous, timeless statements. One soldier of the 101st Airborne Division said, "So they've got us surrounded, the poor bastards," while Brigadier General Anthony McAuliffe said "Nuts" as the official reply to the German demand for the surrender of the Americans.

December 21
D-Day +198

German advances continued into the VIII Corps area, with penetrations as deep as St. Hubert, and Moircy. They had initially bypassed a small town called Bastogne. Enemy air activity increased suddenly. With 39 German planes attacking the Third Army installations in a series of raids, American antiaircraft units claimed eight planes destroyed and three probably destroyed.

The III Corps, now established in the Arlon vicinity, was prepared to attack on the southern flank of the German salient. In the late afternoon, the attack was launched. The 26th Infantry Division gained three or four miles while the 80th Infantry Division captured Merzig and encircled Ettelbrück. Combat Command "A" gained three miles while Combat Command "B" gained five miles in the 4th Armored Division's zone.

Elements of the 28th Infantry Division continued to hold defensive positions in Sibret, five miles southwest of Bastogne, while the 101st Airborne Division (with attached armored and tank destroyer elements) continued to defend the communications center at Bastogne. The 101st was now completely enveloped by the advancing Germans.

The XII Corps moved its headquarters to Luxembourg and prepared to attack to the north toward the German salient.

Elements of the 95th Infantry Division relieved the 2d Infantry in XX Corps' Saarlautern bridgehead.

Weather, once again, prevented the air support from flying anything except limited missions. One hundred twelve sorties were completed and seventeen tons of bombs were dropped, but results could not be observed. During the night, sixty-five enemy aircraft were reported to be flying over the Third Army headquarters.

All commanders of corps were ordered to take immediate and vigorous action to enforce compliance with tire maintenance standards in order to relieve the critical tire shortage.

The VIII Corps requested supply by airdrops for the 101st Airborne Division at Bastogne.

December 22
D-Day +199

According to G-2 estimates, the most favored capability for the enemy was that they could continue their advance to the west, implementing this drive by attacking to the north and south to expand the shoulders of the Bastogne salient. Other considerations were that the enemy could
1. Commit their reserves
2. Attempt to extend their penetration in depth (while bypassing Bastogne)
3. Launch an attack in the Echternach area in an attempt to endanger the east flank of the Third Army.

German opposition stiffened in the III Corps and several local counterattacks were launched. The Germans continued their efforts to capture Bastogne and reported to be regrouping for a fresh assault.

German air activity increased dramatically, with eighty-nine planes making seventy-eight raids on this date. An attack on a supply point at Mancieulles destroyed one hundred thousand gallons of Allied gasoline. Antiaircraft units claimed that they shot eight German planes out of the cold winter skies.

Detailed information was disseminated to all corps and divisions concerning the operations of German soldiers wearing American uniforms and using American equipment. Unnecessary civilian traffic was cleared from all roads. The provost marshal was directed to use his own discretion to clear any main supply route except for the most essential civilian traffic.

Substantial progress was made in the attack launched by III Corps. In the 4th Armored Division, Combat Command "A" advanced to Martelange, thirteen miles south of Bastogne, where it halted to wait for a bridge to be constructed. Combat Command "B" reached Burdon, ten miles from Bastogne.

In the 26th Infantry Division, the 104th and 328th Infantry Regiments advanced to a position just east of the 4th Armored Division. The 101st Infantry Regiment remained in reserve east of Arlon.

In the 80th Infantry Division, the 319th Infantry reached and cleared Heiderscheid, northwest of Ettelbrück, while the 317th Infantry remained in reserve near Walkergange.

The 101st Airborne Division continued to hold out against the Germans surrounding them at Bastogne.

The XII Corps was prepared to attack heavily in a zone running from Ettelbrück (due north of Luxembourg) to Echternach, and then south to Wormeldange (east of Luxembourg).

The 90th Infantry Division completed its withdrawal to the west bank of the Saar River in the XX Corps area while the 377th and 379th Infantry Regiments of the 95th Infantry Division maintained their bridgehead areas across the Saar River at Saarlautern.

A total of 558 sorties were flown by XIX TAC, during which they dropped 157 tons of high explosive bombs (plus large quantities of napalm) on the Germans positions. Twenty-two confirmed and one probable enemy planes were shot down. A majority of the flights were made in the First Army area and over Trier, a city used by the Germans as a jumping off place for their offensive. Patton said he could have captured Trier had not General Bradley gone back on his word and taken the 83d Infantry Division from him at a critical time. Among claims made by XIX TAC were 412 motor vehicles, 26 gun installations, 56 railroad cars, and various other targets.

The command strength of the XIX TAC was increased from four to nine fighterbomber groups in view of the increased need for assistance against the enemy breakthrough.

The Third Army continued its attacks north with III and XII Corps toward Bastogne and St. Vith and northeast in the area around Echternach, while VIII Corps defended the area from Neufchâteau to Recogne, to Bastogne. To the immediate southeast, XX Corps maintained its position.

December 23
D-Day +200

Clear weather arrived, aiding tremendously in halting the German Ardennes Offensive. General Patton attributed the good weather to the prayer that he had requested from the Third Army Chaplain Colonel James O'Neill.

The Germans continued their heavy pressure on Bastogne, but at the same time showed anxious concern over the pressure being exerted on them by the southern advance of the III Corps. In the Trier-Merzig area, enemy activity increased, with heavy night attacks being launched. The 4th Armored Division met with stiff resistance at Chaumont and the 26th Infantry Division met head-on with stubborn resistance in the III Corps zone. More than one hundred German planes bombed and strafed installations in the Third Army's area. Antiaircraft shot down sixteen of them and claimed six more as probables.

The 80th Infantry Division captured Tadler, southeast of Bastogne, while to the west the 26th Infantry Division advanced about four miles, keeping its 328th and 104th Infantry Regiments abreast during the drive and keeping its 101st Infantry Division in reserve. On the corps' west flank, the 4th Armored attacked directly north toward Bastogne, capturing

Hanville and Warnach. The 4th Reserve Combat Command captured Bigonville.

The VIII Corps continued its mission, defending from Neufchateau to Bastogne.

Another successful day was completed by the XIX TAC. They flew 493 sorties, shooting down 23 confirmed and 4 probable enemy aircraft while losing only 11 of their own. They dropped 54 tons of high explosive bombs and expended the largest amount of fragmentary bombs and napalm of any day of the month. Among their claims were 26 tanks and armored vehicles, 250 motor vehicles, and 36 gun positions.

Thirty-two tactical reconnaissance missions were scheduled to cover the entire battle area.

One hundred and sixty-one plane loads of supplies were dropped to the 101st Airborne Division's troops surrounded in Bastogne. Two hundred fifty additional planes were waiting for good weather in order to leave England on the same type of mission.

The Military Police became a primary force in the maintenance of security and the apprehension of suspected spies and saboteurs, especially in the form of German soldiers in American uniforms (an action which requires an immediate death penalty). To meet this need, an emergency issue of twelve hundred fragmentation hand grenades was ordered for the Military Police.

Experiments with a submarine bolt driving gun showed highly satisfactory results for sealing the doors of pillboxes and 20 were procured from the British Royal Navy for Third Army use.

December 24
D-Day +201

"Order of Battle" facts concerning the German's capabilities indicated that while they had so far committed 9 Panzer divisions and 14 infantry divisions during the Ardennes Offensive, they still possessed strong reserves and the necessary means for transportation of them. It was considered that the enemy was capable of redisposing their forces and reinforcing them in an effort to regain lost momentum or in order to launch another powerful attack in the areas from either Echternach or Trier-Merzig. It was estimated that the forces opposing the Third Army totaled 88,500 troops, with 63,000 troops against the First Army.

The Germans resisted stubbornly in both Heiderscheid and Kehman (both in the III Corps area). In addition, the Germans continued a buildup of forces in the VIII Corps area around St. Hubert. When the Germans withdrew to the north bank of the Sauer River, they offered only spotty resistance in the XII Corps area, with very little action in the XX Corps zone.

Strafing and bombing by the Germans increased. Out of 143 German aircraft making 94 raids on the Third Army, antiaircraft fire shot down 17 and claimed 6 as damaged.

In the 26th Infantry Division, the 328th Infantry advanced to Eschdorf and Arsdorf with leading elements of the 317th and 319th Infantries making their way eight miles northwest of Diekirch. The 318th Infantry made their advance to a point near Tintange. The 4th Armored Division's units advanced to positions near a point four miles from Bastogne.

In the VIII Corps area, there was little change. The 101st Airborne Division kept up their defense of Bastogne, keeping open the vital communications center there.

The advance continued in the VII Corps area. The 11th Infantry of the 5th Infantry Division made its way six miles west of Echternach, and the 10th Armored Division's Combat Command "A" captured Mostroff. The 35th Infantry Division completed refitting at Metz and prepared to move north to assume a frontal position.

In the XX Corps area, the 90th and 95th Infantry Divisions maintained their positions, holding their bridgeheads in the Saarlautern area while the 6th Armored Division closed together at Metz for refitting. The Seventh Army took over the responsibility for the positions vacated by the 6th Armored and 103d Infantry Divisions.

The fighterbombers of the XIX TAC flew 652 sorties, killing 19 Germans planes confirmed and 2 probables. Additionally, they claimed a total of 558 motor vehicles, 117 tanks and armored vehicles, and 115 railroad cars either damaged or destroyed. They cut 15 railroad lines and attacked 12 troop concentrations. They lost 13 planes and 11 pilots.

A request was made for 1,200 gallons of white paint and an equal amount of paint thinner to be used for painting helmets, raincoats, and leggings for snow camouflage. In a measure to rectify the immediate need for snow tunics, a total of 2,185 yards of white cloth were requisitioned from local French civilian sources. The yardage was delivered to a salvage repair company where the personnel completed 700 tunics in a single day.

The engineers had the prime responsibility for camouflaging vehicles and tents. Pattern painting of vehicles and tents was accomplished by the use of the residue from the manufacture of acetylene gas (a lime-like substance found in dump piles in a dry state) which was mixed with water and then applied with brushes. In the days of Tom Sawyer, this mixture was called white wash. The white coat provided was harmless to metal or canvas.

December 25
D-Day +202

There was no alteration in G-2's estimation of enemy capabilities.

There was bitter and vicious fighting throughout the III Corps zone as the Germans made a last ditch attempt to prevent further encroachment on the southern flank of his penetration into the First Army's zone. It was believed that the Germans were planning a concentrated attack along the Sure River. At Bastogne, Von Rundstedt's forces launched two heavy attacks in an effort to capture the communications center there. The Germans also maintained an aggressive defense and improved positions north of the Sauer River in the XII Corps area. In raids by German aircraft, eleven were destroyed out of 103 planes and 11 more were claimed by antiaircraft fire as probables.

The 26th Infantry Division drove north, taking Eschdorf, while the 80th Infantry Division captured Ringel. The 4th

Armored Division pushed slowly against stubborn resistance, with Combat Command "A" capturing Tintange and Combat Command "B" capturing Remichampagne, Chaumont, and Hollange.

The 101st Airborne Division continued to repulse the heavy attacks by the Germans.

Support by elements of the 10th Armored Division continued in conjunction with the 5th Infantry Division. They cleared Echternach, Haller, and Walbillig, and encircled Befort.

The 4th Infantry Division prepared to readjust its position, continuing to assemble and reorganize its troops while the 35th Infantry Division moved from Metz to take positions on the front lines.

In the XX Corps, the 90th and 95th Infantry Divisions patrolled aggressively while the 6th Armored Division prepared to move to the XII Corps zone to relieve the 10th Armored Division.

The XIX TAC flew 599 sorties in a day of heavy activity. They had kills on 756 motor vehicles and 74 tanks and armored vehicles.

A Third Army surgeon volunteered to be flown into Bastogne in an L-5 plane, taking with him a basic surgical instrument set and medical supplies, including whole blood, penicillin, plasma, morphine, and dressings.

Every available means was being used by the Germans to disrupt the supply and communications of the Third Army units. A delay in the delivery of supplies to the III Corps was caused by sabotage on the rail line between Longy and Arlon.

December 26
D-Day +203

Hampered by snow, ice, bitter cold, and attacks on both flanks by the Germans, the 4th Armored Division made contact with the garrison at Bastogne. The Germans also failed to prevent the arrival of reinforcements for the defense of Bastogne. The actual contact was made at Assenois, two miles south of Bastogne, by elements of Combat Command "B."

The 4th Armored Division then established a supply line to Bastogne, assuring that the town was longer isolated.

In the western portion of the German salient, Panzer spearheads swung northwest, with a large enemy buildup in the Rochefort-March-Hotton area. Tactical reconnaissance indicated a considerable decrease in enemy vehicular traffic during daylight hours in the Bastogne area. The XIX TAC had inflicted very high vehicular and supply losses on the Germans and they were taking cover.

General Patton issued Amendment No. 1 to the Commanding Generals of III, XII and XX Corps, dated December 21, formalizing the verbal orders that he had issued previously. The amendment provided that

1. The III Corps would pass control of the 80th Infantry Division to XII Corps effective 2000 hours on December 26
2. The XII Corps was to assume control of the 80th Infantry Division and to move Combat Command "A" of the 9th Armored Division to III Corps area immediately
3. The XII Corps was to pass the 35th Infantry Division control to III Corps and the 10th Armored Division control to XX Corps
4. The XX Corps was to pass control of the 6th Armored Division to XII Corps, assume control of the 10th Armored Division, and move the 35th Infantry Division to III Corps.

The XIX TAC had another busy day, with 558 sorties in 59 missions. They dropped 157 tons of bombs, and escorted medium and heavy bombers. They destroyed or damaged 412 motor vehicles, 34 armored vehicles and tanks, 26 gun positions, 61 buildings, 2 bridges, 2 supply dumps, and 83 stacks of ammunition. They also hit 3 marshalling yards and 14 rail lines. While the XIX TAC lost 15 planes, they killed 22 German planes with 1 probable and 11 damaged.

Two surgical teams with three days' medical supplies were flown into Bastogne by glider.

December 27
D-Day +204

The Germans began to shift their armor into the northwest portion of their salient. This action actually assisted the Allies in their attack. By lengthening their tenuous supply lines, the Germans made it easier for the XIX TAC and the Third Army to seriously impair their supply situation. Many German vehicles with little or no gasoline were captured in Celles.

The Germans were repulsed in their attempt to regain the high ground they had lost north of Ringel. In the XII Corps, they were cleared out of the area around Eppeldorf and Echternach. The German air activity dropped sharply, with only seventy-four planes making thirty-five raids on the Third Army. The Third Army antiaircraft claimed three of these destroyed and eight probables.

The 26th Infantry Division continued their forward advance, capturing Kaundorf, Mecher-Dunkrodt, and Bavigne, while the 35th Infantry Division captured Surre, Boulaide, and Baschleiden. The 4th Armored Division conducted mopping up operations to the south and southwest of Bastogne, with Combat Command "A" capturing Sibret; Combat Command "B" capturing Hompre and Salvacourt; and Reserve Combat Command entering Bastogne.

The XIX TAC flew 544 sorties in 57 missions. Claims for the day were 434 motor vehicles, 97 tanks and armored vehicles, 336 railroad cars, 15 locomotives, 3 bridges, 42 gun installations, and 11 supply dumps either destroyed or damaged.

Additional snow camouflage became increasingly necessary. Requests were made to ComZ for an additional twelve hundred gallons of both paint and thinner and for fifty thousand yards of white muslin and fifty-thousand snow suits. ComZ replied that no white cloth was available, but suggested the possible use of five thousand mattress covers, from which 10,000 suits could be made. Arrangements were made to deliver the mattress covers from the depot at Reims.

A total of 652 patients were evacuated from Bastogne.

Military government personnel to the south evacuated more than three thousand German civilians from Saarlautern and Wallerfangen, and approximately twenty-five hundred other scattered villagers of the Saar River area. They were moved into concentration areas to the rear of regimental lines both for security reasons and to simplify control problems.

December 28
D-Day +205

The Germans made two desperate attacks against Bastogne in an attempt to prevent the further widening of the corridor punched through by the 4th Armored Division. Tactical reconnaissance indicated considerable enemy movement headed east toward the Bastogne corridor. The Germans unsuccessfully attempted to recapture Ringel, and their air activity came to a virtual standstill. After suffering heavy losses, they sent over only eight sorties against the Third Army.

The 26th Infantry Division captured Nothum and rapidly approached the Wiltz River.

The 17th Airborne Division assumed defense of the Meuse River, while the 28th Infantry Division regrouped in the VIII Corps.

The 4th Infantry Division maintained its positions along the Moselle River in the XII Corps area, while limited advances were made by the 80th Infantry Division to the Sure and Sauer Rivers.

The 90th and 95th Infantry Divisions, along with the 10th Armored Division, continued organization and defensive improvements in the XX Corps area.

Despite unfavorable weather, the XIX TAC managed to make 196 sorties, dropping 62 tons of bombs on the German forces. Special attention was given to rolling stock, with 56 locomotives and 325 railroad cars being destroyed or damaged. Rail lines were cut in 3 places and 2 large oil tanks were destroyed. There was no enemy air activity in the Third Army's area of operations.

There was an increasing emphasis on the Third Army security, due to a report that there existed special German assassin squads wearing U.S. Army uniforms whose missions were to kill the top Allied generals.

The possibility of using carrier pigeons as a return means of communication was investigated.

December 29
D-Day +206

Determined enemy resistance continued in the III Corps area, with enemy tank and troop concentrations observed by tactical reconnaissance in the Houffalize-Noville area.

The Third Army antiaircraft shot down ten of eighty-eight Germans planes during a raid.

Marvie was captured by the 101st Airborne Division, which had reverted to the III Corps control.

The 87th Infantry Division closed in the VIII Corps area, while the 11th Armored Division assumed positions on the front northeast of Neufchâteau.

Little activity was noted in the XII Corps area.

The XX Corps maintained both its patrols and positions along the Saar River.

The XIX TAC flew, but found many fewer targets than at anytime since the initial German penetration. They did find and destroy a V-1 launching site at Dierfeld and lost six planes and five pilots during the day.

The normal handling of American dead was hampered by the receipt of German soldier's bodies. They not only wore American uniforms, but also had American identification tags. In cases where identity could not be established by normal methods, photographs were taken as an additional aid to identification.

A salvage repair company received five thousand mattress covers and immediately began the manufacture of snow camouflage suits.

December 30
D-Day +207

While continuing to build up forces on the east flank of Bastogne, the Germans launched an attack with an estimated two battalions of infantry and forty tanks, where they successfully attacked and recaptured Lutrebois. Other attacks against the Third Army were unsuccessful.

The 26th Infantry Division continued its slow advance while the 35th Infantry Division, assisted by the 4th Armored Division, repulsed a counterattack between Marvie and Villers.

The 11th Armored Division in the VIII Corps area advanced to Remange, and the 10th Infantry Regiment of the 5th Infantry Division captured Riesdorf, seven miles northwest of Echternach in the XII zone.

The 379th Infantry Regiment of the 95th Infantry Division obtained their limited objective by seizing a bridgehead in the Saarlautern area.

The XIX TAC flew 92 sorties, making claims on 165 motor vehicles, 62 tanks and armored vehicles, 22 locomotives, and 468 railroad cars.

A new system was placed into effect by the Military Police for handling absent-without-leave personnel (AWOL). Each Military Police battalion maintained a collecting center through which AWOLs were returned under guard to corps units. AWOLs from Third Army units were held for these unit guards, while AWOLs from other armies, the Army Air Force, and from ComZ units were cleared through the AWOL collecting center to the ComZ AWOL center. This system was expected to be more efficient than the former method of handling AWOLs through replacement channels, which frequently permitted the offender to renew his absence without leave before he could be returned to his unit for disciplinary action.

December 31
D-Day +208

In one week, during which the enemy plan of attack appeared to undergo radical revision due to the Third Army's smashing counteroffensive, the following significant Order of Battle facts were highly visible

1. The Germans had all of their armor in action, all of the original Panzer reserve in the west being either committed or dis-

posed close to the battle area. To meet the pressure caused by the Third Army, the German resorted to his well known shuttle system, moving Panzers from inactive areas to the fiercely contested Bastogne area

2. German infantry reinforcements were far below estimated capability of six to eight divisions a week

3. Several new Volksgrenadier divisions committed to battle proved to be third-rate troops.

These facts indicated that the enemy faced the alternative of either breaking out of the Ardennes salient or retiring behind the Siegfried Line. In the words of General Patton, the Germans had, "...shot their wad."

In the III Corps, the towns of Wardin, Neffe, and Lutrebois were captured—Lutrebois being taken for the second time.

In the VIII Corps area, the 11th Armored Division captured Houmont and Chenogne, while the 87th Infantry fought against extremely heavy resistance from Moircy to St. Hubert.

To the south, the 95th Infantry Division took two more city blocks in the Saarlautern bridgehead area.

XIX TAC flew 296 sorties and dropped 128 tons of high explosive bombs, claiming 125 motor vehicles, 68 railroad cars, 4 bridges and 17 buildings. Also attacked were 9 marshalling yards, with 17 railroad lines being cut. No losses were sustained by the XIX TAC.

During the operations to relieve Bastogne to date, 35 battalions of field artillery participated in the establishment of the solid contact with the Bastogne forces. Beginning on December 22, these battalions expended a total of 94,230 rounds of ammunition.

CHAPTER 6

January, 1945

The month of January would involve the Germans desperate attempts to stop the Third Army's rapid northward advance from the Bastogne area and their undertaking of a costly withdrawal into the Siegfried Line. By the end of January, the gamble of the Ardennes Offensive would prove to be the complete undoing of the German forces. They would be driven back to their original starting point of the blitzkrieg to hide behind their lines of defense.

January 1
D-Day +209

The Germans continued to reinforce at Bastogne, sensing that failure to complete their mission would doom them to complete failure for future capabilities.

G-2 estimates from the Third Army indicated that the Germans could

1. Attack the shoulders and/or the base of the Bastogne wedge
2. Attack in force along the entire perimeter of the wedge
3. Implementing the first two capabilities and attack to the south at the western portion of the Third Army's wedge.

The German Luftwaffe reached its operational peak, with 308 hostile aircraft attacking the Third Army units. At Metz, 25 planes made diving attacks, strafing parked P-47s, destroying twenty and damaging 17. Sixteen of the enemy aircraft were shot down by antiaircraft artillery. Although the Ger-

mans attacked and damaged some Third Army supply installations and field artillery positions, they paid for it with 63 of
their planes.

There was no change in the XX Corps area.

Beginning with 69 divisional and corps artillery battalions,
and growing to 77 battalions later, the Third Army expended
the largest volume of artillery fire in its history. For the next
week, these battalions would fire a total of 401,393 rounds of
ammunition.

Despite some shortages, such as overshoes, mess gear, and
shelter halves, the supply system was generally considered
satisfactory. Gasoline was arriving in substantial quantities.

The Third Army's strength to date was 353,655 troops; in
addition were 25,336 troops of Advance Section ComZ; 37,033
of the Ninth Air Force, 2,271 of the French, and 2,344 miscellaneous troops in or near the army area. The total—420,639
troops—had to be supplied with rations.

The XX Corps continued to maintain their lines and train
troops.

The XIX TAC flew 469 sorties in excellent weather. They
accounted for destroying or damaging 195 motor vehicles,
274 railroad cars, and 42 tanks and armored vehicles. Photographs indicating routes available to the Germans for their
expected withdrawal from Bastogne were forwarded to command headquarters by Photo Reconnaissance.

January 2
D-Day +210

An attack coordinated between the 26th and 35th Infantry
Divisions continued, but little was gained.

Senonchamps and the high ground north of the town were
taken by Combat Command "A" of the 9th Armored Division,
while Mande St. Etienne was captured by Combat Command
"B."

The situation remained unaltered in the XII Corps area.

In the XX Corps area, the Germans were cleared from an
area west of a junction of the Roselle and Saar Rivers near

Volklingen and Werbeln. The XIX units rotated and maintained the Saarlautern bridgehead.

The XIX TAC flew 407 sorties in 42 missions. They shot down 5 German planes (losing seven of their own) and claimed damage or destruction of 55 armored vehicles and tanks, 180 motor vehicles, 323 railroad cars, and 12 locomotives.

A shortage of "K" rations was alleviated by the receipt of 439,200 rations at the Verdun depot, with emergency shipments then being transported to individual units. Fresh meat and butter were in short supply.

A total of twnty-seven improved, mechanized flamethrowers were designed and manufactured specially for mounting on medium tanks.

January 3
D-Day +211

G-2's estimation of German strength on the Third Army's front was 93,000 troops, the equivalent of 12 divisions, and 290 tanks or assault guns. On the basis of prisoner-of-war statements, it was considered that the Germans still had a powerful striking force capable of employment against the Third Army. The shuttling of a Volksgrenadier division from the Seventh Army front to the Third Army front indicated that the Germans were having difficulty in producing infantry to replace the heavy losses sustained in their December offensive against the Third Army.

Only one German plane appeared in the sky over the Third Army units.

The 26th and 35th Infantry Divisions gained positions to attack around the town of Berle, while the 6th Armored Division was making only slow progress against bitter resistance.

The 101st Airborne Division succeeded in repulsing a strong counterattack by both tanks and infantry at Longchamps, about three miles north of Bastogne.

The 17th Airborne Division relieved the 11th Armored Division, with the 11th Armored Division assembled northeast of

Neufchâteau, and the 28th Infantry Division assumed command of the sector around the Meuse River.

The 4th, 5th, and 80th Infantry Divisions of the XII Corps continued their active patrolling, with no change in front line positions.

In the XX Corps area, the 90th and 95th Infantry Divisions made some small local gains, while the 10th Armored Division continued its program of rehabilitation and troop training activity.

Poor flying weather prohibited any activity by the XIX TAC.

The supply of coal became critical due to the increased consumption caused by the uncommonly cold winter conditions. Advance Section of ComZ was informed that the army needed fifteen thousand tons of coal during January and that the twenty-five hundred tons that was scheduled for delivery from January 7 to January 14 should be increased to four thousand tons.

January 4
D-Day +212

G-2 interpreted the failure of the Germans to build up their offensive power in the Third Army salient with the reinforcements believed available to them as an overall assumption of a defensive attitude.

Letter of Instruction No. 12 from Twelfth Army Group stated that the Third Army would continue their attack to the northeast to seize Houffalize and bring into effect a junction with the First Army in the Houffalize area. Additionally, they were to destroy the Germans trapped in the Third Army's zone of operation; continue the attack toward St. Vith; protect the right flank of the First Army; and lastly continue to defend the line of the Saar, Moselle, and Sauer Rivers.

A special request was received in Third Army headquarters by the Germans in the VIII Corps area. They asked that the VIII Corps artillery cease firing on an important crossroad which was located near an enemy hospital. After a thorough investigation, General Patton decided to hold his fire in that sector. To insure the validity of the situation, he sent officers through the enemy lines to ascertain that these roads were being used exclusively for hospital traffic. It was a fine example of civilized warfare.

The XIX TAC were again grounded by adverse weather conditions.

The Third Army released necessary materials to be used for repairs to the Sixteenth-century walls of the University of Pont-à-Mousson. The French had reported that the university had been wantonly fired upon by the Germans during the fighting in September.

January 5
D-Day +213

The Germans continued their attempts at counterattacks against the Third Army's VIII Corps, also using intense artillery fire and infiltration tactics against the III Corps front.

The 26th Infantry Division in III Corps continued to reorganize and strengthen its positions while the 35th Infantry Division fought against enemy pressure, clearing the town of Lutrebois. The 6th Armored Division (on the corps' west flank) consolidated its front after joining flanks with both the 101st Airborne Division and the 35th Infantry Division.

In the VIII Corps area, the 101st Airborne Division continued with its defense of Bastogne while the 17th Airborne Division was being strongly counterattacked.

The situation remained relatively unchanged in the XII Corps area with the exception of the 5th Infantry Division, which relieved elements of the 80th Infantry Division east of the Alzette River, allowing the 80th Infantry to launch an attack to the north, securing a bridgehead across the Sure River.

There was little change in the XX Corps area.

The XIX TAC flew 191 sorties, directed primarily at marshalling yards and enemy airfields. They did manage to hit 127 railroad cars during operations.

A directive issued to hospital units instructed that evacuation and/or transfer of patients must be coordinated to insure proper meals for them. Provided that their condition warranted it, incoming patients were to be given a hot meal no matter at what hour they were received. This directive also applied to the feeding of ambulance drivers.

January 6
D-Day +214

The favored capability considered by the Third Army's G-2 Section was that the Germans would pull out of the western portion of the salient to assume a defensive position on the more favorable ground extending northeast from Houffalize to St. Vith. Due to this consideration, it was suggested that the Third Army advance to the northeast and/or east. Enemy air activity continued to be very light, with only four planes reported over the entire Third Army area.

Activity on the III Corps Front lessened somewhat, allowing the 26th Infantry Division to consolidate its positions. The 35th Infantry continued to push their attack in the northwest part of its zone, and there was no change in the position of the 6th Armored Division.

In the VIII Corps area, the 101st Airborne Division continued their defense of Bastogne, the 17th Airborne Division strengthened its positions, and there was no change in the lines of the 11th Armored Division. The 87th Infantry Division cleared Tillet, eight miles west of Bastogne, and the 28th Infantry Division patrolled along the Meuse River sector.

In the XII Corps, the towns of Goesdorf and Dahl were captured and elements of the division neared positions short of Nocher. A tank destroyer battalion knocked out two enemy tanks in a night attack by first illuminating the tanks with 60mm mortar flares and then opening fire on them.

The 90th Infantry Division was relieved of assignment with the XX Corps and moved control to III Corps, while the 94th Infantry Division was assigned to the Third Army in relief of the 90th Infantry Division.

The XIX TAC was socked in.

The Third Army headquarters was visited by Paul V. McNutt, chairman of the War Manpower Commission, and Maury Maverick, vice chairman for labor production. They were given a tour of army supply installations in the area of Nancy.

The Twelfth Army Group indicated that the Third Army was to receive about thirty-five percent of cold weather clothing available in the ETO. These items included shoe packs, socks, ponchos, mittens, and mufflers.

January 7
D-Day +215

Significant order of battle facts indicated that the enemy had abandoned further offensive operations in the Ardennes salient, screening their withdrawal of armor and infantry by use of local diversionary attacks.

On the III Corps' eastern flank, the 26th Infantry Division patrolled to the Wiltz River and improved its positions. The 35th Infantry Division held its front against some heavy counterattacking and relieved some of its elements. The 6th Armored Division, on the western flank, improved its positions while fighting off some small counterattacks.

In the VIII Corps, fighting was heavier to the north and west of Bastogne. Although the 101st Airborne Division had no change in its front, the 17th Airborne Division managed to advance about two miles along its front. The 513th Infantry Regiment of the 17th Airborne Division captured Flamierge, six miles northwest of Bastogne. The 87th Infantry Division continued its attack at Tillet while the 26th Infantry Division continued its defense of the Meuse River sector.

The 80th Infantry Division gained some limited objectives east of Goesdorf, consolidating its positions around the town of Dahl. Elsewhere in the XII Corps, there was little change.

In the XX Corps, the 94th Infantry Division completed its relief of the 90th Infantry Division.

The XIX TAC could fly neither their fighters nor bombers due to poor weather.

A definite policy was established by Third Army headquarters, concerning the handling of Allied nationals who had collaborated with or served with the Germans. When captured, these persons were to be handled and processed as

143

POWs. The disposition of exceptional cases was to be made by the army provost marshal in accordance with instructions from higher headquarters. Combat commanders were not authorized to accept the parole of French, Belgian, Netherlands, nor Luxembourg nationals who had served with German forces.

The rear echelon of the Third Army Headquarters began a move to Esch.

Civil Affairs Section issued intelligence reports citing many cases of looting of food, horses, cattle, blankets, clothing, and other civilian property by German troops who had participated in the Ardennes Offensive.

January 8
D-Day +216

An operational directive confirming previous verbal orders was issued by General Patton. In part the orders stated that

1. The 94th Infantry Division was assigned to the XX Corps
2. The III Corps was to assume control of the 90th Infantry Division, pass control of the 4th Armored Division, and to attack on January 9 to the southeast of Bastogne
3. The VIII was to seize Noville and Houffalize or to continue to the northeast in the direction of St. Vith and to maintain contact with the First Army;
4. The VIII Corps was to continue defense of the Meuse River line, assume control of the 4th Armored Division, and attack on January 9 to capture Noville and high ground around Houffalize
5. The XII Corps was ordered to continue its mission of clearing the Germans west of the Moselle andSaur Rivers and to attack north on Army order
6. The XX Corps was ordered to continue its present mission. There was no alteration in corps' boundaries.

Attacks were launched on schedule at 1000 hours on January 9. In accordance with orders from SHAEF, the 9th Armored Division and the 28th Infantry Divisions were assigned to XV Army and places in SHAEF's reserve.

Another day of overcast and cloudy skies prohibited air activity.

The railhead located at Audun-le-Roman continued to be the principle ammunition supply source for the Third Army units. Point Number 38 at Mamer served both III and XII Corps. Point Number 39 at Mellier served VIII Corps.

Reconnaissance was completed, stockage planned, and ammunition diverted by rail to the area of Bastogne in order to establish a new point for the support of VIII Corps.

January 9
D-Day +217

G-2 issued a report stating that, "While the enemy's overall defensive attitude increased and indications of a retrograde movement continued in the western projection of his salient, there was still no conclusive evidence of a general withdrawal. It was indicated that the enemy was pursuing his familiar policy of selling space for time at as high a cost as possible." The possibility of an enemy thrust toward Luxembourg and Metz was given serious consideration.

The advance begun by III Corps at 091000 (1000 hours, January 9) and was supported by all of the corps artillery. The 26th Infantry Division reached and captured high ground overlooking the town of Wiltz, while the 90th Infantry Division moved forward to attack and capture Berle and Trentelhof. The 35th Infantry Division made small advance in its divisional left flank and maintained contact with the 6th Armored Division between Marvie and Lutrebois.

The 101st Airborne Division in the VIII Corps advanced two miles and captured Recogne, northeast of Noville. The 17th Airborne Division maintained contact with the 101st, while the 87th Infantry Division attacked around Tillet. The 4th and 11th Armored Divisions made slight gains, keeping prepared to attack in any direction, wherever it might be needed the most.

No change in XII Corps.

The Twelfth Army Group informed the Third Army that a directive from SHAEF indicated that the Third Army might be forced to hold back its attack on the Bastogne area and divert divisions to the Moselle River area, southeast of Luxembourg, to meet a possible attack by the Germans at that point. In General Patton's opinion it was another case of the higher command seeing phantom devils where none existed.

Although weather was bad, the XIX TAC managed to send out twenty-four sorties in escort of bomber missions.

A special shipment of winter clothing totaling seven hundred tons waited for the Third Army at Le Harve. General Lee of ComZ requested that the Third Army use its own trucks to go to the harbor to pick up the supplies. Unfortunately, the Third Army trucks were being used to fight a war, while the trucks in ComZ were being used to move office equipment and typewriters to more plush surroundings.

January 10
D-Day +218

G-2 estimates indicated the belief that German effective strength at the front of the Third Army's lines was 74,000 troops, the equivalent of about 9 divisions, and about 220 tanks or assault guns. This estimate represented a decrease of 19,000 troops and 20 tanks/assault guns in one week's time. While the Germans did succeed in maintaining a flow of infantry replacements, the indications were that these covered only a partial amount of the heavy losses that they had sustained.

Small advances were experienced by almost all units within the III Corps area, even against heavy German artillery reaction. The 6th Cavalry Group, flanked by both the 90th and 35th Infantry Divisions, captured Betlange, Watrange, and Harlange and then proceeded toward Tarchamps. The 35th Infantry Division captured Villers-le-Bonne-Eau and Lutremange. Although the 6th Armored Division made no advance, it furnished fire support for the 35th Infantry Division's advance.

In the VIII Corps, the 87th Infantry Division cleared Tillet and Bonnerue using a heavy smoke screen laid by supporting artillery.

In the XII Corps' area (while the 4th, 5th, and 80th Infantry

Divisions patrolled), the 2d Cavalry Group captured Machtum.

Good weather allowed the XIX TAC to fly. During operations totaling 325 sorties, 182 tons of general-purpose bombs were dropped on the poor old krauts. In the day's operations, either damaged or destroyed were 246 motor vehicles, 14 tanks or armored vehicles, 145 railroad cars, and 4 bridges.

A train wreck occurred at Messancy, destroying all but thirteen out of forty-four railroad cars loaded with ammunition destined for Supply Point Number 39. Most of the ammunition either exploded or burned. Two full days of a round-the-clock work by both a platoon of a truck company and an ammunition company were required to salvage the maximum amount of ammunition.

Conservation measures were initiated and supply discipline emphasized at hospital units due to a critical shortage of both blankets and litters.

Plans for increased production and supply of camouflage snow suits were completed. Manufacturing facilities had been located which had an estimated capacity of ten thousand suits per week. Completed suits for use by the Third Army troops were expected to also come from ComZ.

A total of 1,806 displaced persons were in camps in the Third Army's zone of operations.

January 11
D-Day +219

With the Germans definitely on the defensive, the Third Army's G-2 Section considered it highly likely that they had completely written off the Ardennes Offensive. Also, it was considered that the Germans would defend and delay while preparing to regain the initiative by an assault in a different sector. Reports persisted that the enemy was preparing for an offensive in the Saarlautern-Saarbrücken area.

In the III Corps, the 90th Infantry Division captured Doncols and Sonlez against heavy artillery concentrations, while the 35th Infantry Division (in conjunction with Task Force

Fickett) captured Lutremange and advanced over one mile against little resistance.

The 101st and 17th Airborne Divisions prepared for an attack and consolidated their positions in the VIII Corps area. The 87th Infantry Division continued its attack on the western end of the Ardennes Bulge, capturing Vesqueville and St. Hubert.

There was no air activity by XIX TAC.

The 8th and 9th Armored Divisions were attached to the Third Army, but only for the purposes of supply and administration. As usual, the Third Army was not being given the authority to fight a war of movement.

Approximately 500,000 troops were being supplied with rations by the Third Army. Included in this total were 367,700 Third Army troops; 31,562 ComZ troops; 42,198 Ninth Air Force troops; 3,066 French troops; and 3,233 miscellaneous troops (including an estimated 52,171 POWs, civilian laborers, casuals, and attachments).

Patton informed his corps' commanding generals that the supply of "K" Rations was critical over the whole of the ETO and that this type of ration should be supplied only to combat troops.

Civil Affairs arranged for an emergency shipment of eight hundred tons of coal for Arlon and moved five hundred pounds of yeast from Luxembourg City to Mersch for the making of bread.

January 12
D-Day +220

On the III Corps' west flank, the 6th Armored Division captured Wardin and made contact with the 35th and 90th Infantry Divisions at Bras. This successful attack created a pocket of German troops which was then mopped up by both the 26th Infantry Division and Task Force Fickett.

In the VII Corps area, north of Bastogne, the 101st Airborne Division patrolled aggressively; the 17th Airborne Division advanced about two miles; the 11th Armored Division relieved elements of the 17th and 101st Airborne Divisions; and the 28th Infantry Division maintained defensive positions on the Meuse River while the 87th Infantry Division continued to reduce the western end of the Bulge.

There was no change in the XII Corps area or in the XX Corps area.

Bad weather precluded any action by the XIX TAC.

An enemy rocket of an unidentified type landed in the area around a semimobile laundry located with the 104th Evacuation Hospital in the city of Luxembourg. It injured seven men, three of them seriously, and caused damage to two vans and one tractor.

Fifty truckloads of clothing from Advance Section ComZ were unloaded at the Third Army depot at Longwy. The shipment included 51,666 field and combat jackets of various types, which alleviated the shortage which had existed for several months. Prospects were that the Third Army would receive from 5,000 to 6,000 camouflage snow suits per division within three weeks.

Responsibility for equipping the 9th Armored Division was delegated to the Third Army.

January 13
D-Day +221

The 26th Infantry Division continued its aggressive patrols in the III Corps area, with the 90th Infantry Division advancing to the Wiltz River. In the southeast, near Bastogne, the 35th Infantry Division mopped up the remaining enemy in the pocket created by the meeting of the 6th Armored Division and the 90th Infantry Division.

The 101st Airborne Division's 502d Parachute Infantry Regiment cleared a forest three miles northeast of Bastogne, with leading elements reaching a point just south of Noville. In the 11th Armored Division, the outskirts of Noville were reached by Combat Command "A," with Combat Command "B" advancing to a point one mile southwest of Bertogne. The 17th Airborne Division succeeded in cutting off the St. Hubert-Houffalize highway and capturing both Ruette and Givry.

Listed in reports as a noteworthy example of effective air-ground coordination was an VIII Corps artillery reconnaissance mission. Upon completion of the mission the pilot was asked to verify a report of enemy armor moving south, into Houffalize. The pilot then located a mixed column of sixty vehicles, both armored and general purpose, moving into the town. The VIII Corps artillery adjusted their guns according to the information received from the pilot and started a three battalion time-on-target concentration on the Germans. The pilot also vectored in a squadron of fighterbombers to bomb and strafe the enemy column. Meanwhile, he circled the area, locating two enemy antiaircraft batteries on which he adjusted two 155mm gun battalions. Destruction of the enemy column was thorough.

There was no alteration in XII Corps.

In the XX Corps only two limited objectives were accomplished, those being the occupation of Tettingen and Butzdorf.

In total, 551 sorties were flown by XIX TAC, cutting 25 railroad lines and claiming 137 motor vehicles, 168 railroad cars, and 40 factories.

The Third Army personnel assisted in the repair of electric power lines throughout the Grand Duchy of Luxembourg. By this date power had been restored to nine out of thirteen communes of Redange Canton and work was progressing in other areas (Cantons are similar to small states or counties).

January 14
D-Day +222

On the west flank of the III Corps, the 6th Armored Division cleared Senonchamps.

In the VIII Corps area, the 101st Airborne Division consolidated its positions. An attack launched by all of the combat commands of the 11th Armored Division resulted in the capture of Cobru.

Front lines of the XII Corps were rotated while patrolling continued.

In the XX Corps, the 94th Infantry Division repulsed a heavy counterattack, continued its own attack, and then captured the town of Borg. Minor advances were made in the Saarlautern bridgehead by the 95th Infantry Division.

Total claims of 7 enemy aircraft, 410 motor vehicles, 52 armored vehicles/tanks, 74 railroad cars, and 10 locomotives were made by the XIX TAC after flying 633 sorties.

General Patton attended a conference at Twelfth Army Group headquarters concerning supply requirements. Also in attendance were Lt. Gen. Breton B. Somerville, commanding general of the Army Service Forces; Lt. Gen. John C. H. Lee, commanding general of ComZ; Lt. Gen. Omar N. Bradley, commanding general of Twelfth Army Group; and Maj. Gen. Leven H. Campbell, chief of ordnance. General Lee wore his special helmet with his rank painted on both the front and back.

The Third Army reached a strength of 370,456 men. Even though the command was at peak strength, and despite a steady flow of reinforcements, the actual Table of Organization requirements were not being met.

The critical shortage of coal persisted. Supply points were ordered to reduce the coal ration from 4 to 2 pounds per man per day. Army and corps headquarters were requested to reduce coal consumption by 50 percent, but the supply for hospitals remained unchanged. A total of 104 tons of medical supplies arrived by train from ComZ, bringing many items which had been in critical short supply.

January 15
D-Day +223

The 90th Infantry Division beat off several counterattacks and with its 358th Infantry Regiment overtook Nieder Wampach, capturing 300 prisoners and losing only 2 casualties. On the west flank of III Corps, Combat Command "A" took the high ground near Longvilly while Combat Command "B" captured the town of Arloncourt. The 320th Infantry took both Oubourcy and Michamps.

While the 101st Airborne Division was capturing Noville and Vaux, the 327th Glider Infantry coordinated with Combat

Command "B" of the 11th Armored Division to clear most of the wooded area east of Noville. The Reserve Combat Command (assisted by Combat Command "B") captured Compogne, Rastadt, and Vellereux, pushing the VIII Corps as far southwest as about three miles outside of Houffalize.

The army headquarters was relieved of control of the 4th Armored Division when it was assigned to XII Corps. Otherwise, there was no change in the XII Corps.

During another limited objective operation in the XX Corps, the 94th Infantry Division captured Wies and Nenning. The 95th Infantry Division continued to patrol, while the 10th Armored Division continue its rehabilitation and training exercises.

XIX TAC flew 472 sorties with today's feature being railroads. They cut 41 rail lines, bombed and blocked 7 railroad tunnels, and caught 1 train in the middle of a tunnel just as it entered, sealing it off completely.

One problem brought on by the extremely cold weather was that of firing small arms. Without gloves, it was possible to freeze a finger to a trigger, but with gloves it was difficult to squeeze that trigger. The ordnance section came up with a new device which they had copied from a similar piece of equipment taken from some captured German soldiers. The device was a trigger adapter which fitted into the trigger housing of rifles, machine guns, and other small arms. It made possible the operation of the trigger without removing gloves or mittens. The device was designed and contracts were placed with local civilian firms for the manufacture of ninety thousand pieces.

One-inch steel cable, used on tank recovery vehicles, became extremely scarce. Since it was virtually impossible to obtain this cable through army supply channels, contracts were let with local steel mills in the vicinity of Esch and Luxembourg for enough cable to satisfy the army's need.

January 16
D-Day +224

G-2 estimated that the Germans were more determined than

ever to continue their defend and delay tactics in the remaining positions of the Ardennes salient. This was surmised from tactical reconnaissance and other reports of heavy artillery concentrations on the ridge lines northeast and south of Houffalize. Mounting pressure on the Eastern Front by the Russians made large-scale commitment of new forces highly improbable.

Information was received from Twelfth Army Group that the First Army would revert to the command of Twelfth Army Group from the Twenty-first Army Group (Montgomery). This indicated that the most precarious aspects of the Battle of the Bulge were over.

In the III Corps, the 26th Infantry Division patrolled aggressively while the 35th Infantry Division remained in reserve. The 90th Infantry Division captured Ober Wampach and Schimpach. To the northeast, the 6th Armored Division was assisted by the 359th Infantry Regiment in the clearing of Longvilly.

The XII Corps remained stable.

In the XX Corps, the 95th Infantry Division maintained position; the 94th mopped up around Tettingen and Butzdorf; and the 10th Armored, being relieved from XX Corps, was attached to Sixth Army Group; and began movement from the Metz area.

When 504 sorties were flown by XIX TAC, German planes flew to meet them. Out of the contact, 14 Germans were shot down and 5 Americans were lost.

During operations, the Third Army captured Ober Wampach, Schimpach, Longvilly, Mabompre, Wicourt, Rachamps, Hardigny, and Bourcy.

Because of ice and snow, almost all of the Third Army's tracklike vehicles became virtually immobilized. The problem of obtaining traction on highly slippery terrain was solved by the welding of manganese steel lugs on every fifth block of steel track and replacing every fifth block of rubber track with a steel block equipped with such a lug. This simple application greatly increased the effectiveness of armor during winter conditions.

A chemical maintenance company worked on the adaptation of white phosphorous hand grenades for use as rifle grenades. The modification was made by attaching an adapter on the bottom of the grenade body.

Third Civil Affairs estimated that 62,805 refugees were in the army's zone of operations, an increase of 10,300 in one week.

In notes written by General Patton concerning the Ardennes Offensive, he stated that:

...the Third Army utilized a total of 17 divisions and lost (in killed, wounded, and missing) a total of 24,598 men. In the same period the Germans utilized 20 divisions and lost a total of 18,051 in POWs and enemy buried by us. Their estimated casualties, excluding nonbattle, for this period amount to 103,900 as follows: 16,400 POWs; 24,200 killed; and 63,200 wounded. We believe that these figures are low....the fighting quality of American troops never reached a higher level than in this operation. Neither intolerable weather nor the best troops in the possession of the Germans were able to stop them nor prevent their supply.

January 17
D-Day +225

The Third Army considered this date to be the official closing of the Bastogne campaign. G-2 estimated that the Germans were now beginning a new campaign of retiring under pressure. They were still capable of attacking at any point in the bulge in an effort to contain Allied pressure. German strength was estimated at 54,500 combat effectives (the equivalent of about 6 divisions) and 170 tanks/assault guns.

In accordance with instructions from SHAEF, the Third Army was relieved by the Twelfth Army Group of operational responsibility for the defense of the Meuse River line south of Givet and the operational control of any troops turned over to them for the Bastogne mission. The Third Army was still responsible for the task of removing all roadblocks, mines, and demolition charges placed in defense of the Meuse River line.

The 10th Armored Division passed from control of XX

Corps to 6th Army Group and began movement from its assembly area at Metz.

Slight advances in the Bourcy-Hardigny area were made by the 101st Airborne Division. Elsewhere in the VIII Corps, the 17th Airborne Division began relief of the 11th Armored Division; the 11th Armored Division in turn relieving the 101st Airborne Division, which started movement to corps reserve.

A very heavy harassing and interdiction artillery program was conducted on this date and subsequently upon all escape routes available to the Germans leaving the Ardennes area. This program was fired by all available artillery of the III, VIII, and XII Corps. In addition, artillery from the First Army participated heavily within its own zone.

The XIX TAC listed only limited claims because of poor visibility.

Operations began at the coal mines at St. Avold for the production of coal for the Third Army. The production estimate was 50 tons per day, with an additional fifty and seventy-five tons per day output expected within two weeks.

January 18
D-Day +226

In the III Corps, the 26th Infantry Division maintained its positions; the 35th Infantry Division departed from the corps area and was en route to Metz. The 90th Infantry Division continued patrolling. The 6th Armored Division consolidated its positions and patrolled east of the Bourcy-Longvilly road.

While the 17th Airborne and 11th Armored Divisions were in preparation for renewal of the attack, the 101st Airborne Division closed in the VIII Corps reserve at Isle-le-Pry. The 76th Infantry Division was assigned to VIII Corps.

The 8th Infantry Regiment (4th Infantry Division) cleared the town of Bettendorf while the 87th Infantry Division attacked Wasserbillig at the junction of the Sauer and Moselle Rivers. In the 5th Infantry Division, the 2d Infantry Regiment captured Diekirch and cleared Erpeldange. The 10th Infantry advanced north of the Sauer River to the north and east of Diekirch.

In the XX Corps, the 94th Infantry Division fired 12,476 rounds of ammunition at the Deutschlanders.

The XIX TAC encountered bad weather, which kept them on the ground.

The Third Army was visited by Leon Henderson, President Roosevelt's advisor on foreign economics.

Seven hundred tons of special winter clothing had been delivered by ComZ to Longy. The shipments included shoe packs, socks, ponchos, mittens, and mufflers.

Arrangements were made with ComZ for the direct exchange of recoil mechanisms, tubes, equilibrators, traversing mechanisms, and the major artillery parts of which the Third Army was critically short.

January 19
D-Day +227

Units in the VIII Corps area regrouped and were preparing for a renewal of the attack. The 17th Airborne and 11th Armored Divisions held their forward positions while the 101st Airborne Division began moving from the Third Army zone to that of Seventh Army.

The 101st and 104th Infantry Regiments of the 26th Infantry Division were relieved by the 28th Cavalry Squadron in the III Corps area. Some units of the 6th Cavalry Group went into corps reserve; the 90th Infantry Division pushed out fifteen hundred yards; the 6th Armored Division maintained positions; and the 35th Infantry Division remained in corps reserve.

The 87th Infantry Division and the 2d Cavalry Group patrolled aggressively, while the 5th Infantry Division repulsed a strong counterattack at Bastendorf and then captured the town. The 4th Armored Division fought around Diekirch and Bettendorf, extending its positions into part of the 5th Infantry Division's zone. The 12th Infantry Division captured Longsdorf.

The XIX TAC flew 149 sorties, but only light claims were made due to poor visibility.

Third Army strength was listed at 350,296 men with a total of 34,000 understrength. Most of the shortage was in infantry divisions, particularly in rifle companies.

A request for fourteen million rations was submitted to Advance Section ComZ for the period of February 1 to 28. Requirements were estimated at 9.8 million "A" rations; 1.05 million "C" rations; 1.05 million "K" rations; and 2.1 million 10-in-1 rations.

In an effort to expedite the shipment of medical supplies, not more than two freight cars of medical supplies would be attached to any one hospital train destined for the general area in which a particular army medical depot was located. Less than carload shipments would be placed in hospital train litter cars destined for the same areas.

January 20
D-Day +228

In the area that remained in the Ardennes bulge, the Germans were generally withdrawing as the Third Army advanced, but they retained the capability of defending and delaying when encountering favorable terrain, particularly the high ground of the Our River. It was expected by G-2 that intensification of the inclement weather would aid the German's delaying tactics while they withdrew most of their forces behind the Siegfried Line.

After almost a full month of quietness and virtual acquiescence, the XX Corps began a schedule of violent, sustained artillery firings aimed predominantly at the Saarlautern bridgehead.

A new type of long-range, medium-caliber projectile was being fired by the Germans. The weapon was characterized by an exceptionally quick fuse action, a high order of fragmentation, and by six fins at its rear and paralleling its height. It indicated the development of what was termed as non-rotating flight. Although no conclusive opinion could be reached by ordnance technical intelligence personnel as to the identity of the weapon, today's information would probably classify it as a missile.

On the III Corps' front, the 26th Infantry Division reached the high ground north of the Wiltz River and cleared the town of Grumelscheid. The 90th Infantry Division captured Allerbronn, Chifontaine, and Hamiville; the 6th Armored Division cleared Troine and the 35th Infantry Division moved to the Metz area for training.

Combat Command "A" of the 11th Armored Division reached Buret in the VIII Corps zone, while the 87th Infantry Division and the 2d Cavalry Group patrolled and held positions in the XII Corps area. Also in the XII Corps, the 80th Infantry Division advanced through Burden to Bourcheid and Welscheid, clearing all three towns.

The 94th Infantry Division in the XX Corps area repulsed some small counterattacks while the 302d Regiment cleared a pocket of resistance between Nenning and Tettingen.

Only ten sorties were flown by the XIX TAC.

Signal construction troops completed the open wire lead from Luxembourg to Ettelbrück, with plans to extend the lead through Clervaux to St. Vith. Constructed at the time when there was heavy fighting in the Ardennes, the cable was damaged frequently by artillery fire. Intermittent trouble occurred on these lines because shell fragments would penetrate the rubber shell, leaving holes too small to be seen from the ground by the naked eye. Rectification of the damage had to be completed by checking the wire closely by hand.

A request was made for two hundred thousand colored eyeshields for issue to troops to prevent snow blindness.

A supply of five million units of insulin was obtained for use in the Grand Duchy of Luxembourg and arrangements were completed for obtaining foot-and-mouth disease serum from Switzerland.

January 21
D-Day +229

G-2 conclusions submitted to headquarters indicated that

1. The Germans had no effective Panzer divisions in reserve on the Western Front
2. They had no infantry reserves to spare on the Western Front
3. They might be attempting to build up an armored reserve with divisions drawn from the Ardennes Offensive
4. The offensive thrust south of the Moselle River was for the purpose of containing the Western Front while attempting to prevent destruction by the Russians in the east.

In the III Corps area, the towns of Wiltz, Noertrange, Niederwitz, Bruhl, and Brachtenbach were captured.

In the XII Corps, the 87th Infantry Division patrolled; the 4th Armored Division captured Fouhren; the 2d and 10th Infantry Regiments of the 5th Division captured Lipperscheid; and in the 80th Infantry Division, the 318th and 317th Infantry Regiments captured Bourscheid, reaching the Sure River.

Poor weather conditions kept the XIX TAC grounded.

All in all, the Third Army kept advancing, capturing a total of 19 small towns.

January 22
D-Day +230

After clearing Wiltz, the 6th Cavalry Group and the 26th Infantry Division advanced northeast on the III Corps eastern flank, moving up the Clerf River and capturing Weischerdange. In the 90th Infantry Division, the 359th and 357th Infantry Regiments captured Donnage, Stocken, Romlange, Boxhorn, and Asselborn. Also captured by the 6th Armored Division were the towns of Esselborn and Eischweiler.

The 2d Cavalry Group and the 87th Infantry Division protected the right flank of the XII Corps while the 4th, 5th, and 80th Infantry Divisions attacked to the north and east. The 12th Infantry Regiment of the 4th Infantry Division pushed past Fuhren to an area west of Vianden and the 80th Infantry Division attacked and occupied Masseler at the junction of the Wiltz and Sure Rivers.

With weather finally permitting, the XIX TAC had a very big day. Making up for lost time, they flew as many planes as possible. The total for the day was 627 sorties, with 1,177 motor vehicles destroyed, and 536 more damaged.

First Army's ammunition supply point No. 128 at the town of Bras (which had been captured by the Germans) was recaptured by the Third Army. The Germans had prepared the stacks of ammunition for demolition, but only a small amount of materiel had actually been destroyed. Because the area was believed to be booby-trapped and mined, one ammunition clearing company and three bomb disposal squads were assigned to inventory the stock and to clear the area before it was to be reopened for use.

January 23
D-Day +231

In accordance with an operational directive dated January 19, revisions of boundaries and readjustment of divisions were begun.

1. The 87th and 4th Infantry Divisions were relieved from XII Corps and assigned to VIII Corps
2. The 76th Infantry Division was relieved from VIII Corps and assigned to XII Crops
3. The 95th Infantry Division was relieved from XX Corps and assigned to VIII Corps
4. The 17th Airborne Division was relieved from VIII Corps and assigned to III Corps
5. The 26th Infantry Division was relieved from III Corps and assigned to XX Corps
6. The 90th Infantry Division was relieved from III Corps to be assigned to VIII Corps.

The net result of these reliefs and assignments was to strengthen VIII Corps on the left flank with five divisions, leaving XII Corps on the right flank with four divisions, and III and XX Corps with two divisions each.

The XIX TAC continued their attacks, destroying or damaging 164 motor vehicles and 29 gun positions.

The advance of the Third Army continued with the capture of Trois Vierges, Binsfeld, Merkols, Biwisch, and Massen.

The 35th Infantry Division began moving from Metz to the Seventh Army.

Artillery was reorganized in accordance with the directive of January 19. One medium and two heavy artillery battalions were detached from III Corps; two medium and one heavy artillery battalions were detached from XII Corps; and all six of them were attached to the VIII Corps.

Because stocks of SAE-10 engine oil were critically low, ComZ indicated that all army trucks would use SAE-30 oil to the fullest extent.

January 24
D-Day +232

A G-2 estimate of enemy strength indicated 40,500 troops (the equivalent of 5 divisions) against the Third Army's front. A total strength of 130 tanks/assault guns was estimated. G-2's consideration was that it was not necessarily the strength of the Germans that was the major obstacle to the Third Army but the extremely rigorous terrain combined with the severe winter weather. The favored capability of the Germans was that they would withdraw into fortifications of the Siegfried Line.

The 26th Infantry Division seized positions along the Clerf River; the 90th Infantry Division captured Hupperdange; and the 6th Armored Division captured Holler, Breidfeld, Drinklange, and Wilwerdange.

The 94th Infantry Division in the XX Corps area entered the town of Berg, where they met with both the dragonteeth of the Siegfried Line and mine fields. The mine fields were cleared by advance elements of the division.

The XIX TAC flew 213 sorties, destroying or damaging 137 motor vehicles and 29 gun installations.

General Patton attended a conference in the office of Lieutenant General Omar N. Bradley, with Lieutenant General Courtney H. Hodges and certain members of their respective staffs. The purpose of the meeting was the coordination of the upcoming attacks by the First and Third Armies against the Siegfried Line.

January 25
D-Day +233

In the XX Corps, the 26th Infantry Division continued to advance while the 90th Infantry Division captured Fischbach, Clervaux, Kochery, and Reuler and the 6th Armored Division captured Weiswampach.

Advancing toward both the northeast and east, the 17th Airborne Division reached the vicinity of Espeler, six miles southwest of St. Vith, in the VIII Corps area.

Patrolling in the southern flank of the XII Corps, the 2d Cavalry Group and the 76th Infantry Division held a quiet part of the front, due west of Trier. The 4th, 5th, and 80th Infantry divisions, in line with one another, advanced slowly against stubborn resistance. The 317th Infantry Regiment of the 80th Infantry Division crossed the Clerf River, clearing Lellingen and Pintsch.

The XIX TAC flew 198 sorties, shot down 2 German planes, and destroyed or damaged 240 motor vehicles.

January 26
D-Day +234

Continuing with its advance along the ridge between the Clerf and Our Rivers, the 26th Infantry Division captured Marnach and Munshausen. The 90th Infantry Division captured Lieler, while the 358th Infantry Regiment relieved units of the 6th Armored Division.

Following the adjustment of the III-VIII Corps boundary, the 90th Infantry Division was passed to the control of VIII Corps. While elements of the 11th Armored Division remained in reserve, the 87th Infantry Division began relief of the 17th Airborne Division.

While the XII Corps patrolled, there was little change in the XX Corps area.

A total of 219 motor vehicles, 145 railroad cars, and 13 armored vehicles were damaged or destroyed in 189 sorties flown by the XIX TAC.

January 27
D-Day +235

G-2 Section indicated that the Germans were attempting to contain the Western Front with both the Siegfried Line and their minimum forces while at the same time attempting to stabilize their Eastern Front. Reports also indicated that at least one of the two panzer armies in the west was being shifted to the east.

The 26th Infantry Division captured Hosingen; the 6th Armored Division captured some high ground east of the Our River; the 17th Airborne Division moved into III Corps zone. Following its relief by the 87th Infantry Division, the 17th Airborne Division attacked and captured Dorscheid.

In the XII Corps, the 2d Cavalry and 76th Infantry Division patrolled. To the north, the 4th Infantry Division was relieved by the 80th and 5th Infantry Divisions. The 5th Infantry Division also captured Consthum and Holzthum, while the 80th Infantry Division captured Bockholz.

The XIX TAC was grounded by bad weather.

Arrangements were made to ship special rations (as they became available) to hospital units. Items included turkey, fresh eggs, and oranges.

January 28
D-Day +236

The Battle of the Bulge officially ended on this date, with all of the ground which had been lost to the Germans having been regained. Some Third Army units were already fighting in the Siegfried Line, with heavy losses inflicted upon the enemy, both in personnel and materiel. More than twenty-two thousand POWs were captured.

In the XII Corps, the 5th Infantry Division cleared Putscheid and Fennberg, securing a line one mile west of the Our River.

Seventy sorties were flown by the XIX TAC as escort for IX Bomber Command. No armed reconnaissance missions were flown.

During the day the towns of Roder, Marbourg, Kalborn, Putscheid, and Bubingen were captured.

January 29
D-Day +237

The VIII Corps began a new phase of operations by crossing the Our River. The 87th Infantry Division moved on the left, two regiments of the 4th Infantry Division advanced in the center, and the 90th Infantry Division progressed on the right. During the day the VIII Corps captured Hemmers, Elcherath, Lommersweiler, and Setz.

The town of Roder was cleared by the 17th Airborne Division in the III Corps area, while the 6th Armored Division extended its patrols up and down the Our River.

Little changed in the XII Corps, except that Task Force OBOE was created from armored infantry elements of the 4th Armored Division. The task force relieved the 319th Infantry Regiment of the 80th Infantry Division.

The XIX TAC flew 512 sorties aimed predominantly at transportation, bombing and strafing 745 motor vehicles and 268 railroad cars.

The Twelfth Army Group was requested to obtain dog teams and sleds to assist in the evacuation of patients through deep snow being encountered by the Third Army Divisions. As the result of experiments made by the XII Corps, plans were initiated to provide litters with snow runners.

January 30
D-Day +238

Occupying a very narrow zone on the southern flank of the III Corps, the 6th Cavalry Group established an outpost line on the high ground east of Hosingen while the 17th Airborne Division and the 6th Armored Division continued their clearing of the Germans on the west side of the Our River.

The VIII Corps was experiencing increasing resistance. In the 90th Infantry Division area, the 358th and 359th Regiments secured a solid one running a mile and a half east of the Our River, capturing Auel. The 4th Infantry Division made some small advances east of Hemmeres. The 87th Infantry Division continued its attacks to the east, capturing Schlierbach and Rodgen and clearing Andler, Schonberg, and Atzerath.

The XII Corps experienced no heavy fighting. The 5th, 76th, and 80th Infantry Divisions merely maintained their positions and patrolled aggressively.

In the new zone of the XX Corps, the 26th Infantry Division consolidated its positions, while the 94th Infantry Division maintained its positions.

Although two flight missions were sent up, they were recalled by the XIX TAC due to bad weather. The bad weather continued and all operations were called off for the day.

January 31
D-Day +239

At the end of January, G-2 estimated that the Germans opposing the Third Army numbered forty-two thousand combat effectives (the equivalent of five-and-a-half divisions) and ninety-five tanks/assault guns. Although this represented an increase of fifteen hundred troops from the last estimate, it also represented a decrease of thirty-five tanks/assault guns. Even though some reinforcements were reaching the Germans, no new divisions were being identified. Every indication was that the Germans were fully occupied with the Eastern Front, letting the Western Front fend for itself. It was becoming apparent that they were relying on the three factors of the Siegfried Line, favorable terrain, and the severe winter conditions.

Defensive positions were patrolled in the III and XII Corps.

In the XX Corps, a limited objective attack was made by the 302nd Regiment of the 94th Infantry Division, while the 26th and 94th Infantry Divisions generally patrolled aggressively.

In the VIII Corps, things were more active. Advances of one mile were made by the 358th and 359th Regiments of the 90th Infantry Division, capturing Heckhalenfeld, Winterspelt, and Eigelscheid. In the 4th Infantry Division, the 12th Regiment captured Elcherath, Ihren, and Weppler, while the 8th Regiment crossed the Our River and advanced about three miles. The 87th Division captured Heum and Laudesfeld, while the 11th Armored Division remained in the assembly area.

Bad weather prevailed for the day, preventing the XIX TAC from engaging the enemy in any activity.

CHAPTER 7

February, 1945

During the month of February, the Third Army would come to grips with two problems which would prove to be as formidable as the Germans: terrain and weather.

Although both posed great hindrances, they would be finally overcome by the spirit and indomitable determination of the men of the Third Army. In spite of rugged terrain and flood-swollen, swiftly flowing rivers, the engineers built bridges and the infantry and armor went forward.

During February, Third Army engineers built more bridges than at any other time in their 281 days of combat. One great advantage finally gained was the supply situation improved by both railroad and air transportation.

February 1
D-Day +240

According to a directive from the Twelfth Army Group, the 8th Armored Division was relieved from assignment to 15th Army, relieved from attachment to the 3d Army (for supply and administration), and was then assigned to the Ninth Army. The Twelfth Army Group also directed the Third Army to move the 95th Infantry Division to 9th Army. The move of the 95th Infantry Division was to be done in absolute secrecy.

A plan of attack was devised by General Patton using troops assigned to XII Corps, but the proposal was suspended by

Twelfth Army Group. General Bradley wanted to make the decision as to where the main effort would be made against the Siegfried Line.

Maintaining their defensive positions, the 17th Airborne and 6th Armored Divisions, and the 6th Cavalry Group patrolled in the III Corps area.

In the VIII Corps, the 90th Infantry Division's 358th and 359th Infantry Regiments captured both Grublangenfeld and Heckhuscheid towns located four miles east of the Our River. The 4th Infantry Division captured Winterscheid and the 87th Infantry Division captured Manderfeld. The 11th Armored Division remained in an assembly area and the 95th Infantry Division remained in reserve.

The XII Corps maintained their front lines as did the XX Corps.

Only thirty-two sorties were flown by the XIX TAC, all of them being in escort for medium bombers.

A program was initiated for placing an additional two-and-one-half inches of armor plate on the forward hull (glacis plate) of the M4A3 medium tanks. This added plating, obtained from wrecked and salvaged tanks at various collection points, greatly decreased the vulnerability of the smaller, lighter American tanks. The job of welding the plate onto the tanks was completed under local contract to civilian factories.

The supply situation was considered to be generally favorable, although there was a definite shortage of coal. There was also a shortage of 73 octane gasoline for use in artillery liaison planes.

February 2
D-Day +241

The current opinion of the Third Army's G-2 Section was that not only was the enemy on the defensive throughout the Western Front, but they also lacked any real striking power. The most favored capability afforded to them was to defend in the fortifications of the Siegfried Line and to oppose the Third Army with local, armor-spearheaded attacks. Indications were that the Germans were experiencing extreme supply problems.

In the VIII Corps, the 90th and 87th Infantry Divisions captured Bleailf, Radscheid, Krewinkel, Bertherath, Weckerath, and Losheim. The 95th Infantry and 11th Armored Divisions remained in reserve.

Artillery in the XX Corps area attacked a group of twelve enemy tanks just east of Kreuzweiler with a time on target concentration by seven battalions. The eight-inch howitzers of the artillery were employed extensively and effectively for the attack of pillboxes by both the VIII and XX Corps.

The XIX TAC's fighterbombers flew 414 sorties, aimed mostly at railroad facilities. They cut 29 rail lines and damaged or destroyed 585 railroad cars and 32 locomotives.

Mechanical flame throwers were issued to the 4th and 6th Armored Divisions to be mounted on medium tanks. Each weapon was equipped with two twenty-five gallon tanks. The flame throwers were attached in the common aperture of the tank's machine gun and either of the two weapons could be fired within an interchange time of thirty seconds. The total firing time for the flame throwers was about fifty seconds and it could spit the flaming mixture from fifty to seventy yards.

Because of a sudden thaw, it was necessary to restack 50 percent of all of the ammunition that had been stacked on frozen ground and snow in the Third Army munitions dumps. The mushy ground caused the stacks to topple.

Notification was finally received by the Third Army that they would receive a number of dog sled teams. They were to be flown in from Labrador.

A list of medical supplies for an emergency air drop was prepared and submitted to the Twelfth Army Group. The list was for a total of 15,000 men and had only 14 items, but the stock requested totaled 18,377 pounds and occupied a space of 10,798 cubic feet.

A War Department circular prohibited the issue of D-type rations as a supplement. This type of ration, if ordered on the daily telegram, would be considered as a full ration and was to be shipped in lieu of either "A" or operational-type rations.

February 3
D-Day +242

At a conference between General Patton and four of his corps commanders, it was decided that the XII Corps would initiate an attack on the night of February 6-7 aimed at Bitburg. The VIII Corps would continue their drive toward Prüm.

It was quiet in the III Corps with the 6th Armored and 17th Airborne Divisions and the 6th Cavalry Group patrolling and maintaining their positions.

Preparing for limited objective attacks in the XX Corps area, the 94th Infantry Division patrolled and consolidated its positions. The Third Cavalry Group and the 26th Infantry Division also patrolled. The XX Corps' artillery continued with its program of 155mm howitzer fire to harass and interdict the enemy's extreme rear echelons.

Air operations by the XIX TAC were limited by the weather to only three uneventful escort missions.

Captured enemy stores in Saarlautern provided the Third Army with many items which were in critically short supply. Some of the issues from this new source were 1,200 plumbing fixtures, paint and putty, 225 truckloads of packing materials, 17 ten-ton loads of lumber dunnage, and a ten-ton load of rubber gaskets for both water and gasoline cans.

February 4
D-Day +243

The Order of Battle Facts on this date showed a reshuffling of German Panzer divisions remaining in the west, with a strong trend of movement to the northern sectors of the front and nonappearance in contact with the Third Army. From these facts, G-2 determined that the Germans were disposing their armor to give the maximum local counterattacking strength and that they were reshuffling their infantry divisions to meet the most urgent need for such troops in threatened sectors.

The VIII Corps continued its attack on the general line of Neuendorf-Prüm-Prosfeld.

The III Corps regrouped in accordance with a change of the III-XII Boundaries.

The XII Corps regrouped while they used searchlights to illuminate their nighttime battlefields. Two lights were emplaced in defiladed sites near Canach, throwing strong beams of light across the Moselle River in the direction of the German lines. The use of lights drew absolutely no artillery fire. It was the first time that the Third Army used lights in lieu of natural moonlight.

No change in the XX Corps.

Bad weather kept the XIX TAC from any operations, with the exception of two planes which performed weather reconnaissance.

February 5
D-Day +244

While the 17th Airborne patrolled the Our River, the remaining elements of the III Corps completed their regrouping operations.

In the VIII Corps, the 11th Armored Division completed the relief of the 90th Infantry Division. The 90th Infantry Division then occupied positions in a new zone and its 359th Infantry Regiment cleared Habscheid. The 4th Infantry Division captured Brandscheid and Schlausenbach, while the 87th Infantry Division launched an attack into the Siegfried Line at 0400 hours.

The XII Corps continued to patrol.

Other than a small counterattack against the 94th Infantry Division (which was easily thrown back), there was little activity in the XX Corps.

The XIX TAC had bad weather and no flying.

Tanks used by cavalry reconnaissance squadrons were being converted from M59 to M24. These conversions not only created a faster, more maneuverable tank, but also exchanged a new 75mm gun in place of the old 37mm Pop Gun.

Authorization was granted to reestablish local mail and telephone services in Luxembourg City, Esch, and other urban centers of southern Luxembourg.

February 6
D-Day +245

In the III Corps, a limited attack was launched by the 507th Parachute Infantry Regiment of the 17th Airborne Division in conjunction with the 6th Armored Division. They crossed the Our River while the 6th Cavalry Group maintained positions and patrolled the river banks.

In the VIII Corps, the 11th Armored Division reached a point about eight miles southwest of Prüm, one of the Third Army's immediate objectives. The 90th Infantry Division, after clearing Habscheid, regrouped and consolidated its positions. The 4th Infantry Division attacked and captured Sellerich, Herscheid, Hontheim, and Wascheid. On the northern flank of the corps area, the 87th Infantry Division advanced about one mile, maintaining contact with the First Army. The 4th Armored Division attacked and captured Bettel.

At 0100 hours, in the XII Corps, the 5th Infantry Division crossed the Sauer River, gaining 1,000 yards in the attack. The 80th Infantry Division attacked a little later, at 0300 hours, and they also crossed the Sauer River. In preparation for the attack, artillery of both the III and XII Corps fired a total of 29,000 rounds in 280 firing missions aimed at German artillery positions, 137 German command posts, and 102 German occupied towns.

In the XX Corps, the 26th and 94th Infantry Divisions patrolled.

A total of 214 sorties were flown by the XIX TAC. They either damaged or destroyed 272 motor vehicles, 13 armored vehicles/tanks, 245 railroad cars, and 30 buildings.

Under the direction of the military government, the civilian labor available to the Third Army produced bib-type Red

Cross aprons to be worn by stretcher-bearers in Third Army divisions. The aprons proved extremely valuable as they seemed to prevent sniper fire at the personnel wearing them.

February 7
D-Day +246

In accordance with orders from SHAEF, the Twelfth Army Group was to secure the Roer River dams and clear the enemy from the area west of the line from the Roer River to Gemund, Schleide, and Frauenkron. They were to attack on their left flank to support the operation of the Twenty-first Army Group (Montgomery) and take advantage of any weakening of the enemy to improve the position of the Third Army. (The orders were, once again, very clearly designed to give most of the support to Montgomery and to relegate the Americans in general [and the Third Army in particular] to a secondary role.)

Until further orders, the Third Army was to continue with its probing attacks and maintain defensive positions.

The 17th Airborne and 6th Armored Divisions enlarged the bridgehead across the Our River in the III Corps area.

The 4th Infantry Division captured Obermerlen in the VIII Corps while the 87th Infantry Division continued to coordinate its attack with the First Army.

Other than enlarging bridgeheads across the Our and Sauer Rivers, the XII Corps experienced only small advancements. The exception was the 80th Infantry Division, which captured Wallendorf.

No fighter bomber sorties were flown by the XIX TAC due to poor weather.

The Third Army informed Twelfth Army Group that there was a very serious railcar shortage due to the additional burden on the Third Army for the required movements of food for minimum civilian needs and coal for military needs.

February 8
D-Day +247

The Third Army, advancing astride the Moselle River, encountered a long succession of rain-swollen and heavily defended streams. The streams, which were normally very mild and usually averaged one-hundred to two-hundred feet across, were converted into raging torrents by heavy rains and melting snows. The water was checked for speed and was found to be flowing at a velocity of around sixteen feet per second. On the far shores of these dangerous streams, the Germans were strongly emplaced in pillboxes and natural rock formations. The assault troops were very often not harmed by the Germans at all; instead, they were often killed simply by the force of the heavy currents. The churning water overturned many of their floats and boats and drowned a great many soldiers. Many of the bodies of those men were never found because of the swift currents. Bridge construction troops were forced to work under the double handicap of the streams and artillery fire. In spite of these handicaps, Third Army troops got across.

The main effort of the Third Army was still concentrated around Prüm, coordinated with the effort of the First Army to the north. In the VIII Corps, the 4th Infantry Division captured Condrenbret and Hermespand. In the 87th Infantry Division, the 345th Infantry Regiment captured Olzheim, with tank destroyers using direct fire to knock out four pillboxes and five machine gun nests.

In the XX Corps, the 26th Infantry Division captured fortified houses in Fraulautern and Saarlautern-Roden.

There were 30 locomotives, 452 railroad cars, 43 tanks/armored vehicles, 173 motor vehicles, and 153 buildings either damaged or destroyed by the XIX TAC in the 314 sorties they flew. They lost a total of 3 planes.

It was noted in official reports that overshoes were superior to shoe packs in wet weather. The shoe packs were not watertight around the seams.

The first dog sled team arrived for use in evacuating the wounded in deep snow. However, they were never used—by the time they had arrived, the snow had melted.

February 9
D-Day +248

G-2 estimated that only one change was evident in the previously considered German capabilities—the Germans might use armored divisions currently out of contact to counterattack in threatened portions of the front.

Along the southern flank of III Corps, the 6th Cavalry Group continued their patrolling. The 17th Airborne Division patrolled their bridgehead across the Our River. The 6th Armored Division gained a mile, joining their two bridgeheads. One of them was a Bailey bridge, with tanks and tank destroyers getting on it immediately after it was completed and using it constantly.

In the VIII Corps, the 90th Infantry Division consolidated their gains of the previous day, seizing the high ground overlooking the Alf River. To do this they used tank destroyers to knock out ten pillboxes and three machine gun positions. To the north, the 4th Infantry Division drove eastward toward Prüm. The 87th Infantry Division captured Neundorf.

The 5th Infantry was enlarging its bridgehead in the XII Corps area. They had crossed the Sauer River and driven inland to a depth of eight hundred yards and a width of two miles. Tank destroyers attacked German pillboxes and assisted in the capture of several hundred German prisoners.

The XX Corps was involved primarily in limited objective attacks, clearing the Banholz woods just south of Sinz.

In 192 sorties, the XIX TAC managed to drop 91 tons of bombs and attack 15 military installations and 8 marshalling yards. They also cut 14 rail lines and destroyed or damaged 161 railroad cars.

P-47s dropped a total of 800 K rations and 800 D rations to some advanced elements of the 80th Infantry Division across the Our River.

February 10
D-Day +249

Amendment No. 1 to the operational directive dated February 3 once again changed the Corps boundaries. The boundary between III and VIII Corps was rescinded. The boundary between VIII and XII Corps was designated as the former boundary between III and XII Corps without change.

Road conditions were extremely poor. This condition sorely handicapped the movement of supplies and equipment to front lines. Due to the quick thaw, the roads became muddy and sloppy with the massive vehicular movement of the corps. These conditions necessitated the lessening of road use and the increased movement via railroad lines. Troops who were isolated from supply by wheeled vehicles were supplied by airdrop, and consideration was thoughtfully given to the use of pack horses in the VIII Corps area. With the road conditions causing such a strain on the engineers, work was required of the POWs. A total of 3,000 civilian laborers and 550 POWs were used to maintain and reconstruct the roads.

In the III Corps the 6th Armored Division began relieving the 17th Airborne Division. The III Corps passed from the Third Army to control by the First Army, and the VIII Corps took over their zone.

The 11th Armored Division, in the southern portion of the VIII Corps, cleared a number of pillboxes, while the 90th Infantry Division captured Weinsfeld, three miles southeast of Prüm. The 4th Infantry Division attacked Prüm from the west.

The XII Corps enlarged their bridgehead and cleared Biesdorf.

South of Sinz, in the XX Corps area, heavy fighting continued. The 94th Infantry Division repulsed some counterattacks, with tank destroyers knocking out four enemy tanks. Troops of the 26th Infantry Division had their first experience with an attack at night under the artificial moonlight of searchlights. They occupied several blocks of buildings in Saarlautern, Roden, and Fraulautern.

The XIX TAC flew 136 sorties despite bad weather. The fighter bombers destroyed or damaged 37 motor vehicles; 131

railroad cars, 4 bridges, and 17 buildings. They attacked a total of 13 towns.

Through operations of Civil Affairs, bus service was reestablished between Bettborn and Luxembourg City. Electrical power was restored to Bouzonville, Veckring, Kedange, and 11 other smaller towns and communes.

February 11
D-Day +250

The 6th Armored Division patrolled the area that was formerly occupied by the 17th Airborne Division in the VIII Corps. The 11th Armored Division attacked and captured Harspelt and Sevenig. The 90th Infantry Division attacked, advanced one mile, and captured Watzerath. To the north the 4th Infantry Division's 22d Infantry Regiment entered the western section of Prüm, while other units of the 4th Infantry encircled it. The 87th Infantry Division consolidated positions and prepared for a new attack.

In the XII Corps' area, the 76th Infantry Division enlarged its bridgehead across the Sauer River, due east of Echternach.

Activity in the XX Corps was limited to patrolling by the 94th Infantry Division and the attacking of Saarlautern by the 26th Infantry Division.

In the sky, the XIX TAC flew 171 sorties. They damaged or destroyed 210 railroad cars, 21 buildings, and 11 locomotives.

Large shipments of bulk gasoline from ComZ increased the amount of fuel on hand to a total of 4.5 million gallons. Due to warmer weather, approximately three days' supply of coal and coke were on hand.

February 12
D-Day +251

In the VIII Corps, the 6th Cavalry Group was fighting around Viaden on the west side of the Our River; while to the north, Combat Command "B" of the 11th Armored Division relieved elements of the 6th Armored. The 6th and 11th Armored and the 90th Infantry Divisions patrolled. The 4th Infantry Division's 22d, 8th, and 12th Infantry Regiments cleared Prüm. The 87th Infantry Division remained in its position.

In the XII Corps, the 5th Infantry Division captured Ferschweiler and Ammeldingen.

There was no alteration in the XX Corps. The 10th Armored Division closed in the area around Metz following its move from the Seventh to the Third Army.

No missions were flown by XIX TAC.

An inspection tour of Clervaux was made by Prince Felix of the Grand Duchy of Luxembourg. He expressed deep satisfaction and appreciation for the assistance given by army detachments at work assisting civilians in the duchy.

February 13
D-Day +252

In the southern and central parts of the VIII Corps, the 6th Cavalry Group and the 6th and 11th Armored Divisions maintained their positions. The 90th Infantry Division regrouped with the 359th Infantry Regiment going into reserve. Preparing for an attack, the 4th Infantry Division organized positions along the high ground west of Prüm. On the corps' northern zone, the 87th Infantry Division organized its positions.

The XII Corps continued its enlargement of bridgeheads.

No change in the XX Corps.

No XIX TAC flights due to bad weather.

About thirty tons of ammunition were dropped by parachute in the vicinity of Belialf as an experiment. Its purpose was to determine the possibilities of supporting VIII Corps by airdrop if all rear supply routes became entirely impassable due to bad road conditions and/or lack of rail transportation.

Reports indicated that throughout the Third Army, full cooperation was extended to military authorities by local civil governments of Luxembourg, France, Belgium, and Germany.

February 14
D-Day +253

There was no alteration in the VIII Corps area. From south

to north, the divisions were deployed in the following order of: 6th and 11th Armored and 90th, 4th, and 87th Infantry Division.

The 4th Infantry Division remained in reserve in the southern part of the XII Corps. The 76th Infantry Division expanded bridgeheads and reduced pillboxes. The 5th Infantry Division attacked, while the 80th Infantry Division fought and kept in contact with the 5th.

Positions in the XX Corps were maintained by the 26th Infantry Division, while the 94th Infantry Division launched a limited-objective attack around Sinz.

The XIX TAC was grounded for the third day in a row.

Bad road conditions forced supplies to be airdropped to the VIII Corps' units. Among the supplies dropped were sixty thousand K rations; fifteen thousand gallons of gasoline; fifteen hundred gallons of diesel fuel; one thousand rifle grenades; one thousand trip flares; and forty-five hundred rounds of high explosive 80mm mortar ammunition.

The Third Army was visited by Major General Paul R. Hawley, chief surgeon, ETO. He conferred with the Third Army surgeon and visited the Third Army hospitals.

February 15
D-Day +254

The VIII Corps continued with no change.

The 4th Infantry Division remained in reserve in the XII Corps. The 5th Infantry Division reached the outskirts of Schankweiler, taking the high ground overlooking the Enz and Prüm Rivers. The 80th Infantry Division advanced to the northern edge of the woods northeast of Biesdorg.

In the XX Corps there was little change. The 10th Armored Division conducted rehabilitation and training exercises.

Finally able to fly, the XIX TAC dropped 108 tons of bombs during 190 sorties. They attacked 21 towns and 9 marshalling yards.

The narrow-gauge railroad from Luxembourg City was placed into operation to the east to supply the 5th Infantry Division. Included in the supplies immediately shipped were

25,850 gallons of 73-octane gasoline for use in artillery liaison planes.

February 16
D-Day +255

Continuing with VIII Corps' advance, the 4th Infantry Division repulsed a counterattack around Hemespand, while the 11th Armored Division destroyed three pillboxes and a roadblock. Interrogation of a POW gained some valuable information concerning an upcoming counterattack directed at Prüm. With this information in hand, the VIII Corps began firing a heavy harassing program at 0955 hours upon all known enemy artillery locations and continued with it until 1015 hours. The planned enemy counterattack never developed.

Only 34 sorties were flown by the XIX TAC, but it was reported that the bombing of a bridge killed at least 150 Germans.

The Third Army generally continued to group its forces in preparation for the pending major offensive.

February 17
D-Day +256

Attacks were renewed in the VIII Corps' area by the 11th Armored and 90th Infantry Divisions and the 6th Cavalry Group. The 11th Armored went forward two miles, entering Leidenborn and clearing Grosskapmenberg. The 90th Infantry Division advanced one mile to capture Kesfeld, neutralized two pillboxes, and captured thirty prisoners.

While reducing pillboxes, the 76th Infantry Division advanced about a half mile toward the junction of the Sauer and Prüm Rivers in the XII Corps zone.

Limited objectives were the order of the day in the XX Corps, with the 26th Infantry Division capturing six additional fortified houses in Saarlautern.

Bad weather kept the XIX TAC on the ground.

Supply of the VIII Corps continued to be a problem, due to the thawing weather.

Arrangements were made to contract for five thousand tons of crushed rock for road building in the XX Corps area.

Throughout the Third Army zone of operations, Civil Affairs and military government personnel were actively engaged in supplying fodder to areas suffering from a shortage. During a four week period, more than a million pounds of fodder were transported to Junglinster to fulfill the food requirements of cattle in the area.

February 18
D-Day +257

In the VIII Corps the 11th Armored Division met with only sporadic resistance, advanced about two miles, and cleared Leidenborn. To the north the 90th Infantry Division overran a German regimental command post located southeast of Kesfeld. They also captured Masthorn, Over-Uttfield, and Nie-der-Uttfield. The 6th Cavalry Group captured Waldhof-Falkenstein, helping to enlarge its bridgehead.

The 2d Cavalry crossed the Moselle River and captured Wincheringen on the southern flank of XII Corps. While some elements of the 76th Infantry Division relieved partial elements of the 5th Infantry Division, other units advanced toward the junction of the Sauer and Prüm Rivers. To the north the 80th Infantry Division captured Hommerdingen.

Limited objectives remained the prime function in the 26th Infantry Division in the XX Corps area. The 26th used tank destroyers to knock out a tower situated across the Saar River which had been used by the Germans as both an observation post and a machine gun nest. The 94th Infantry Division, to the north, gained a mile to the east of Sinz. The 10th Armored Division moved near the front to an assembly area in preparation for an upcoming attack.

Only fourteen sorties were flown by the XIX TAC, accumulating only negligible results.

In the 6th Armored Division a report was filed concerning the M4A3 tanks that had been previously fitted with additional armor on the forward hull (glacis plate). The report stated that a direct hit had been made on the hull of one tank by a German 75mm shell, which penetrated only the additional armor. The shell had separated the middle section of plate from the forward hull. The additional armor had allowed the tank to continue to function and it succeeded in knocking out the German tank which had originally fired the direct hit. Crew members, whose lives had been saved by the plate, praised the modification with affirmative adjectives (which came as no surprise).

February 19
D-Day +258

The divisions of the VIII Corps were lined up north to south in the following order: 87th, 4th, and 90th Infantry Divisions; the 11th and 6th Armored Divisions; and the 6th Cavalry Group. In the corps' area, the towns of Sengerich, Herzfeld, and Lasthorn were either captured or cleared. A treadway bridge was built over the Primmer River just south of Leidenborn by the 90th Infantry Division.

The divisions of the XII Corps were placed 4th Armored Division; 2d Cavalry Group; 76th, 5th, and 80th Infantry Divisions from south to north respectively. Towns captured by the Corps's divisions were Halsdorf, Stocken, Neidersgegen, Freilingen, and Nusbaum.

In the XX Corps the 26th Infantry Division attacked on a small scale. The 94th Infantry Division and the 10th Armored Division launched a coordinated attack around Sinz. The 10th captured Kirf and Palzem while the 94th captured Faha, Munzingen, and Oberleuken.

In spite of bad weather, the XIX TAC flew 279 sorties. However, the weather conditions did keep them from having anything except marginal results. They destroyed 6 German planes and damaged 10 others. On the ground, they damaged or destroyed 185 railroad cars and 95 vehicles.

Intelligence reports from G-2 indicated to General Patton's staff that the residents of the occupied German towns of Ginsingen and Niedaltdorf were very much interested in ending the war and returning to normal life. They cooperated completely with the Third Army personnel.

February 20
D-Day +259

Combat Command "B" of the 6th Armored Division secured high ground north of Waldhof-Falkenstein, captured Langfuhr, and improved its bridgehead over the Our River. The 11th Armored Division captured Rischeid, cleared fifty-three pillboxes, and gained one mile. The 4th and 87th Infantry Divisions consolidated their positions and otherwise remained inactive.

The 2d Cavalry Group, fighting in the XII Corps, built two footbridges across the Moselle River while the 76th Infantry Division consolidated its positions and secured the high ground west of the Prüm River. The 5th Infantry Division cleared Halsdorf and established a line on the Prüm River overlooking Wettlingen, a town seven miles south of Bitburg. Bitburg was the primary objective of the attack. The 80th Infantry Division went two miles across the Enz River and captured Obersgegen, Korperich, and Seimerich. The 4th Armored Division remained in reserve.

At the Saarlautern bridgehead in the XX Corps, a counterattack was repulsed by the 26th Infantry Division. The 94th Infantry and 10th Armored Divisions continued their coordinated attacks into the Moselle-Roer River triangle. The 94th infantry captured Kollesleucken, Orscholz, Weiten, and Freudenburg, with leading elements only three miles from the Saar River. The 10th Armored Division captured Meurich, Korrig, Wehr, Helfant, Dilmar, Rehlingen, Sudlingen, Rommelfangen, Ditlingen, and Fisch.

The 174 sorties flown by the XIX TAC ended with 2 enemy command posts attacked and 257 vehicles destroyed or damaged.

February 21
D-Day +260

General Patton personally and verbally ordered the XX Corps to attack and seize the key German communications center of Trier.

The 6th Cavalry Group consolidated its positions east of Viaden in the southern sector of VIII Corps' area. While doing this, the 6th Armored's Combat Command "B" managed to gain two miles and capture Reipeldingen, Dasburg, and Daleiden. The 11th Armored Division consolidated its positions, with its Reserve Combat Command taking Reiff and Eschfield. The units in the 90th Infantry Division cleared Binscheid, Hickeshausen, Halenbach, Euscheid, and Strickscheid. Task Force Spiess (headquarters, 773d Tank Destroyer Battalion, four tank destroyer gun platoons, one tank destroyer reconnaissance company, 90th Infantry Division reconnaissance troop, one light tank company, one infantry rifle company, one infantry antitank company, and one engineer platoon) covered the 90th Infantry Division's right flank and mopped up. All in all, the corps reported that from January 29 to February 21 they had destroyed a total of 936 pillboxes. The 6th Armored accounted for 72, the 11th Armored 171, the 90th Infantry 391, the 4th Infantry 223; and the 87th Infantry 79.

The 2d Cavalry Group and the 76th Infantry Division in the XII Corps maintained positions and patrolled. The 5th Infantry Division cleared the ground up to the Prüm River. The 80th Infantry Division captured Lahr, Huttingen, and Geichlingen. Bridgeheads of the 80th Infantry Division and the 6th Cavalry Group were joined across the Our River at Roth.

In the XX Corps the 26th Infantry Division maintained its positions. The 94th Infantry and 10th Armored Divisions continued their joint attack into the Siegfried Line. Combat Command "A" of the 10th Armored reached a point six miles from the city of Trier, with the Reserve Combat Command clearing Temmels and Fellerich.

The XIX TAC flew 504 sorties in support missions. They damaged or destroyed 318 vehicles, 28 armored vehicles/tanks, 575 railroad cars, and 14 gun positions.

Circumspectly, the Third Army had a good day. The XX Corps cleared most of the triangle formed by the Moselle and Saar Rivers, and elements of the VIII and XII Corps struck from north and south respectively. All of Saarburg was cleared with the exception of one lone castle. In addition, 23 other towns were captured.

February 22
D-Day +261

In the VIII Corps the 6th Cavalry Group advanced about one-and-a-half miles, reaching a place about three miles northeast of Vianden. In the 6th Armored Division, Combat Command "A" captured Affler after crossing the Our River. Combat Command "B" captured Olmscheid and Irrhausen, seizing the high ground overlooking the Enz River. The Reserve Combat Command of the 11th Armored Division repulsed a strong counterattack, advanced two miles, and reached the Manner River. The 90th Infantry Division cleared Lichtenborn, Heilbach, and Kopscheid. The 4th Infantry Division was finalizing preparations for their attack.

In the XII Corps the 2d Cavalry Group patrolled along the corps' southern boundary. The 76th Infantry maintained positions and the 5th Infantry Division patrolled in zone. The 80th Infantry Division gained two miles along its front and the 4th Armored Division moved to a jump off point, preparing for an attack in conjunction with the 80th Infantry Division.

The XX Corps' 26th Infantry Division held its bridgeheads, while the 94th Infantry Division and the 10th Armored Division, both to the north, continued reducing the Moselle-Saar River triangle. An examination of the captured German positions in the triangle disclosed that nineteen of their artillery pieces had been destroyed or damaged beyond repair by the corps' counterbattery fire. An additional sixteen pieces had been overrun and captured intact by the rapid drive of the XX Corps' advances.

The XIX TAC lost 2 of their own planes and shot down 3 German planes while flying 358 sorties. They accounted for damage or destruction of 18 marshalling yards and the cutting of 78 railroad lines. Escort missions were flown for 25 formations of medium bombers making a widespread attack aimed primarily at rail activity.

February 23
D-Day +262

In the VIII Corps the 6th Cavalry Group cleared Berscheid, Karlshausen, Scheitenkorb, Bauler, Herbstmuhle, Rodershausen, and Koxhausen. The 6th Armored Division captured Leimbach and Muxerat and secured the high ground overlooking Neuerburg at the junction of the Enz and Wahl Rivers. The 90th Infantry Division captured Uppershausen, Plascheid, Emmelbaum, Niederpierscheid, Berkoth, Krautscheid, Ringhuscheid, and Lauperath. Task Force Spiess captured four German self-propelled guns. The 4th and 87th Infantry Divisions and the 11th Armored Division patrolled.

In the southern part of the XII Corps, the 2d Cavalry Group and the 5th and 76th Infantry Divisions maintained positions. To the north the 80th Infantry Division received fire support from the 4th Armored Division. The 4th Armored made some slight gains, clearing Sinspelt and Niedergeckler and capturing a bridge over the Enz River before the Germans could destroy it.

In the XX Corps the 26th Infantry Division defended and maintained its bridgeheads at Saarlautern. The 94th Infantry Division managed to cross a total of six battalions over the Saar River at Serrig to expand the bridgehead there. The 10th Armored Division captured Ockfen, then expanded their bridgehead to a depth of one mile and a width of two miles.

Six planes were lost by the XIX TAC in 572 sorties. They had fine weather and plentiful targets. They destroyed or damaged 724 vehicles, 269 armored vehicles/tanks, 1,308 railroad cars, 19 gun positions, 135 buildings, and 36 locomotives.

ComZ was informed of a critical shortage of hot patches for tires in the Third Army units. Also aggravating the situation was a shortage of both tires and innertubes. A total of twenty thousand patches were requested at once and five thousand additional each week.

February 24
D-Day +263

In a swinging movement to the north, the 6th Cavalry Group continued advancing. They captured Scheurn, Altscheuern, Berraden, and Fischbach, also knocking out sixteen pillboxes. In the 6th Armored Division, Combat Command "B" moved south and exchanged positions with the 6th Cavalry Group. They also cleared Neuerburb and knocked out seven pillboxes with their tank destroyers. The 11th Armored Division made no attacks. The 90th Infantry Division gained two miles and captured Oberpierscheid. The 4th and 87th Infantry Divisions remained inactive.

The 5th Infantry Division, in the XII Corps, attacked across the Prüm River, where they secured two small bridgeheads. In the 76th Infantry Division, one unit (the 304th Infantry Regiment) attacked through the 5th Infantry Division's zone to capture Holstrum. The 80th Infantry Division (with Combat Command "B" borrowed from the 4th Armored Division) advanced two miles and captured Outscheid, Brimigen, and Niederranden.

In the southern part of the XX Corps, the 26th Infantry Division continued with limited objectives. Some elements of the 94th Infantry Division advanced two miles east of the Saar River, while a number of tanks and tank destroyers were brought across into the bridgehead. The 10th Armored Division increased their bridgehead's size. Engineers of both the 94th Infantry and 10th Armored Divisions worked at a fever pitch to construct bridges to bring across main supporting weapons.

Fighter bombers of the XIX TAC made claims of 253 vehicles, 47 armored vehicles/tanks, 597 railway cars, 2 supply dumps, and 8 marshalling yards destroyed or damaged. The work required 327 sorties in 47 missions.

Artillery liaison-type aircraft proved to be essential in the supplying of the 5th Ranger Battalion attached to the 94th Infantry Division. In the face of heavy enemy machine gun fire, the pilots flew 56 sorties to drop ammunition, rations, medical supplies, and blankets to the troops who were in advanced positions near Serrig. Reports from VIII Corps indicated that ninety-five percent of the supplies dropped by parachute to the Rangers were retrieved and found to be in good condition. The five percent lost consisted mostly of gasoline containers which burst upon impact.

In the Grand Duchy of Luxembourg, evacuees were being returned to their homes. From February 17 to February 24, about 600 out of 3,750 refugees in Esch had been allowed to reenter their homes in the northern cantons. Many of these refugees were requested by the Luxembourg government for the purpose of rehabilitation work in the vicinity of Ettelbrück.

February 25
D-Day +264

G-2 reported that although there was no indication of a mass collapse or surrender by the Germans at this time, there was evidenced a noticeable loss of control and a disintegration of morale among the forces against the Third Army's front lines. Other significant facts were that six of the eight remaining Panzer divisions in the west were either committed or actually in tactical reserve in the northern sectors of the Western Front, and, lastly, the Germans lacked replacements for the heavy losses that they were continually sustaining against all armies on all fronts.

In preparation for further movements to the east, the VIII Corps engaged its units in patrolling.

An air observation post in the 76th Infantry Division located a large troop concentration and adjusted the fires of an organic artillery battalion onto it. Thirty vehicles were destroyed and more than one hundred casualties were inflicted. To the north, in the XII Corps area, the 5th Infantry Division continued its attack by seizing high ground overlooking the Nums River. The 10th Infantry Regiment took Dockendorf, Messerich, Bettingen, and Ingendorf. A hard-driven attack by the 4th Armored Division gained seven miles and seized bridges intact over both the Prüm and Nims Rivers. This attack drove to a vicinity only two miles outside of the northern limits of Bitburg. The 80th Infantry Division then followed the 4th Armored Division and mopped up and captured Echtershausen, Mettendorf and Hamm and entering Mauel.

The 26th Infantry Division maintained its positions in the bridgehead at Saarlautern in the XX Corps.

Several 105mm howitzers and the 90mm guns of tank destroyers were frequently employed by divisions in coordination to attack and reduce pillboxes. The artillery was first adjusted upon the pillbox, then the tank destroyer attacked the pillbox with direct fire methods to effect penetrations and force the personnel into the open. They thereupon, the artillery immediately fired for effect against the personnel.

The XIX TAC flew 434 sorties. Their count for the day was 250 vehicles, 97 tanks/armored cars, 21 locomotives, 692 railroad cars, 67 buildings and 26 marshalling yards damaged or destroyed. A total of 23 rail lines were cut. Out of the day's activities, they lost only one plane.

February 26
D-Day +265

The Twelfth Army Group ordered the Third Army to hold the 90th Infantry Division in reserve to be available to SHAEF. The division was not to be committed without the authority of that higher headquarters.

The VIII Corps continued with its refitting and preparation for the continuance of their attack.

In the XII Corps the 2d Cavalry Group continued fighting in Wasserbillig. The 76th Infantry Division continued to clear the high ground overlooking the Nims River and advanced as far as the outskirts of Wolsfeld and Kaschenback. The 5th Infantry Division went through Niederstedem and Oberstedem, captured a bridge intact at Birtlingen, and cleared Stahl. The 4th Armored Division captured Matzen and Mattenheim (roughly four miles northeast of Bitburg. To the north, the 80th Infantry Division moved forward six miles, relieving some elements of the 4th Armored Division along the Prüm River and clearing Maeul in the process.

The 26th Infantry Division rotated its units in the XX Corps area while the 94th Infantry Division enlarged its Saar River bridgehead cleared a forest southeast of the town and mopped up an enemy pocket at Beurig. In the 10th Armored Divison, the troops of Combat Command "B" captured Zerf; Combat Command "A" crossed the Saar River at Serrig; and the Reserve Combat Command followed the 94th Infantry Division across at Saarburg.

Poor weather hampered the XIX TAC. They flew only five missions, two of which were weather reconnaissance. The other three were armed reconnaissance missions east of the Rhine River. Two locomotives were destroyed and 6 were damaged. They also hit 40 railroad cars.

February 27
D-Day +266

The 6th Cavalry Group in the VIII Corps advanced one mile to capture Waxweiler. In the 6th Armored Division, Combat Command "A" advanced about a mile and a half, crossed the Prüm River, and cleared Pintesfeld. The 4th Infantry Division patrolled but made no attack. The 345th and 346th Infantry Regiments of the 87th Infantry Division advanced about one thousand yards to the high ground southeast of Ormont. The 11th Armored Division remained in the corps' assembly area.

In the southern part of the XII Corps, the 2d Cavalry Group patrolled. To the north three regiments of the 76th Infantry Division moved southeast toward Trier. In the 5th Infantry Division, the 10th Infantry Regiment advanced about two-and-a-half miles and captured Scharfbillig, Rhol, and Esslingen. The 11th Infantry Regiment captured Motsch and Masholder and advanced about three miles. Still farther to the north, the 4th Armored Division mopped up in its area after a rapid advance. The 4th Armored Division's elements captured Fliessem, Niederweiler, and Bickendorfg. The 76th Infantry Division was used to aid the XX Corps in its mission of capturing Trier. The 80th Infantry Division consolidated gains, cleared five towns, and patrolled aggressively.

In the XX Corps, the 26th Infantry Division widened its zone

to take over positions previously held by the 3d Cavalry
Group. The 3d Cavalry moved north and attached to the 94th
Infantry Division. The 94th Infantry Division advanced
about one mile to the northeast while the 10th Armored Division went forward about four miles, reaching an area just six
miles south of Trier.

The artillery contingents of both the VIII and XII Corps
combined their guns to conduct a coordinated antiflak program of continued neutralizing firings upon four heavy antiaircraft batteries on the route of approach of twelve hundred
heavy bombers of the Eighth U.S. Air Force. The firings were
conducted for about ninety minutes as the bombers flew into
Germany and were repeated on the return flight.

Poor flying conditions limited the XIX TAC to 112 sorties.
With low, overcast skies, the planes were kept from strafing
the Germans. A total of 36 tons of bombs were dropped with
only partially observed results, although it was known that 4
marshalling yards were damaged and 6 locomotives were
destroyed.

There was a very great lack of civilian medical personnel
and facilities in the Third Army's area and that situation was
causing an excessive burden on the military medical units. To
eliminate this, military government public health officers reestablished and improvised hospitals, relocated civilian doc-
tors, and salvaged medical supplies.

February 28
D-Day +267

The 6th Cavalry Group increased its bridgehead to a depth
of five hundred yards in the VIII Corps area, completely
crossing all of its troops. The 6th Armored Division cleared
Merlscheid, Lunebach, Pronsfeld, Dackscheid, and Eilscheid.
The 4th Infantry Division renewed its attack, driving one mile
east of the Prüm River and capturing Kleinlangenfeld. The
87th Infantry Division encountered heavy resistance, but still
managed to advance about five hundred yards and reduced
pillboxes as they went forward. The 11th Armored Division
remained in the assembly area.

The 2d Cavalry Group patrolled in the XII Corps while the 76th Infantry Division drove southward toward Trier. The 76th Infantry's elements cleared Hohn, Butzwerler, Welsch-billing, Desheim, Ittel-Kyll, and Eisenach. The 5th Infantry Division gained about two miles to the high ground overlooking the Kyll River. In the process they captured Idenheim, Trimport, Sulm, and Dahlem. The 4th Armored Division pushed on one mile to the east, between the Nims and Kyll Rivers and captured Irsch. The 80th Infantry Division gained two miles between the Prüm and Ehlenz Rivers and captured Ehlenz, Schleid, and Obersweiler.

There was no alteration in the 26th Infantry Division's situation in the southern section of the XX Corps. The 10th Armored Division captured Lampaden, Pellingen, and Wiltingen. Elements of the 10th Armored advanced to positions within a mile west of Trier.

Overcast conditions again kept the number of sorties down in the XIX TAC. They flew 239, but they were mostly as escorts for medium bombers. Several German planes were encountered in the operations with losses of 4 confirmed, 2 probably destroyed, and 3 damaged. There were no losses for the XIX TAC.

A report concerning the use of searchlights for night artillery firings indicated that it was generally a success, although some combat commanders observed certain limitations. When searchlights shined at 45-degree angles on low clouds during the night to create artificial moonlight, the Germans (when located in buildings or trenches) could observe the movement of the Third Army troops. Interrogated POWs, stated that the Germans enjoyed a number of the advantages from the lights that the Third Army also received. Used in the river crossings of the XII and XX Corps' zones, the searchlights, in the words of one commander, "...lifted the doughboy from a blind, groping ineffective to an efficient, confident, and aggressive soldier."

CHAPTER 8

March, 1945

During the month of March, the Third Army would cross over the Rhine River and bring the war to the German's own backyard. The Third Army, in conjunction with other Allied armies, would inflict such terrible and disastrous defeats upon the Germans that they would have no hope of ever regaining any initiative toward victory. Highlights of the Third Army's advance would be

1. The smashing of the Siegfried Line
2. The trapping of thousands of Germans in the Palatinate Campaign
3. The first assault crossings of the Rhine River in modern history;
4. The penetration into Central Germany.

March 1
D-Day +268

The 6th Cavalry Group, 6th Armored Division, 4th Infantry Division, the 87th Infantry Division, and Combat Command "A" of the 11th Armored Division were on the line from south to north in the VIII Corps area. The 11th Armored Division was in corps reserve and the 90th Infantry Division was in SHAEF reserve. The 6th Cavalry Group, in the south, advanced about a mile and a half to the east and cleared Greimelscheid, Lambertsberg, Hargarten, and Plutscheid. The 6th Armored Division advanced a mile and a half east of the

Prüm River. The 87th Infantry Division, on the northern flank, captured Ormont, about a mile and a half to the east.

The XII Corps consisted of the 2d Cavalry Group, 76th Infantry Division (with the 318th Infantry Regiment of the 80th Infantry Division attached), 5th Infantry Division, 4th Armored Division, and 80th Infantry Division. They were in line in that order from south to north. The 76th Infantry Division advanced toward Trier, clearing the pocket in the Sauer River east of Echternach, capturing Edingen, and advancing about two miles. The 2d Cavalry Group cleared Rospoet and Steinheim. The 5th Infantry Division maintained positions along the west bank of the Kyll River. The 4th Armored Division moved north about a mile between the Nims and Kyll Rivers, clearing Malbergweich and Sefferweich. They secured the high ground near Seffern, about five miles north of Bitburg.

The divisions of the XX Corps continued to maintain their positions in the Saarlautern bridgehead. To the north the 94th Infantry Division cleared Paschel, Schomerich, Hentern, Lampaden, and Obsersehr. Some leading elements of the 10th Armored Division entered Trier from the southern route and succeeded in cutting the road leading from the city to the northeast. They also managed to seize a bridge intact. During the attack on Trier, the 609th Tank Destroyer Battalion captured 474 POWs. The 376th Infantry Regiment of the 94th Infantry Division cleared Oberemmel, Kommlingen, Krettnach-Obermennig, and Wiltingen.

A total of 485 sorties were flown by the XIX TAC. They dropped 188 tons of bombs; shot down 7 German planes; and lost 3 planes of their own. Low cloud cover caused limited visibility, but they still were able to claim destruction or damage to 111 motor vehicles, 29 tanks/armored cars, 12 locomotives, 40 railroad cars, and 63 factories.

In total, the month of March began with the Third Army entering Trier, clearing twenty-nine towns, and capturing 47 and a half square miles of territory.

The supply situation was generally quite good and the strength of the Third Army was 304,690 troops.

A decision was made to reduce the number of ammunition supply installations. Previous experience had indicated that the flow of supplies (especially critical items) could be more closely controlled with a minimum of installations.

March 2
D-Day +269

It was learned that General Model had been elevated to the rank of German commander-in-chief of the Western Front, replacing General Von Rundstedt. According to G-2 Section's estimation, this news indicated that the Nazis were insistent upon an uncompromising political high command on the Western Front and that (to that end) they were *Nazi-fying* the high command as they had done on the Eastern Front. Model was known as an ardent Nazi.

The 6th Cavalry Group advanced two miles in the VIII Corps area, reaching the high ground overlooking the Nims River. Just to the north, the 6th Armored Division captured Heisdorf, Wetteldorf, Schonecken, Niederlauch, Oberlauch, Dingdorf, Heisdorf, and Winringen. During this fighting, they also seized a bridge intact at Schonecken and forded the Nims River at Wetteldorf. The 4th Infantry Division cleared Weinsheim and Niederprum. The 87th Infantry Division advanced about a mile in the northern section of the corps' zone.

The 2d Cavalry Group crossed the Sauer River in the southern zone of the XII Corps, gain four miles and capturing both Grewenich and Herresthalerhof. The 76th Infantry Division went four miles forward and cleared Trierweiler, Sirzenich, Neuhas, Niederweiler, and Fusenich. The 5th Infantry attacked under the cover of darkness and encountered only scattered small arms and mortar fire. The 5th Infantry took Huttingen and Metterich. Farther south, the 4th Armored Division captured Seffern during a mile-and-a-half advance to the north. The 80th Infantry Division made some small advances, capturing Heilenbach and making contact with the 6th Cavalry Group of the VIII Corps.

In the XX Corps the 26th Infantry Division maintained its Saarlautern bridgehead. The 94th Infantry Division cleared pillboxes and gained about one-half mile. The 10th Armored Division cleared Trier as well as the area between Saarburg and Trier, where two small pockets of Germans remained. Some elements of the division advanced to the Kyll River, about three-and-a-half miles northeast of Trier.

The XIX TAC flew 577 sorties through murky weather. They had good results on targets of all types. Among their claims were 204 motor vehicles, 29 locomotives, 8 barges, 115 factory buildings, 9 fuel tanks, and 1 supply depot damaged or destroyed. They also cut 29 rail lines and 4 highway cuts and shot down 5 German planes. The TAC lost only 3 planes.

March 3
D-Day +270

G-2 reports indicated that there was a very great decline of the morale of the German soldiers facing the Third Army. This was evidenced by the fact that since February 28, 6,589 German POW's had been processed into U.S. Army cages.

The Twelfth Army Group finally released the 90th Infantry Division from SHAEF reserve to the Third Army control. The only problem was that within the same directive, they took the 6th Armored Division from Third Army control and placed it into SHAEF Reserve.

In the VIII Corps the 6th Cavalry Group captured Reuland and Huscheid, both about a mile east of the Nims River. Before being relieved by the 90th Infantry Division, the 6th Armored Division captured Giesdorf and gained an advance of about two-and-a-half miles. Immediately after the relief, the 90th Infantry Division attacked viciously and captured Niedehersdorf and Seiwerath. To the north the 11th Armored Division passed through the 4th Infantry Division's zone and then attacked and captured Fleringen. The 4th Infantry had captured Rommersheim, Weinsheim, and Gondelsheim just before the 11th passed through its zone.

In the XII zone the 2d Cavalry Group captured Mesenich, Langsur, Liersberg, Igel, and Zewen-Oberkirch. In the 76th Infantry Division, the 304th Infantry Regiment crossed the Kyll River, secured a bridgehead, and cleared Hosten and

Orenhoffen. The 5th Infantry Division cleared Gondorf and repulsed a counterattack. The 4th Armored Division assembled in the vicinity of Bitburg in preparation for their upcoming attack. The 80th Infantry Division moved forward about one half mile east of Seffern.

In the XX Corps the 26th Infantry Division patrolled. Both the 10th Armored and the 94th Infantry Divisions consolidated their gains of the preceding days and mopped up in their zones to the west bank of the Rewer River.

An overcast sky prevented some of the 540 sorties of the XIX TAC from being completely successful. The majority of the sorties were flown in corps support. Among claims for the day were 224 motor vehicles, 38 tanks/armored vehicles, 245 railroad cars, 2 bridges, 16 gun positions, 95 factory buildings, 22 towns, 11 marshalling yards, and 1 troop concentration.

Plans were being made at Lucky Forward for the supply of a twenty division attack to the Rhine River.

March 4
D-Day +271

The 6th Cavalry Group in the VIII Corps advanced four miles in the face of strong resistance. They captured Neustrassburg, Balesfeld, Neuheilenbach, Wawern, and Burbach. The 90th Infantry Division maintained contact with the 6th Cavalry Group and advanced to the west bank of the Kyll River, capturing Oberhersdorf, Eigelbach, and Kopp in the process. The 11th Armored Division advanced about 4 miles to a place a mile and a half west of the junction of the Kyll and Oos Rivers. To the north the 4th Infantry Division continued its attack, capturing Schwirzheim, Oos, and Duppach. The 87th Infantry Division captured Scheid, Hallschlag, and Schonfeld.

In the XII Corps the 2d Cavalry Group assembled in reserve in the southern portion of the corps' area. In the 76th Infantry Division, the 304th Regiment captured Speicher, Preist, and Orenhoffen; the 395th Regiment patrolled; the 10th and 11th Regiments expanded their Kyll River bridgehead and captured Philippsheim, Baden, Erdorf, Dudeldorf, Ordorf, and Pickliessem; and the 2d Regiment patrolled west of the Kyll River. The 4th Armored Division attacked through the 5th Infantry Division's bridgehead positions and passed quickly through Gindorf and Steinborn. The 80th Infantry Division's 318th Infantry Regiment made contact with the 6th Cavalry Group (VIII Corps) near Balesfeld, and assumed the high-ground positions west of the Kyll River.

The 26th Infantry Division patrolled in the southern portion of XX Corps. The 65th Infantry Division closed in an assembly area. The 94th Infantry Division maintained positions. The 10th Armored Division cleared Pfaizel with its Combat Command "B," and both its Reserve and Combat Command "A" crossed the Rewer River in two places, driving in bridgeheads about a half-mile deep.

Poor weather limited the effectiveness of the XIX TAC. They flew only six sorties—two for weather reconnaissance and 4 for Corps support. The only claims for the day were one rail out and one locomotive, one factory building and five railroad cars damaged or destroyed.

In an effort to relieve tactical units of the growing task of maintaining large numbers of security guards, local police units were organized throughout the Third Army area by the Military Government Section.

March 5
D-Day +272

According to G-2 reports, German POW disclosures definitely showed that the Germans were using makeshift combat commands composed of stragglers, supply troops, and convalescents. The enemy faced a tactical situation that normally would indicate a withdrawal, but it was known that Hitler would never voluntarily relinquish territory and that the Germans repeatedly suffered serious defeats because of this stubbornness to yield untenable positions. It was estimated that German forces facing the Third Army totaled about forty-five thousand combat effectives and about fifty tanks. According to the estimation of G-2, it was time to let the Third Army strike the killing blow to Germany's heart; but SHAEF had other ideas.

Letter of Instruction No. 16 was received from the Twelfth Army Group. Outlined in the letter were the orders that

1. Twenty-first Army Group (Montgomery) would engage in operations which had the objective of closing to the Rhine River and seizing a bridgehead over the Rhine River north of the Ruhr
2. The Sixth Army Group was to remain on the defensive
3. The Twelfth Army Group (with the Third Army) was to clear the enemy of the area west of the Rhine and north of the Moselle Rivers to insure the security of the main lines of communication to the north, with the front of the southern zone (Third Army) to remain on the defensive.

All in all, the American armies were again called on to support Montgomery and his flurry of inactivity in the north.

In the VIII Corps, the 6th Cavalry Group moved to assembly in the northern portion of the corps' zone. The 90th Infantry Division closed completely to the Kyll River, capturing Lissingen, Birresborn, and Morelenbach. The 11th Armored Division captured Scheulern, Kalenborn, Roth, and Nieder-Bettingen. The 87th Infantry Division continued to attack, crossing the Kyll River and capturing Lissendorf, Gonnersdorf, and Stadtkyll.

The 76th Infantry Division attacked in an attempt to enlarge its bridgehead over the Kyll River. They gained about one-half mile both to the north and west. The 4th Armored Division continued toward the Rhine River. Combat Command "B" disrupted German communications and gained fifteen miles; Combat Command "A" began another route to the south. Unfortunately, bad roads and demolished bridges forced them to move north to follow Combat Command "B." The 4th Armored captured Seinsfeld, Steinborn, Meisburg, Kyllburgweiler, Oberstadtfeld, Salm, and Wallenborn during the day's operations.

The XX Corps was mostly involved with relief and regrouping activities.

There were no flights for the XIX TAC because of bad weather.

The Third Army captured its two-hundred-thousandth German POW. He was received at the army enclosure located at Arlon, where he was photographed with a sign around his neck proclaiming him the two-hundred-thousandth Prisoner of War. The photograph was censored at higher headquarters, claiming that the Third Army had abused the man's rights and degraded him under the Geneva Convention Rules of War.

March 6
D-Day +273

On the southern flank of the VIII Corps, the 90th Infantry Division advanced about three miles east from its Kyll River bridgehead and enlarged it both north and south. They also captured Densborn, Gerolstein, Buscheich, Peim, and Gees. In the 11th Armored Division, Combat Command "A" crossed the Kyll River. The 4th Infantry Division closed up to the Kyll River, with its 22d Infantry Regiment crossing it. The 87th Infantry Division captured Feusdorf, Junkerath, and Birgel.

In the XII Corps the 76th Infantry Division pushed forward three miles from its bridgehead and cleared Herforst and Binsfeld. To the north the 5th Infantry Division gained seven miles, having been motorized just a day before. They cleared Oberkail, Spangdahlem, and Dahlem. In the 4th Armored Division's zone, Combat Command "A" was trying to make up its 17-mile separation from Combat Command "B," which was nearing the town of Mayen. The 80th Infantry Division maintained its positions.

In the XX Corps, the 65th Infantry Division continued its relief of the 26th Infantry Division. The 94th Infantry Division maintained its positions. The 10th Armored was busier, moving forward a mile and a half and clearing the towns of Mertesdorf and Ehrang.

Bad weather kept the XIX TAC grounded.

Throughout the occupied sections of Germany, the Third Army found that foodstocks were generally adequate for the civilian population. When shortages were encountered, redistribution of surplus stocks from other localities sufficed for the minimum needs of the people.

March 7
D-Day +274

It was estimated that about twenty-five thousand German effectives were located in a pocket north of the Moselle River. The Germans were considered to be capable of local offensive action within the pocket as an effort to effect the relief of the trapped forces and to cut the communications of the Allied forces encircling it. There was no evidence yet indicating that the German High Command had yielded in its determination to continue resisting as long as it could continue an adequate form of control. G-2 estimated that locally, however, the high command's control had either vanished or was impotent and that the will and capability of the combat troops to continue fighting was disintegrating.

The 90th Infantry Division employed all three of its regiments to enlarge its Kyll River bridgehead and to capture Rockeskyll, Essingen, Neroth, Betteldorf, and Berlingen. The 11th Armored Division continued its attack in the north, advancing rapidly and capturing Kirchweiler, Dockweiler, Dreis, and Kelberg. In support of the 11th Armored's advance, the 4th Infantry Division captured Hillesheim, Boldorf, and Lammersdorf. Also in the 4th Infantry Division, the newly motorized 8th Regiment advanced five miles to the east and captured Alendorf, Mirbach, Ripsdorf, Dollendorf, Hundersdorf, Bigel, Wiesbaum, and Esch. The 6th Cavalry Group kept in contact with the First Army and patrolled.

The 76th Infantry Division continued to advance in the XII Corps. The 2d Cavalry Group cleared Rodt, Scheidweiler, and Zemmer. The 4th Armored Division continued its rapid advance, completely unchecked by the Germans. Combat Command "A" was closing the gap between it and Combat Command "B." In the 5th Infantry Division, the towns of Gransdorf and Schwarzenborn were captured. The 80th Infantry Division gained about one mile.

The 65th Infantry Division completed its relief of the 26th

Infantry Division in the XX Corps area, including the Saarlautern bridgehead. While the 26th Infantry Division remained in position, the 94th Infantry Division repulsed some counterattacks in is's zone. The 10th Armored Division gained 10 miles after crossing the Kyll River just northeast of Trier. Combat Command "A" passed through the 76th Infantry Division's zone while Combat Command "B" captured Quint and Ehrang. The Reserve Combat Command crossed the Kyll River and made a short advance to the northeast.

The XIX TAC was grounded again due to poor weather.

It was estimated that a total of 73,405 refugees and 3,442 displaced persons were encompassed in the Third Army's zone of operations.

March 8
D-Day +275

The chief measures of defense utilized by the Germans at this time were mine fields and roadblocks. Counterattacks and other aggressive means of resistance were being abandoned for methods which would permit more hasty withdrawals.

The 11th Armored Division was operating far in advance of other VIII Corps units. The 11th's Combat Command "B" made contact with the 4th Armored Division east of Mayen and captured Brohl while Combat Command "A" advanced and captured Mayen, which had been previously bypassed by the 4th Armored Division's Combat Command "B". The 90th Infantry Division continued following the 11th Armored Division, with its 357th Infantry Regiment spearheading through Kelberg. In the 4th Infantry Division, the 8th Infantry had been motorized and was far in advance of both the 12th and 22d Regiments. The 22d Regiment captured Kerfen, Leudersdorf, Uxheim, and Hoffeld. The 87th Infantry Division, while keeping in contact with the V Corps of the First Army, gained thirteen miles in the northern portion of the corps zone. The 6th Cavalry Group began passing through the 4th Infantry Division's zone, while to the rear the 6th Armored Division remained in SHAEF's reserve.

The 2d Cavalry Group (attached to the 76th Infantry Division) screened the southern flank of the XII Corps. After clearing out Gladbach, Landscheid, Burg, and Heeg, the 385th Infantry Regiment of the 76th Infantry Division crossed the Salm River and drove toward Grosslitgen. Also in the 76th's zone, the 304th Infantry Regiment drove up to the Salm River, took the town of Greverath, and prepared to cross the river. The 5th Infantry Division had already gotten its 2d and 11th Infantry Regiments across the Salm River. In the 4th Armored Division's zone, both Combat Command "A" and "B" took ground north and west of Koblenz, capturing Bassenheim, Wolken, Kobern, Rubenach, Mulheim, Karlish, Druft, Plaidt, Miesenheim, Saffign, and Kettiog. The 11th Infantry Regiment (attached to the 4th Armored Division from the 5th Infantry Division) near the whole of the 4th Armored. The 80th Infantry Division had little to do, having been pinched out of the action by the northerly attack of the 5th Infantry Division.

In the XX Corps, the 65th Infantry Division patrolled in Saarlautern at the bridgehead and throughout the southern portion of the corps' zone. The 26th Infantry Division relieved part of the 94th Infantry Division, allowing it to regroup its forces. The 10th Armored Division went forward and captured Erlenbach and Rievenich.

There were only three weather reconnaissance sorties flown by the XIX TAC and they were all uneventful. Bad weather precluded any attack sorties.

March 9
D-Day +276

German concern regarding their exposed positions south of the Moselle River was very much expressed by the appearance of a Volksgrenadier division in the Cochem area.

The Twelfth Army issued orders transferring the 87th Infantry Division from the Third to the Seventh Army. Later, these orders would be revoked and the 4th Infantry Division would be transferred in lieu of the 87th.

Rapid advances were being made by all units of the VIII.

Between the VIII Corps and the First Army, a large number of Germans were trapped in an area which was called the Eifel Pocket. The Third Army would spend much time in the following days reducing the troops in this area.

Infantry units following the armor of both the VIII and XX Corps gained 266 square miles of territory on this day, experiencing the largest gains of any day since the lightning advance by the Third Army in August and early September.

The 11th Armored Division was being followed up quickly by the 90th Infantry Division as some of its elements neared Mayen. The 11th Armored Division captured Brohl and Andernach, reaching the Rhine River. While the 11th Armored Division was rapidly driving forward for a total of twenty-five miles, the 90th Infantry went forward a similar distance. The 6th Armored Division began their movement to Dieuze, to join with the Seventh Army.

On the southern flank of XII Corps, the 76th Infantry Division gained three miles. The attached 2d Cavalry Group screened the corps' southern flank while the 76th captured Bruch, Bergweiler, Musweiler, Hupperath, Schladt, and Minderlittgen. The 4th Armored Division made short gains, capturing Hambuch, Dunfus, and Montenich. The 5th Infantry Division gained nine miles and mopped up and captured Battenfeld and Manderscheid. The 80th Infantry Division, by now far to the west, maintained positions while preparing for an attack.

In the XX Corps the 65th, 26th, and 94th Infantry Divisions continued with their reorganizations while maintaining their positions. The 10th Armored Division continued with its attack, capturing Wittlich. In the rear of the corps' zone, the 16th Cavalry Group closed in an assembly area around Veckring.

Operating in very adverse weather, the XIX TAC cooperated fully with the advancing ground units. They attacked special military targets where visibility permitted, flying a total of 309 sorties. They destroyed or damaged 104 railroad cars, 37 factory buildings, 4 oil storage tanks, 42 motor vehicles, and 11 locomotives. They suffered no losses.

Generally, infantry units of the VIII and XX Corps made excellent gains following the armored elements which had finally penetrated to the Rhine River.

March 10
D-Day +277

As the Third Army began increasing their pace of advance, the number of POWs taken increased dramatically. This situation created a serious transportation problem for all of the corps units. From March 3 to March 10, Third Army had taken 11,608 POWs, 446 of whom had been admitted to Third Army hospitals.

In the VIII Corps, the 11th Armored Division cleared Germans from their zone to the west bank of the Rhine River. The 6th Cavalry Group continued its contact with the First Army and advanced in the rear of the 11th Armored Division. The 90th Infantry Division completed its mopping up and then went into an assembly area five miles northwest of Mayen. To the rear the 4th and 87th Infantry Divisions were already in their assembly areas. With the exception of the city of Koblenz, the entire zone of VIII Corps was cleared of the enemy. The 6th Armored Division cleared the Third Army area en route to the Seventh Army. The 4th Infantry Division was relieved of attachment with the Third Army, being attached to the Sixth Army Group to the south.

In the XII Corps, the 4th Armored Division cleared ground along the west bank of the Rhine River and along the northern bank of the Moselle River. They captured Gondorf, Wirfus, Guls, Winningen, Kobern, Illerich, Greimersburg, Carden, Landkern, and Brohl. The 5th Infantry Division gained three miles west of the Lieser River. The 89th Infantry Division, to the rear, began relieving some elements of both the 5th and 76th Infantry Divisions. The 90th Infantry Division finished their mopping up and moved into their assembly area. The 80th Infantry Division was pulled back to the vicinity of Luxembourg en route to XX Corps after being relieved from the XII Corps.

In the XX Corps the 65th, 26th, and 94th Infantry Divisions

patrolled, awaiting orders to attack. The 10th Armored Division gained five miles forward and captured Bombogen, Clusserath, Schleich, Polich, Kremae, Clausen, Pohlbach, Kirsch, Longuich, Riol, and Casel. The 16th Cavalry Group moved forward and began to relieve elements of the 3d Cavalry Group.

The XIX TAC flew 337 sorties, dropping 60 tons of bombs on the hapless Germans. They also provided column cover for the 4th Armored Division during its rapid advance. Some special targets were attacked and a large number of psychological warfare leaflets was dropped for the Germans to read during their leisure time. Damaged or destroyed during the operations were 129 motor vehicles, 8 locomotives, and 23 gun installations.

Overall, the XII Corps moved vigorously in an attempt to catch up with the VIII Corps, while XX Corps was being reinforced for an upcoming large-scale attack.

March 11
D-Day +278

By now, things were looking grim for the Germans. The Allies controlled the west bank of the Rhine River and had a substantial bridgehead on the east bank in Remagen. Four German armies (First Paratroop, Fifth Panzer, Fifteenth and Seventh Armies) had been decisively beaten. One of the most crushing blows was in the Eifel Pocket, where at least half of the combat strength of the German Seventh Army had been destroyed. Many of the Third Army staff believed that had they been allowed to encircle that same Seventh Army and cut them off at the Argentan-Falaise Gap, they would not have been required to fight them again in the Eifel Campaign. At any rate, and in spite of Montgomery's August debacle at the Argentan-Falaise Gap, the Germans were definitely in trouble and the Third Army was not about to let them escape again.

In the VIII Corps the 11th Armored Division cleared all of the Germans in its zone while the 6th Cavalry Group patrolled. To the rear the 4th Infantry Division began its movement from VIII Corps to the Seventh Army. The 90th Infantry

Division remained in assembly positions. Only one small pocket of Germans remained in the woods just northeast of Mayen.

Along the Rhine River in the XII Corps area, Combat Command "B" of the 4th Armored Division was relieved by the 11th Infantry Regiment. Combat Command "A" and the Reserve Combat Command maintained their positions and patrolled. The 5th Infantry Division made some good gains southwest of Mayen, clearing Udler, Oberwinkel, Niederwinkel, Immerath, Strotzbusch, Strohn, Faid, and Gevenich. The 76th Infantry Division was relieved by the 89th Infantry Division in zone, and then proceeded to a new zone farther to the south. Meanwhile, the 89th Infantry Division continued with its attack to the northeast in the former zone of the 76th Infantry.

In the XX Corps the 65th, 26th, and 94th Infantry Divisions patrolled and maintained positions.

The 80th Infantry Division closed between the 26th and 94th Infantry Divisions. The 10th Armored Division gained five miles to the northeast, clearing Mehring, Polan, Logen, Lorch, Schleit, Hisserath, Altrich, Platten, Walholz, Wengerohr, Belinger, and Berliner. The 3d Cavalry Group attacked just beyond Riol.

The XIX TAC had a low ceiling but managed to fly 205 sorties in escort of medium bombers. Ten communication centers were attacked.

A German shell, estimated to be 280mm, struck and exploded within ten yards of the building housing Lucky Forward's Forward Echelon in the city of Luxembourg. It killed two enlisted men and caused considerable damage to the building.

To meet the rising need for medical facilities in occupied areas of Germany, improvised hospitals for sick and wounded civilians were established in Waxweiller, Schonecken, Seidingen, Neuerburg, Saarburn, and Bitburg.

March 12
D-Day +279

An amendment sent out by General Patton to his corps commanders altered the corps boundaries.

In the VIII Corps the 87th Infantry Division began movement to the eastern portion of its zone while the 6th Cavalry Group relieved elements of the 4th and 11th Armored Divisions. The 11th Armored Division moved to an assembly area. In the rear of the corps area, the 4th Infantry Division cleared VIII Corps' zone during its move to the Seventh Army.

In the XII Corps' eastern sector, the 4th Armored Division's Combat Command "A" patrolled along the west bank of the Rhine River and the north bank of the Moselle River. The 4th's Combat Command "B" and the Reserve Combat Command went into assembly areas. Elements of the 90th Infantry Division relieved 4th Armored Division elements and patrolled along the north bank of the Moselle River. The 11th Infantry Regiment reverted from 4th Armored Division to 5th Infantry Division control. The 89th Infantry Division gained seven miles, clearing Niederscheidweiler, Diefenbach, Driesch, and Lutzerth. The 76th Infantry Division passed control of the 417th Infantry Regiment to the 10th Armored Division, while advancing to the east, capturing Kinderbeuern, Urzig, Osann, Kesten, Peisport, and Maring.

In the XX Corps the divisions maintained positions during the initial part of the day. Late in the day the 26th, 80th, and 94th Infantry Divisions launched a coordinated attack. All of the divisions gained from two to four miles before the end of the day. The 10th Armored Division continued with its attack to the northeast in the first part of the day and then was relieved by the 76th Infantry Division. At the end of the day, the 10th Armored Division was moving to an assembly area near Trier, preparing to share in the attack with the three infantry divisions. The 3d Cavalry Group patrolled.

The XIX TAC experienced bad weather and flew only 142 sorties. The majority of their flights were in escort for the 9th Bomber Command.

March 13
D-Day +280

Some elements of the XII Corps crossed the Moselle River to join in the coordinated attack to effect contact with the Seventh Army to the south and to envelop the Germans in the Saar-Moselle-Rhine area.

Letter of Instruction No. 17 from Twelfth Army Group informed the Third Army that

1. The Sixth Army Group was to initiate an operation to close to the Rhine River and establish bridgeheads around Mainz and Mannheim
2. Twelfth Army Group was to secure the Remagen bridgehead over the Rhine River, clear the Germans west of the river, and to assist the Sixth Army Group
3. The Third Army was to defend the line of the Rhine River in zone and attack in conjunction with the Seventh Army in order to protect the Seventh Army's flank and rear
4. The Twenty-first Army Group (Montgomery) was to continue operations to secure crossings over the Rhine River north of the Ruhr.

It is little wonder that General Patton's staff seemed to feel as they had again been relegated to the position of step-child in the role of flank defender.

In the VIII Corps, the 6th Cavalry Group patrolled and the 4th Armored Division operated along the Rhine River. The 11th Armored Division was in reserve. The 87th Infantry was moving up to join the other corps near the Rhine River.

The XII Corps front was roughly southwest to northeast. The 4th Armored Division was at the extreme northeastern part of the zone doing some patrolling. The 5th and 90th Infantry Divisions were just to the south and deployed along the northern bank of the Moselle River. Both divisions jumped off at nightfall and followed a two-hour long artillery preparation. They seized bridgeheads across the Moselle River—which they promptly enlarged to about one mile in depth—and consolidated them before the day was done. Farther to the west, the 89th and 76th Infantry Divisions were clearing out some enemy pockets along the northern banks of the Moselle River. As artillery harassed the Germans along their escape routes, the 2d Cavalry Group was relieved from attachment with the 76th Infantry Division and began moving to join the 90th Infantry Division.

The 65th Infantry Division patrolled along the northern part of the XX Corps boundary. The 26th, 80th, and 94th Infantry Divisions attacked through the rough Hunsbruck terrain. They gained two miles, three miles, and one-and-a-half miles respectively. The 80th Infantry Division cleared Greimerath and the 94th Infantry Division captured Holzerath and Schondorf. The 10th Armored Division remained in assembly, near Trier. The 3d Cavalry Group patrolled.

The XIX TAC dropped 88 tons of bombs in 432 sorties. They claimed 140 motor vehicles, 21 armored cars/tanks, 380 railroad cars, 92 factory buildings, and 9 locomotives damaged or destroyed. A total of 8 Germans were shot down, but the XIX TAC fliers suffered no losses.

March 14
D-Day +281

G-2 estimated that there were about 20,500 combat effective troops and 40 tanks facing the Third Army—the equivalent of two- and-a-half divisions.

The 87th Infantry Division took over the patrolling duties along the Rhine River in the VIII Corps area, after relieving the remaining units of the 4th Armored Division. After their relief, the 4th Armored Division started its movement to control of the XII Corps. The 6th Cavalry Group patrolled on the VIII Corps front, to the north and south of Andernach. The 11th Armored Division remained in its assembly area.

The 5th and 90th Infantry Divisions continued with their attack to the south in the XII Corps. The 5th Infantry Division cleared Lutz and Tries; the 90th Infantry Division captured Herschwiesen, Oppenhausen, Udunhausen, Morshausen, Beulich, and Macken. Preparing for an attack, the 4th Armored Division moved into an assembly area. To the west the 76th and 90th Infantry Divisions continued with their mopping-up operations north of the Moselle River.

The 65th Infantry Division patrolled in the southern portion of XX Corps. A one-mile gain was made by the 26th Infantry Division; and the 80th Infantry Division advanced up to three miles, clearing Bergen and reaching Weiskirchen on the edge of the Waldern Forest. The 10th Armored Division remained in assembly in the northern section of the corps area, and the 3d Cavalry Group patrolled.

During 482 sorties, the XIX TAC dropped 80 tons of bombs. Destroyed or damaged were 244 motor vehicles, 19 tanks/armored vehicles, 315 railroad cars, 3 supply dumps, 17 locomotives, and 135 factory buildings. The XIX TAC lost only 1 plane to the 10 German planes that were shot down.

Reports by Third Army hospital units concerning cold-injury cases indicated that 1,197 cases were treated, of which 817 were diagnosed as trench foot and the remainder as frostbite. Of the trenchfoot cases, 7.5 percent were returned to duty; 63 percent were transferred to a convalescent hospital, and 29.5 percent were evacuated to ComZ. Of the frostbite cases, 8 percent were returned to duty, 51 percent were transferred to a convalescent hospital, and 41 percent were evacuated to ComZ.

March 15
D-Day +282

The Germans were now in a situation very similar to that of the Falaise-Argentan Pocket. The 4th Armored Division had swept across the German rear in the Palatinate triangle bounded by the Rhine, Moselle, and Saar Rivers. The Third Army was once again threatening the complete envelopment of the German's forces on their front and their defensive positions in the triangle. If General Patton or his staff could help it, the chance to decimate the enemy would not escape this second time, as had occurred when General Montgomery failed to close the Argenten-Falaise Gap and allowed the German Seventh Army to live to fight another day.

The 87th Infantry Division crossed the Moselle River in the eastern part of the VIII Corps and captured Dieblich, Dieblicherberg, Niderfell, and Waldesch. The 11th Armored Division remained in assembly and the 6th Cavalry Group patrolled in the northeastern part of the zone.

The combined attack of the 5th and 90th Infantry Divisions continued south of the Moselle River. The 5th Infantry Division gained three miles, clearing Dommershausen, Dorweiler, Kastellaun, Zilhausen, Korweiler, Morsdorf, Lahr, and Buch. The 90th Infantry Division gained four miles, capturing Oppenhausen, Herschwiesen, Bushhoiz, Dieler, Ney, Kratzenburg, Halsenbach, Ehr, Gondershausen, Merinuth, and Beulich. The 4th Armored Division struck quickly from its assembly area, pushing through the 90th Infantry Division's zone and gaining over fifteen miles. The 89th Infantry Division attacked south, across the Moselle River, gained two miles and cleared Bullary, Neef, Nehaan, Senhals, Ellenz, and Poltersdorf. The attack was preceded by artillery barrages for nearly an hour. The 76th Infantry Division relieved the 2d Cavalry Group, and continued with its patrolling along the northern bank of the Moselle River. The 65th Infantry Division carried out patrols in the XX Corps. The 26th Infantry Division advanced to the south, toward Merzig and gained two miles over very rugged terrain. The 80th Infantry Division cleared Waldholzbach, Scheiden, Weiskirchen, and Hausbach. The 10th Armored Division came out of its assembly area near Trier and passed through the 80th Infantry Division, gaining four miles. The 94th Infantry Division gained six miles toward St. Wendel, capturing Gusenburg, Reinsfeld, Mandern, Kell, and Grimburg in its path. The 3d Cavalry Group, in a limited-objective attack, captured Waldrach.

A whopping 643 sorties were flown by the XIX TAC, with the planes dropping 133 tons of bombs on the Germans. A total of 16 towns and 7 marshalling yards were attacked; 393 railroad cars, 219 motor vehicles, 38 tanks/armored vehicles, 15 locomotives were damaged or destroyed and more than 100 German troops killed. Five German planes in the air and 3 on the ground were destroyed, and the XIX TAC lost only 1 plane in the entire of the operation.

The dam again burst, with the Third Army becoming completely fluid and spreading like flood waters on German soil. The 4th Armored Division struck through the 5th and 90th Infantry Division zones and advanced more than 15 miles to the south.

To the south the Seventh Army was striking into the Siegfried Line in a link-up drive to meet the freewheeling the Third Army. They wanted to share in the liquidation of an estimated eighty thousand German troops in the Rhine-Saar area.

During the day, the Third Army had captured 47.5 square miles of territory.

March 16
D-Day +283

According to reports from G-2, German POWs had given information indicating that they were, indeed, very much concerned and obviously fearing the possible envelopment and destruction or capture of their forces in the Palatinate area by the Third Army. There were four key communication centers on the Rhine River that they worried about losing to the Third Army: Koblenz, Bingen, Mainz, and Worms.

General Patton immediately issued verbal orders for the 4th Armored Division to attack toward Mainz, the 11th Armored Division to attack toward Worms, and the 10th Armored Division to attack toward Kaiserslautern.

In the VIII Corps the 87th Infantry Division advanced on Koblenz, with artillery providing close-in support. The 6th Cavalry Group continued patrolling.

The 4th Armored Division gained a maximum of eighteen miles, and the 90th Infantry Division reduced the enemy in Bad Salzig and Boppard. The 5th Infantry Division gained seven miles and captured Buch, Kastellaun, and Hundheim, mopping up in the rear of the 4th Armored Division. The 89th Infantry Division gained four-and-a-half miles, enlarging its bridgehead over the Moselle River and capturing Burg, Briedel, and Ellenz. The 76th Infantry Division maintained positions, and the 2d Cavalry Group screened the corps' northern flank while maintaining contact with the VIII Corps.

The 65th Infantry Division continued patrolling in the XX Corps zone. The 26th Infantry Division gained two-and-a-half miles toward Merzig, and in the process captured Saarholzbach and Mettlach. The 80th Infantry Division made gains of three miles and captured several small towns. The 94th Infantry Division outflanked the city of Saarlautern. The 10th Armored Division passed through both the 80th and 94th Infantry Divisions and captured Nieder-Losheim, Thailen, and Confeld. In the rear of the corps area, the 12th Armored Division began to assemble following its attachment to the Corps.

The XIX TAC destroyed 20 German planes in the air and 20 on the ground while losing 5 of their own. They flew 625 sorties and dropped 136 tons of bombs; destroying or damaging 550 motor vehicles, 81 tanks/armored vehicles, 398 railroad cars, and 35 locomotives.

A staff conference was called by General Patton. General Eisenhower attended the conference to learn of the supply situation for current and future operations in the Third Army. A total of five days' supply of rations and gasoline, about ten day's supply of Allied products, and ten to thirty days' supply of Classes II and IV supplies were stored in the army area.

March 17
D-Day +284

G-2 Section issued a report on German Panzer movements. The report stated that tactical reconnaissance of the movements from the Remagen area indicated that the Germans were probably going to reinforce against the Third Army with the equivalent of one armored division (about 1,000 troops and 25 tanks). As the Third Army and its armored columns pursued the retreating Germans, the POW numbers increased greatly. During the period from March 11 to March 17, the Third Army took 22,220 prisoners into army cages and 1,144 were admitted to Third Army hospitals, making a total of 23,364 Germans giving up the fight.

The only major activity in the VIII Corps was the action of

the 87th Infantry Division, which was fighting inside the city of Koblenz and clearing the town of Rhens.

The XII Corps spearhead continued to be the old favorite of General Patton, the 4th Armored Division. The 5th and 90th Infantry Divisions closely followed the 4th Armored as it gained six miles going through the town of Bad Kreuznach. The 11th Armored Division passed through the 89th Infantry Division's zone and gained more than fifteen miles. In the western sector the 76th Infantry Division maintained its positions north of the Moselle River and the 2nd Cavalry Group continued to screen the flank along the Rhine River.

In the XX Corps the 65th Infantry Division's units averaged about a mile's worth of advance, and the 26th Infantry Division captured both Merzing and a bridge intact across the Prims River. The 80th Infantry Division crossed the Prims River and gained three miles. The 94th Infantry Division cleared Birkenfeld after advancing three miles on its own. The 10th Armored Division pushed forward more than ten miles, while the newly organized 12th Armored Division moved south from its assembly area to share in the attack. The 16th Cavalry Group cleared Prosterath in the northern sector.

The fighterbombers of the XIX TAC flew 190 sorties, claiming 640 motor vehicles, 30 armored vehicles/tanks, and 153 horse-drawn vehicles. They also shot down 2 German planes and damaged 2 more.

The Seventh Army, to the south of the Third Army, was breaking through the Siegfried Line, aiding the Third Army in its opening up of the German frontier.

March 18
D-Day +285

In the VIII Corps the 6th Cavalry Group was relieved by the newly assigned 28th Infantry Division. The large and important city of Koblenz was cleared by the 87th Infantry Division, which also captured both Niederspay and Oberspay.

In the XII Corps the 2d Cavalry Group patrolled and the 90th Infantry Division cleared ground to the south beyond

Bingen. The 4th Armored Division gained ground south of the Nahe River, fanning out to the east and west to reduce the bypassed pockets of Germans in the area. The towns of Sobernheim and Reckerhausen were captured and the town of Bad Kreuznach was completely cleared. The 11th Armored Division gained eight miles in its advance, fording the Nahe River and capturing Meddersheim and Becherbach. The 89th Infantry Division reduced German troops bypassed by the fast-moving armored columns.

The XX Corps was now at a strength as large or perhaps larger than any other corps in U.S. Army history. It consisted of four infantry divisions, two armored divisions, and two cavalry groups. The 65th Infantry Division cleared Dillingen and enlarged its bridgehead at Saarlautern. The 26th Infantry Division went due east of Saarlautern. The 10th Armored Division captured St. Wendel and seized a bridge intact on the outskirts of the town. The 80th Infantry Division, supporting the 10th Armored, gained about sixteen miles and also penetrated St. Wendel. The 94th Infantry Division cleared numerous small towns and took a large number of POWs. The 12th Armored Division, in front of the 94th Infantry Division, pushed themselves forward ten miles in the direction of Kaiserslautern. The 16th Cavalry Group moved toward positions of the 76th Infantry Division and cleared Heidelburg. The 3d Cavalry Group remained in reserve. More than fifty small towns were captured during the day by the XX Corps elements. With the power built up in the XX Corps, they could have thrust viciously and quickly into almost any part of Germany that they wished, but they were held back by both Eisenhower and his British advisors at SHAEF.

The incredible number of 714 sorties flown by the XIX TAC were responsible for destroying and/or damaging 1,033 motor vehicles, 106 armored vehicles/tanks, 49 locomotives, 488 railroad cars, and 416 horse-drawn vehicles. The XIX TAC was becoming increasingly impolite to their German hosts.

In order to facilitate support of the fast-moving tactical situation, tire repair teams were organized to patrol all main and auxiliary supply routes. These teams were equipped with hot patches, tubes, tires, and air compressors. When wheels were available, tires and tubes were premounted for direct exchange. This was the Third Army's version of pit crews similar to the Indianapolis 500. Two racks, no waiting.

March 19
D-Day +286

The 28th Infantry Division maintained positions in the VIII Corps. The 87th Infantry Division cleared the remaining Germans along the Rhine River in their zone and prepared to move south. The 6th Cavalry Group remained in reserve.

The 4th Armored and 90th Infantry Divisions had their direction of attack changed toward the southeast for the purpose of bringing their forces to the banks of the Rhine River in the Mainz-Worms area. The 2d Cavalry Group was attached to the 90th Infantry Division, which captured Horweiler, Aspisheim, Dromersheim, and Sponsheim. The 4th Armored Division cleared a total of sixteen German towns. The 5th Infantry Division cleared its pathway to the Nahe River, capturing Nussbaum, Sobernheim, Walbocheiheim, and Volxheim. The 89th Infantry Division, in the west, mopped the pockets that had been quickly bypassed by the 11th Armored Division. The 11th Armored Division, continuing in its rapid advance, captured 11 towns while going forward 8 miles. The 76th Infantry Division maintained positions.

In the XX Corps the 65th Infantry Division cleared Fraulautern, Saarlautern-Roden, Nalbach, Ensdorf, and Saarwellingen. The 26th Infantry Division gained eight miles, cleaning up resistance in Ottweiler. The 80th Infantry Division continued on its way to the southeast and gained two miles. The 80th followed the 10th Armored Division, which quickly moved twenty miles forward to the outskirts of Kaiserslautern and practically cut off the city of Saarbrucken. The 12th Armored Division moved to the east and ended up five miles north of Kaiserslautern. The 94th Infantry Division, following the 12th Armored, gained fifteen miles. The 16th Cavalry

Group went forward four miles, clearing Morscheid. The 3d Cavalry Group remained in reserve.

The XIX TAC flew 605 sorties without a single loss to themselves. They claimed 816 motor vehicles, 46 locomotives, 46 tanks/armored vehicles, and 367 railroad cars damaged or destroyed. They also removed any need for the Luftwaffe to worry about six of its planes.

March 20
D-Day +287

The 28th and 87th Infantry Divisions patrolled along the Rhine River and in the rear of the VIII Corps area the 6th Cavalry Group remained in its assembly area.

The major action in the XII Corps was along the Rhine River, all the way south to Ludwigshafen. The 76th Infantry Division was transferred to VIII Corps. The 2d Cavalry Group patrolled just south of the 76th Infantry Division. The 90th Infantry Division drove forward and cleared Goshenheim, Marienborn, and Hectsheim. The 4th Armored Division raced thirteen miles forward, clearing Flonheim, Bornheim, Albig, and Alzey. The city of Worms was cleared by the end of the day.

During the day the Germans launched their heaviest air attacks on the Third Army in the entire campaign. Attacks were made against the bridge at Bretzenheim-Bad Münster and primarily against the 4th Armored and 90th Infantry Divisions. The Germans employed a varied assortment of aircraft, using also the new jet-propelled Me-262s. During 61 raids, a total of 314 German aircraft were counted by the Third Army antiaircraft artillery observers. The artillery gunners successfully defended their troops and installations by shooting down 25 of the attacking planes and damaging 11 more.

In the XX Corps the 65th Infantry Division cleared Holz, Wiesbach, and Merchweiler before they were pinched out by the junction of the 26th Infantry Division and the 6th Armored Division from the Seventh Army. The 26th Infantry Division drove forward a quick sixteen miles, making contact with the 6th Armored at Wieselskirchen. The 10th Armored Division advanced rapidly twenty miles and captured Hochspeyer. The 12th Armored Division reached the Rhine River at Ludwigshafen and the 80th and 94th Infantry Divisions both made ten-mile gains in the rear of the 12th Armored. The 6th Cavalry Group mopped up and the 3d Cavalry Group remained in reserve.

Dropping 145 tons of bombs, the XIX TAC flew 655 sorties in close support of the Third Army's swiftly moving columns. Their claims for the day included 859 motor vehicles, 283 horse-drawn vehicles, and 17 German planes.

The burgeoning movement of displaced persons from Germany presented the very real problem of a typhoid outbreak among the people of France. The military government officers met this threat by dusting thousands of displaced persons with DDT before evacuating them to France.

March 21
D-Day +288

Positions in the VIII Corps were maintained by the 28th and 87th Infantry Divisions. After the change of the VIII-XII Corps' boundaries, the 76th Infantry Division was assigned to the VIII Corps, where it continued to patrol. The 6th Cavalry Group remained in its assembly area.

There was a change in the boundary of the XII and XX Corps, after which the 2d Cavalry Group captured Freiweinheim and Gaulsheim. The 90th Infantry Division made a direct attack on Mainz, clearing half of the city against decreasing resistance. Also cleared by elements of the 90th Infantry Division were the towns of Dexheim, Schornsheim, Udenheim, Hahnheim, Selzen, Mommenheim, and Marienborn. To the south, the 5th Infantry Division mopped up. The 4th Armored Division made a fifteen-mile gain and in the process cleared Gimbsheim, Bermersheim, Weihheim, Dalheim, Rhein-Durkheim, Ibersheim, Osthofen, Bechtheim, Mettenheim, Frettenheim, Dorndurkheim, Wintersheim, Dolgesheim, and Elmsheim. The 11th Armored Division relieved some elements of the 4th Armored Division in and around

Worms. The 89th Infantry Division followed the 11th Armored Division and mopped up after them.

In the XX Corps, the 94th Infantry Division reached the Rhine River between Worms and Ludwigshafen. The 80th Infantry Division went ten miles past the city of Kaiserslautern heading east. The 26th Infantry Division moved eastward, also, capturing Kindsbach and generally mopping up. The 10th and 12th Armored Divisions both attacked toward Landau and Speyer to the southwest, to close the last open gap allowing any escape for the Germans in the area.

The XIX TAC had another glorious day of attack against the retreating German rail and road columns. They claimed 287 motor vehicles; 45 armored vehicles/tanks, 49 locomotives, 232 railroad cars, and 10 planes. The XIX TAC lost only 3 planes.

Because of the increasingly large number of POWs being taken by the Third Army units, a directive was issued stating that trucks returning to the vicinity of Trier from supply points at Holzbach and Sothern should collect prisoners from the XII Corps' cage at Meisenheim and the XX Corps' cage at Baltersweiler. They were to be transported to the Third Army POW enclosure near Trier.

March 22
D-Day +289

The commanding general, staff and soldiers of the Third Army were tired of playing second fiddle to the Twenty-first Army Group commanded by General Montgomery. The Twenty-first Army Group was planning to cross the Rhine River with a massive preparation of seventy thousand artillery rounds fired by two thousand guns, an air bombardment utilizing hundreds of heavy bombers and three thousand fighter planes, smoke screens, a multitude of amphibious vehicles, assault craft, bridging material, and an airborne landing in support of 80,000 infantry troops. The earth-shattering event was named Operation Plunder and was to be reported in a speech by Winston Churchill over the British Broadcasting Company (BBC).

While the "Gentlemen up north," as General Patton referred to them, planned to cross the Rhine River on March 23, the Third Army secretly began crossing the river on the March 22. As General Patton wrote of it in his diary, "Without benefit of aerial bombing, ground smoke, artillery preparation, and airborne assistance, the Third Army at 2200 hours, Thursday evening, March 22nd, crossed the Rhine River." The statement was precisely worded not only as a notice of the Third Army's crossing, but also as a slap in the face to Monty. As luck would have it, the speech by Churchill, proclaiming Montgomery to be the first general to cross the Rhine River by assault in modern times, was erroneously broadcast on BBC, even though Patton's Third Army had already crossed the river.

The VIII Corps was ordered to cross the Rhine River south of the Lahn River and to advance generally to the east. It was to assume command of the 89th Infantry Division from the XII Corps and to transfer the 28th Infantry Division to the V Corps of the First Army.

The XII Corps was to cross the Rhine River and advance rapidly to the northeast and then cross the Main River and continue the advance to the northeast. They also were to assume command of the 26th Infantry Division and transfer the 89th Infantry Division to the VIII Corps.

The XX Corps was to move one infantry and one armored division to the eastern portion of XII Corps area and two infantry divisions to the western part of the XX Corps area. They were then to be prepared to follow either the VIII or XII Corps through secured bridgeheads. They were to pass control of the 10th and 12th Armored Divisions to the Seventh Army and assume control of the 6th Armored Division from the Seventh Army.

In the VII Corps the 76th Infantry Division maintained positions the 6th Cavalry Group relieved the 87th Infantry Division and the 87th Infantry Division moved into its assembly area.

In the XII Corps the 2d Cavalry Group patrolled, the 90th Infantry Division extended its front; and the 4th Armored

Division remained in assembly areas. The 5th Infantry Division finished mopping up in the rear of the 4th Armored Division and made an assault crossing of the Rhine River (without benefit of artillery or any of Montgomery's other hardware). The 89th Infantry Division assembled at Sobernheim, fifteen miles southwest of Bad Kreuznach, and the 26th Infantry Division passed to corps control.

The change in the Third and Seventh Armies boundary left all XX Corps units (except the 26th Infantry Division) in the Seventh Army zone. The 11th Armored Division patrolled north and south of Worms. The 80th Infantry Division moved into an assembly area and the 94th Infantry Division continued with its clearing of Ludwigshafen. The 12th Armored Division cleared Bohl while the 10th Armored Division was clearing Landau. The 3d Cavalry Group remained in reserve and the 65th Infantry Division assembled around Neunkirchen.

The XIX TAC flew both support and reconnaissance missions to assist the Third Army's corps. They claimed 55 rail cuts and 876 railroad cars, 210 motor vehicles, 68 locomotives, and 18 gun installations damaged and destroyed.

The deep, accelerated penetrations by the Third Army into the German frontier brought an enormous increase in the amount of supplies and equipment captured from the Germans. Problems involved in the disposing of this equipment had reached such proportions that special procedures had to be established for its handling by the supply sections. Many items, of course, became war booty and assumed the role of souvenirs for the Third Army soldiers.

March 23
D-Day +290

In a special order to soldiers and airmen of the Third U.S. Army and the XIX Tactical Air Command, General Patton announced the first Third Army bridgehead over the Rhine River.

In the period from January 20 to March 22, 1945, you have wrested 6,484 square miles of territory from the enemy. You have taken 3,072 cities, towns, and villages, including among the former: Trier, Koblenz, Bingen, Worms, Mainz, Kaiserslautern, and Ludwigshafen.

You have captured 140,112 enemy soldiers, and have killed or wounded an additional 99,000, thereby eliminating practically all of the German 7th and 1st Armies. History records no greater achievement in so limited a time.

This great campaign was only made possible by your disciplined valor, unswerving devotion to duty, coupled with the unparalleled audacity and speed of your advance on the ground; while from the air, the peerless fighter-bombers kept up a relentless round-the-clock attack upon the disorganized enemy.

The world rings with your praises; better still, General Montgomery, General Eisenhower, and General Bradley have all personally commended you. The highest honor I have ever attained is that of having my name coupled with yours in these great events.

Please accept my heartfelt admiration and thanks for what you have done, and remember that your assault crossing over the Rhine River at 2200 hours last night assures you of even greater glory to come.

In the VIII Corps the 6th Cavalry Group assumed control of the land along the Rhine River which the 87th Infantry Division had been patrolling, allowing the 87th to then move to an assembly area. The 76th Infantry Division patrolled. The 89th Infantry Division passed to the control of the VIII Corps and moved to its new area.

Things were becoming quite busy in the XII Corps. The 5th Infantry Division used assault rafts to attack across the Rhine River (without benefit of aerial bombardment or artillery preparation) quickly exploiting its new bridgehead. The crossing, which was made during the night of March 22-23, was pushed to a depth of 6 miles and to a width of 7 miles by the end of the day. 5th Infantry received no help of artillery firing on targets of opportunity. Alone, with the first wave of the infantry assaults were some amphibious tanks of the 748th Tank Battalion. Twenty-four hours after the 5th Infantry Division had crossed the Rhine, the Luftwaffe struck furiously at them, attempting to wipe out the bridgehead. Both light and heavy anti-aircraft had been quickly set up on the bridgehead, expecting just such an attack. Out of a total of

154 Germans raiding the bridgehead, 18 were known to be shot down and 15 more were probables. Two additional planes were shot down by the XX Corps' antiaircraft gunners when attacks were made against the 12th Armored Division and some field artillery battalions.

In other parts of the XII Corps the Third Army infantrymen, attacking from Oppenheim, met little resistance against them as they cleared Trebur, Wallerstein, Leehim, Erfelden, Dornheim, and Asteheim. A heavy pontoon bridge and a treadway bridge were completed within thirty-six hours of the initial crossing. The 357th and 359th Infantry Regiments drove into the bridgehead and assumed control of the southern half of the bridgehead. The 358th Infantry Regiment assembled in preparation for crossing the Rhine River after having completely cleared Mainz. In the 4th Armored Division, Combat Command "A" crossed into the bridgehead and attacked through the infantry at the close of the day; and Combat Command "B" assembled in preparation to crossing the river. The 11th Armored Division relieved elements of the 4th Armored Division and began to patrol aggressively. The 26th Infantry and 6th Armored Divisions passed control to the corps during the day, with the 6th Armored moving into an assembly area and the 26th Infantry Division patrolling around Mainz.

In the XX Corps the 65th Infantry Division and the 3d Cavalry Group assembled near Neunkirchen. The 80th Infantry Division was already in their assembly area near Bad Kreuznach. The 10th Armored Division continued its attack, making contact with the 14th Armored and 36th Infantry Divisions of the Seventh Army. Through a mutual agreement between the commanding generals of both the Third and Seventh Armies, the 10th and 6th Armored Divisions were exchanged, with the 6th Armored passing to control of the XX Corps. The 12th Armored Division captured Hafsloch and Weingarten after clearing Speyer. Speyer was the last escape route open to the fleeing Germans. After that, the 12th Armored Division passed to control of the Seventh Army. The

94th Infantry Division completely cleared the city of Ludwigshafen.

The XIX TAC flew a massive number of sorties, totaling 775. Unfortunately, they failed to find any highway transportation. Six of the fighterbombers were lost to the Germans, but the Germans got the worst of it, by far. Destroyed or damaged by the XIX TAC were 41 planes, 1,100 railroad cars, 70 locomotives, 162 motor vehicles, 21 tanks/armored vehicles, and all types of military installations.

Because of the extremely heavy demand by combat troops for "K" rations, these units were issued as one hundred percent operation-type rations, while noncombat units were limited to twenty-five percent and hospitals to 50 percent.

March 24
D-Day +291

During the period from March 18 to 24, the Third Army had taken a total of 68,192 POWs.

The 87th Infantry Division in the VIII Corps crossed the Rhine River about five miles south of Koblenz. The 87th's 345th Infantry Regiment captured Braubach, Filsen, and Camp. Its 346th Regiment remained in reserve. To the south the 76th Infantry Division patrolled in support of the 87th Infantry Division. The 89th Infantry Division closed into an assembly area at Lingerhahn and the 6th Cavalry Group maintained positions.

The 4th Armored Division broke out of the Rhine River bridgehead, with both Combat Command "A" and "B" passing through the 5th and 90th Infantry Divisions' zones. They gained twenty miles, driving to Graf Zimmern and Kieestadt. The 5th Infantry Division, meanwhile, continued its enlargement of the bridgehead and cleared Bauscheim, Russelsheim, Konigstaden, and Gross-Gerau. To the south the 90th Infantry Division gained more than five miles in its attack to the east, capturing Buttelborn, Worfelden, Goddelau, Schneppenhausen, Grafenhausen, and Griesheim. By the end of the day, some elements of the 90th were attacking the large industrial city of Darmstadt. Combined, the 5th and 90th Infantry Divisions had enlarged the bridgehead to a depth of nine miles and a width of ten miles. The 26th Infantry Division pulled up to the Rhine River, with its 101st Infantry Regiment crossing into the bridgehead late in the day. The 6th Armored Division, now with the XII Corps, crossed into the bridgehead area. At the same time that the 2d Cavalry Group was patrolling, the engineers of the XII Corps completed a floating treadway bridge across the Rhine River in the lower part of the corps' zone.

The elements of the XX Corps continued to operate well within the Seventh Army's zone, following the Third and Seventh Armies' change of boundary. The 65th and 80th Infantry Division and the 3d Cavalry Group were in assembly areas. The 11th Armored Division proceeded into an assembly area, following its change in assignment from XII to XX Corps. The 16th Cavalry Group conducted patrols along the Rhine River during the day. The 94th Infantry Division was relieved around the Ludwigshafen area by the Seventh Army and began movement to the north.

During the day 374 motor vehicles, 27 tanks/armored vehicles, 329 railroad cars, and 32 locomotives were claimed by the XIX TAC after they strafed the Germans and very rudely dropped a total of 62 tons of bombs on them.

General Patton walked across a pontoon bridge built by his engineers and stopped in the middle. He whipped out his pecker and proceeded to piss into the Rhine River, saying, "I've waited a long time to do that. I didn't even piss this morning when I got up so I would have a really full load. Yes, sir, the pause that refreshes." When he reached the eastern bank of the river he faked a fall, rose with two hands of German soil and remarked, "Thus William the Conqueror", in emulation of the victor of the Battle of Hastings in 1066.

March 25
D-Day +292

According to G-2, things were looking pretty black for the Germans. They could hardly scrape together anything at all to reinforce their positions which were becoming more untenable as the days passed. It was estimated that a force about the size of one division was all that the Germans could put in front of the Third Army. They made their heaviest air attack to date against the XII Corps Rhine River bridgehead with their depleted Luftwaffe. Two hundred and thirty German planes attacked the bridges, installations, and troop concentrations in the corps area. American antiaircraft artillery destroyed 29 of the planes for sure, with another twenty-three claimed as probables.

The VIII Corps bridgehead established by the 87th Infantry Division was enlarged to a depth of three miles and a width of eight miles, and the division captured Osterspai, Braubach, and Lykershausen. The 89th Infantry Division captured Dorscheid. The 76th Infantry Division maintained its positions on the west bank of the Rhine River and furnished fire support to attacking elements. The 6th Cavalry Group maintained its positions while, at the same time, engineers completed another treadway bridge at Boppard.

The 4th Armored Division kept up its incredible pace, advancing thirty-five miles. Both its Combat Commands "A" and "B" bypassed Darmstadt and Combat Command "A" captured a bridge intact over the Main River, near Grossauheim. They repulsed several small counterattacks aimed at the bridgehead. At Aschaffenburg, Combat Command "B" captured a railroad bridge intact over the Main River. The 5th Infantry Division continued with its attack to the north, clearing ground up to the Main River and the 90th Infantry Division drove northeast six miles and cleared Darmstadt. They also captured Griesheim, Grafenhausen, Worfelden, and Langen. The 16th Cavalry Group relieved the 2d Cavalry Group and the 6th Armored Division captured both Raunheim and Kelsterbach.

Units of the XX Corps were pulled north from the Seventh Army zone. By the end of the day, the 65th, 80th, and 94th Infantry Divisions; the 11th Armored Division; and the 3d Cavalry Group were in their assembly areas in the rear areas of the XII Corps.

The XIX TAC flew a massive 700 sorties in both reconnaissance and support missions. They damaged or destroyed 527 motor vehicles; 36 armored vehicles/tanks, 61 locomotives, 27 gun positions, 1,067 railroad cars, 2 bridges, and German troop losses were 150. The XIX TAC lost only two planes.

The city of Darmstadt, an important communications center, was completely cleared and bridgeheads in the VIII Corps area were consolidated.

The Third Army captured and registered its three-hundred thousandth POW at their enclosure at Trier.

All appointments to civilian posts of authority were being made on a temporary basis by the military government. In numerous localities, officials first chosen were removed when investigation revealed that they had connections with the Nazi Party or when their performance of the duties of the office proved that they were either incompetent or inefficient. In many villages and small towns, it was learned that non-Nazi officials had been permitted to retain office after 1933 because of their importance to the local governments and due to the high regard in which they were held in their communities.

March 26
D-Day +293

In the VIII Corps the 87th and 89th Infantry Divisions consolidated their bridgeheads, and between them they captured Dachsenhausen, Oberlahnstein, Desighofen, Gemmerich, Kasdorf, Ruppertshofen, Himmighofen, Winterwerb, Kelbach, Dahlheim, Klaub, St. Goarshausen, Lierscheid, Struth, Bornich, Kestert, Weyer, Nochern, and Weisel. The 76th Infantry Division maintained its positions and the 6th Cavalry Group assembled in preparation to cross into the Rhine bridgehead.

By now, all major units of the XII Corps were well beyond the Rhine bridgehead. The 4th Armored Division continued to spearhead the corps' attack. The 26th Infantry Division followed the 4th Armored Division closely. The 6th Armored Division captured a damaged railroad bridge on the Main River and pushed infantry elements across into the city of

Frankfurt. Other elements of the 6th Armored captured Sch-wanheim, Kelsterbach, Raunheim, Sachsenhausen, Offen-bach, and Niederrad. At the request of the 6th Armored, the corps' artillery fixed on and fired on both the telephone ex-change and the main power plant in Frankfurt. The 2d Cav-alry Group patrolled.

The XX Corps units moved up near the Rhine bridgehead, in preparation for an upcoming attack, but all remained in assembly areas. The only exception was the 16th Cavalry Group, which patrolled the west bank of the Rhine River.

Without losing a single plane, the XIX TAC claimed 361 motor vehicles, 13 locomotives, and 119 railroad cars dam-aged or destroyed.

The distance between railway off-loading points and the Third Army supply areas became so great that it was with extreme difficulty that the supplies were moved forward us-ing the available truck transportation. A request was made for air delivery of two-hundred thousand gallons of gasoline per day for three days at airfields at Darmstadt and Buttel-born. An answer was received that these airfields would be available to receive air supply shipments on March 27. Deliv-eries were to begin with two hundred planes.

March 27
D-Day +294

Six days after the Third Army had begun its initial assault across the Rhine River, the Germans had still not produced any divisional size units to oppose them.

Orders were received from the Twelfth Army Group that very shortly the Third Army would have operational control of three new units: the 70th and 71st Infantry Divisions and the 13th Armored Division. One stipulation was added—the 13th Armored and the 70th Infantry Divisions could not be used beyond the Rhine River.

The VIII Corps continued to log steady progress. Between the two of them, the 87th and 89th Infantry Divisions cap-tured Frucht, Hinterwald, Schweighausen, Sulzbach, Dien-thal, Bergnassau-Scheuern, Kehlbach, Niederbachheim,

Singhoffen, Lollscheid, Pohl, Holzhausen, Reichenberg, Zorn, Lipporn, Welterod, Munchenrothm, and Espenscheid. The 6th Cavalry Group entered the bridgehead area, passed through the 87th Infantry Division's zone, and attacked to the east. The 76th Infantry Division, on the west bank of the Rhine, maintained its positions.

The XII Corps continued with its rapid gains. The 4th Armored Division, attacking to the northeast, captured Ostheim and Weckesheim, approximately twenty miles northeast of Frankfurt. The 90th Infantry Division supported their advance, crossed the Main River, and captured Bischofsheim, Bruchkobel, Niederdorfelden, Wachenbuchen, and Mittelbuchen. The 26th Infantry Division cleared Hanau and moved east to join with other elements in its control. The 5th Infantry Division was fighting inside Frankfurt and managed to clear half of the city. At the same time, engineers built three complete bridges across the Main River near there. The 6th Armored Division prepared to renew its attack and along the southern bank of the Main River, the 2d Cavalry Group was patrolling.

Just south of Mainz, the 80th Infantry Division attacked across both the Rhine and Main Rivers, clearing Kastel and Hocheim. The 11th Armored Division moved north and prepared to cross in the rear of the 80th Infantry Division, which was just reaching Wiesbaden.

The XIX TAC flew a moderate 408 sorties in support of advancing ground troops. Their kills for the day included 1,027 motor vehicles, 25 armored vehicles/tanks, 290 railroad cars, 19 locomotives, and 5 planes.

Lucky Forward moved from Luxembourg to Idar-Oberstein. It was the first time that General Patton commanded from German soil.

March 28
D-Day +295

The Third Army's steady advances were paced by the fast-moving favorite of General Patton, the 4th Armored Division.

The POW count for all of the Third Army on this date was twenty-two thousand.

The VIII Corps was moving fast across German soil. The 6th Cavalry Group made contact with the 9th Armored Division of the First Army and assumed positions previously held by the 9th Armored. After the 9th Armored withdrew within First Army's boundary, the 76th, 87th, and 89th Infantry Divisions moved forward about fifteen miles and cleared numerous small towns in the rear of the spearheading 6th Cavalry Group.

The 4th Armored Division, still the leading edge of the XII Corps, gained thirty miles and reached both Engelrod and Lauterbach with its combat commands. Elements of the 90th Infantry Division both mopped up behind the 4th Armored and maintained positions. Their engineers also completed a pontoon bridge across the Main River near Dornigheim. The 26th Infantry Division moved into blocking positions on the corps' southern flank. The 2d Cavalry Group assembled in the vicinity of Babenhausen.

After the XX Corps assumed the central portion of the Third Army's zone, there ensued a major reshuffling of divisions. The 5th Infantry and 6th Armored Divisions were passed to control of the XX Corps; the 11th Armored Division passed to control of the XII Corps; and the 71st Infantry Division passed to control of the XX Corps from the Seventh Army.

The 6th Armored Division, the vanguard of other XX Corps units, gained twenty miles after crossing the Main River. At Frankfurt the 5th Infantry Division was met by moderate resistance by German air-raid wardens, firemen, police, and only a few regular troops. The 11th Armored Division passed through the zone of the 80th Infantry Division to a position just east of Hanau. The 80th Infantry Division expanded its bridgeheads across both the Main and Rhine Rivers to a depth of ten miles. They also cleared Erbenheim, Bierstadt, Delkenheim, Florsheim, Igstadt, Auringen, and Wiesbaden. The 94th Infantry Division passed control to the Seventh Army with the 6th Armored Division coming under the control of the XX Corps. The 6th Armored Division gained fifteen miles for the day, clearing Enkheim and Bergen. The Third Cavalry Group went into its assembly area, and the 16th Cavalry Group maintained its positions west of the city of Wiesbaden.

In the flying of 307 sorties, the XIX TAC furnished cover for the advancing columns of the Third Army and claimed 649 motor vehicles, 21 tanks/armored vehicles, 16 locomotives; and 53 horse-drawn vehicles.

With little in front of them, the Third Army advanced pretty much at will, unchecked by any resistance from Germans in any of the three Corps areas. The XII Corps reached points approximately two hundred miles from Berlin.

March 29
D-Day +296

As they now stood, the corps in the Third Army included:
VIII Corps:
76th Infantry Division
87th Infantry Division
89th Infantry Division
XII Corps:
26th Infantry Division
71st Infantry Division
90th Infantry Division
4th Armored Division
11th Armored Division
XX Corps:
5th Infantry Division
65th Infantry Division
80th Infantry Division
6th Armored Division

The VIII Corps continued with its advance to the east, with the 87th Infantry and 6th Cavalry Group advancing twenty miles.

In the XII Corps the 4th Armored Division had to slow down according to a directive in order to let the infantry catch up. The 90th Infantry Division moved forward ten miles to the northeast, clearing Grosskarben, Kilianstaden, and Heidenbergen. The 11th Armored Division cleared Roghenbergen and Ruckingen and advanced eight miles to the north. The 2d

Cavalry Group relieved the southern parts of the 26th Infantry Division and the 71st Infantry Division continued to move from the Seventh Army to the XII Corps area.

In the XX Corps the 5th Infantry Division began policing the city of Frankfurt. The 6th Armored Division gained twenty miles just east of Giessen, and the 80th Infantry Division captured Bad Nauheim and Delkenheim. The 65th Infantry Division was still in its assembly area west of Frankfurt. The 16th Cavalry Group crossed the Rhine River to assume screening positions on the corps' left flank.

Bad weather prevented flying by the XIX TAC.

Plans for the supply of the Third Army units east of the Rhine River were being hurried, with air deliveries of gasoline being given the highest priority.

Active measures were taken by the military government to protect against civilian looting. In Koblenz thirteen persons were arrested and held for trial by military government courts.

March 30
D-Day +297

The VIII Corps units pushed up to the eastern limits of their zone, where they were then pinched out from any further advance. They spent their time mopping up enemy pockets in their zone, taking thirty-four hundred prisoners in the course of the day.

The XII Corps continued with its attack, and was much farther east than any other Third Army corps. The 4th Armored Division resumed its attack, gaining twenty miles to the northeast. The 90th Infantry Division also made gains of twenty miles as it followed the 4th Armored Division. The 11th Armored Division moved ten miles, capturing Gelenhausen. The 2d Cavalry Group provided right flank protection and the 71st Infantry Division, in the rear, closed to an area southeast of Frankfurt. The 26th Infantry Division gained ten miles, advancing directly behind the 11th Armored Division and captured Liesenwald and Budingen.

The 5th Infantry Division remained in Frankfurt, clearing

and policing the city. The 6th Armored Division made advances as far as thirty miles to an area about six miles south of Kassel. The 3d Cavalry Group followed behind the 6th Armored; farther to the rear, the 65th Infantry Division gained about 10 to 15 miles, mopping up as they went. The 16th Cavalry Group was clearing a forest twenty miles northeast of Frankfurt.

Poor flying weather kept the XIX TAC down to only 167 sorties.

Air deliveries of gasoline to support the Third Army began to arrive on this date. A total of 216,000 gallons arrived at four airfields—162,500 at Ober Olm; 5,500 at Buttelborn; 3,000 at Ailertchen; and 45,000 at Limberg.

March 31
D-Day +298

A total of 31,715 POWs were taken during the past week within the Third Army boundaries.

An operational directive was issued by Third Army headquarters, reading in part:

> The 70th Infantry Division is to be responsible for the Third Army area "Rhine River, Boppard, Braunshorn, Stromberg, Bad Kreuznach, Oberndorf, and Oppenheim," all inclusive. After effecting necessary coordination therein with the Army Provost Marshal and Army G-5, the division will guard all bridges; maintain law and order, both civil and military; regulate and control traffic on main supply routes; guard all public utility and military government installations; protect army supply points and installations; and be prepared to assemble for movement outside of the Army area on twenty-four hour notice.

The 13th Armored Division was given the same responsibility for the area loosely defined as "...from Trier to Saarlautern and the 1939 German border." In addition, it was to provide one battalion or the equivalent to garrison the city of Koblenz.

In the VIII Corps, the 76th, 87th, and 89th Infantry Divisions and the 6th Cavalry Group continued to mop up in their zone.

In the XII Corps Hersfeld was cleared by elements of Combat Command "B" of the 4th Armored Division, while the major portion of the Combat Command attacked to the east, abreast with Combat Command "A." Following the 4th Armored, the 90th Infantry Division gained twenty miles, captured Starklos, and mopped up isolated pockets of resistance. The 11th Armored Division sliced their way to the east, gaining thirty miles to the north and east of Fulda. The 11th Armored was followed by the 26th Infantry Division, which mopped up the area. The 2d Cavalry Group stayed to the rear, screening the Corps' right flank. The 71st Infantry Division remained in their assembly area.

In the XX Corps the 6th Armored Division was within three miles of Kassel, while some of its units seized a bridgehead over the Fulda River. The 3d Cavalry Group advanced thirty miles, reached the west bank of the Fulda River, and patrolled. The 5th Infantry Division policed in the city of Frankfurt and the 16th Cavalry Group mopped up a whole forest of Germans twenty miles northwest of Frankfurt.

The XIX TAC finished the month of March by flying a total of 580 sorties. They claimed as damaged or destroyed 685 motor vehicles, 47 tanks/armored vehicles, 722 railroad cars, and 94 locomotives.

Gasoline shipments to air delivery fields were increased, with gallonages being received as follows: fifty thousand at Over Olm; fifty-four thousand at Buttelborn; ninety-six thousand at Frankfurt-Eschborn; and 235 thousand at Limberg.

The Advance Section of ComZ notified the Third Army that they planned to retain all captured medical supplies in the army area and use them in captured German hospitals, displaced persons camps, and POW camps.

CHAPTER 9

April, 1945

When the month of April began, the Third Army had units advanced as far as sixty miles east of the Rhine River. The German Panzers were on their last legs, unable to either resist or defend against the Allied forces. The German Panzers were destroyed or captured, their replacement system was broken down, and their communications systems were destroyed. Their complete and utter collapse was hanging by a single thread. With no remorse and with unremitting pressure, the Third Army continued on its way to the absolute destruction of the enemy. Unfortunately, the Third Army would once again be the victim of SHAEF's and Eisenhower's *"fear of they,"* as General Patton put it. They would be turned away from the capture of Berlin toward the National Redoubt area, which only existed in the mind of Eisenhower and his advisors at SHAEF.

April 1
D-Day +299

Mopping-up operations continued in the VIII Corps, with the 76th, 87th, and 89th Divisions and the 6th Cavalry Group holding the mop handle.

Both the 4th and 11th Armored Divisions continued with their rapid advances. The 4th was twenty miles northeast of Hersfeld at the start of the day. The 11th gained up to twenty-five miles with all three of its combat commands. The 90th

Infantry Division and the 26th Infantry Division followed and cleared the areas behind both the 4th and 11th Armored Divisions. To the rear, the 71st Infantry Division cleared the area from Büdingen to Staden of any German stragglers.

The 65th and 80th Infantry Divisions caught up with the 6th Armored Division in the XX Corps. The 3d Cavalry Group maintained its positions on the west bank of the Fulda River, while at the same time, far to the rear, the 5th Infantry Division remained in and around Frankfurt.

The XIX TAC started the month with 388 sorties, dropping 68 tons of bombs. They claimed 398 motor vehicles, 109 armored vehicles/tanks, 32 locomotives, 236 railroad cars, and 77 German planes damaged or destroyed. The supply situation was satisfactory and two new railheads were opened for business at Heidesheim and Nieder-Ingelheim.

A policy of establishing small ammunition supply points and leap-frogging these installations remained in force. The lack of adequate rail facilities was an important factor in dictating the current system of ammunition supply.

A German toxic gas dump was captured at Hundstadt. Located there were fifty-thousand shells, of which an estimated forty-five thousand were found to be filled with a gas believed to be either adamsite or diphenylchlorarsine.

April 2
D-Day +300

G-2 estimated that the Germans had a strength of sixteen thousand combat effectives and about sixty tanks/assault guns, the equivalent of two divisions. The Germans also possessed favorable terrain southeast of Kassel, between the Fulda and Werra Rivers, and east of the Werra River from Munden to Eisenach.

In the VIII Corps the 76th, 87th, and 89th Infantry Divisions and the 6th Cavalry Group removed all organized resistance in the area.

The 4th Armored Division established another bridgehead, this one located across the Werra River in the XII Corps. The 4th's Combat Command "A" advanced to Stregda and Combat Command "B" reached the town of Goldbach. Later, the 11th Armored Division's Combat Command "A" established still another bridgehead to the south at Ritschenhausen, from which it advanced fifteen miles. The 11th's Combat Command "B" closed to the west bank of the Werra River. The 90th Infantry Division moved forward ten miles, clearing the area behind the 4th Armored Division. The area around Fulda was cleared by the 26th Infantry Division, which continued to follow the 11th Armored Division. The 71st Infantry Division, to the rear, mopped up, and the 2d Cavalry Group screened the corps' southern flank. The 16th Cavalry Group, in an assembly area, prepared to move to the 15th Army zone west of the Rhine River.

In the XX Corps zone the 80th Infantry Division had some elements fighting in the city of Kassel, where they encountered dug-in infantry and tanks, roadblocks, and blown-up bridges. To the southeast the 6th Armored Division crossed the Wehre River and gained twenty miles to the east. The 6th Armored was closely followed by the 65th Infantry Division. The 3d Cavalry Group began its move to the corps' left flank, west of Kassel, and the 16th Cavalry Group passed control from the command of the Third Army. The 5th Infantry Division remained in Frankfurt with its policing duties.

Poor weather limited the XIX TAC to only 73 sorties, but excellent results were obtained even with that small number. Claims for the day were 102 motor vehicles, 55 railroad cars, 9 buildings, and 26 planes damaged or destroyed.

April 3
D-Day +301

An adjustment of the intercorps boundaries gave VIII Corps the central portion of the Third Army's zone, with XX Corps on the north and XII Corps on the south. The 87th Infantry Division moved northeast, going into an assembly area near Friedewald. The 4th Armored Division, 65th Infantry Division, and the 6th Cavalry Group passed to control of the VIII Corps. The 4th Armored continued to advance to the east, with the 65th following on its heels. The 6th Cavalry Group continued to clear the area west of the Fulda River.

The 11th Armored Division, the spearhead of the XII Corps, captured Suhland-Oberhof, with the 26th Infantry Division closing in behind and gaining fifteen miles. When the new intercorps boundaries went into effect, the 90th Infantry Division was inside VIII Corps, in the rear of the 4th Armored Division. The 90th attacked southeast, moving back into the XII Corps area. It gained fifteen miles and capturing Schenkfeld, Vacha, and Berka. The 71st Infantry Division cleared the woods for twenty miles south of Lauterbach. The 2d Cavalry Group screened the southern flank and the 16th Cavalry Group cleared the army zone en route to the 15th Army.

The XX Corps had the 6th Armored Division nearing the city of Mühlhausen. The 5th Infantry Division still policed in Frankfurt. The 76th Infantry Division passed to corps control and began to move across the Fulda River into the corps zone in the latter part of the day. The 3d Cavalry Group protected the left flank and stayed in contact with the 69th Infantry Division of the First Army.

In 219 sorties, the XIX TAC claimed 185 motor vehicles, 32 locomotives, 104 railroad cars, and 23 planes damaged or destroyed.

The Forward Echelon of Lucky Forward moved to Frankfurt-on-Main, a total distance of eighty-five miles from the previous location at Idar-Oberstein.

April 4
D-Day +302

A directive from the Twelfth Army Group set a new boundary for the First and Third Armies. It ran from Kassel to Sommerda.

The 5th Infantry Division was relieved from assignment to the XX Corps, after which they began to move from Frankfurt to Lich. The 70th Infantry Division policed on the west side of the Rhine River and the 13th Armored Division started to move from Idar-Oberstein to an area near Alsfeld.

The 4th Armored Division, in the VIII Corps, captured

Gotha and Ohrdrum and kept right on going to the east. The 89th Infantry Division followed the 4th Armored. The 65th Infantry Division made gains up to twenty miles with its elements clearing Eschwedge and Treffurt. To the rear of the corps area, the 87th Infantry Division moved into an assembly area near Friedewald. The 6th Cavalry Group patrolled along the Fulda River.

The three combat commands of the 11th Armored Division gained about ten miles, staying abreast of one another and leading the XII Corps' attack. The 26th Infantry Division followed the 11th Armored closely. The 90th Infantry Division cleared Eckartshausen, Hohra, Allendorf, and Barchfeld. The 71st Infantry Division completed the clearing of its zone and then moved north to assume positions along the line from Schlüchtern to Fulda.

Another adjustment of the boundary between the First and Third Armies left most of the XX Corps units north of the boundary in the First Army's zone. The city of Kassel, an important communications center, was captured by the 80th Infantry Division. The 80th then continued with its advance after clearing the city of the enemy. To the south the 304th and 385th Infantry Regiments of the 76th Infantry Division continued to the east, while the 417th Infantry Regiment closed in the division's zone. The 6th Armored Division cleared Mühlhausen and then sent reconnaissance elements to the north and east of the city. The 3d Cavalry Group patrolled the corps' flank and maintained contact with the First Army.

The XIX TAC flew 455 sorties, claiming 215 motor vehicles, 53 locomotives, 162 railroad cars, 7 gun positions, 9 buildings, and a whopping 48 Luftwaffe planes damaged or destroyed.

The first trains with rations arrived at the newly opened railheads at Nieder-Ingelheim and Heidesheim. Gasoline received at airfields totalled 517,204 gallons, and operational-type rations totalled 117,348 units. These were both record receipts for one day.

A refrigeration plant in operating condition, with a cold

storage capacity of two thousand tons, was taken over by the Third Army at Frankfurt.

April 5
D-Day +303

Enemy resistance continued to be only scattered to moderate. G-2 Section estimated that the strength of the Germans on the Third Army front was probably about 17,200 combat effectives and about 70 tanks/assault guns, roughly the equivalent of two divisions.

After advancing southeast from Gotha, the 4th Armored Division made some slight gains and then organized its positions to allow the 90th Infantry Division to catch up and clear the rear areas. The 90th Infantry Division, while moving behind the 4th Armored Division, was being relieved by the 87th Infantry Division. After the relief the 90th was to move south into the XII Corps' area. The 89th Infantry Division captured Westhausen, Wiegleben, Hotzelsroda, and Neukirchen. The 6th Cavalry Group cleared the enemy remaining along the Fulda River and then went into assembly area near Berneberg.

Being restrained by Third Army orders, the 11th Armored Division made only slight advances in the XII Corps area. This enabled the supporting 26th Infantry Division to close the gap between infantry and armor. The corps' southern flank was screened by the 2d Cavalry Group, and elements of the 71st Infantry Division moved north in search of German stragglers.

Like both the 4th and 11th Armored Divisions, the 6th Armored Division in the XX Corps was being restrained. It maintained its positions and performed reconnaissance screening maneuvers. The 65th Infantry Division made gains of twenty miles, reaching the rear of the 6th Armored Division's positions. The 80th Infantry Division was relieved by the 69th Infantry Division of the First Army and the 80th moved southeast from Kassel, going into an assembly area in the western portion of the corps' zone. The 76th Infantry Division cleared the Germans to the Werra River, guarding the Third Army's northern flank. The 3d Cavalry Group moved southeast to an assembly area.

The XIX TAC flew 369 sorties, claiming 371 motor vehicles, 25 tanks/armored vehicles, 536 railroad cars, 12 gun positions, and a massive total of 132 planes damaged or destroyed.

A total of three hundred fifty tons of captured medical supplies were uncovered at Lauterbach, and a medical depot with seven hundred tons of supplies was found at Kassel. Because of the boundary change, the supplies were turned over to the First Army.

April 6
D-Day +304

According to a Letter of Instruction from the Twelfth Army Group, the Third Army was ordered to perform a two-phase operation. The first phase one was the complete capture of Kassel, after which the city was to be turned over to the First Army. The Third Army was also to seize the line of Meiningen-Gotha-Langesalza and regroup for a strong offensive action to the east. The second phase of the plan was for the Third Army to advance on order of the Twelfth Army Group to the east in its zone, maintain contact with the Sixth Army Group as far as Bayreuth, and be prepared to continue the advance to either the east or southeast.

In the eastern portion of the VIII Corps, the 4th Armored was still constrained by order of headquarters. With nothing else to do, they reorganized their positions and consolidated their gains from the previous day's activity. The 89th Infantry Division consolidated its positions and prepared for further movement to the east. The 87th Infantry Division completed the relief of the 90th Infantry Division and continued to push eastward, capturing Asbach. The 6th Cavalry Group remained in assembly area near Berneburg. The 65th Infantry Division captured Altengottern, made five miles during the day, and prepared to move south into the VIII Corps zone.

In the XII Corps the 90th Infantry Division completed its move to the south and then attacked to the east with the 359th

Infantry Regiment. The 11th Armored Division advanced its combat commands ten miles during the day. The troops of Combat Command "A" and Combat Command "B" went south to the vicinity of Themar, and at the same time, Reserve Combat Command attacked Vachdorf with reconnaissance elements entering Schleusingen. The 26th Infantry Division followed, clearing stragglers. The 2d Cavalry Group was attached to the 71st Infantry Division, which went into an assembly area at Hof-Bieber.

All of the XX Corps units were now south of the First-Third Army boundary, with the exception of the 6th Armored Division, which maintained a northern flank screen east of Mühlausen. Elements of the 76th Infantry Division moved to the vicinity of Langesalza. All elements of the 80th Infantry Division closed in their assembly area, preparing to resume the attack. To the rear the Third Cavalry Group closed in their assembly area.

Poor weather cancelled XIX TAC activity.

April 7
D-Day +305

The 5th Infantry Division passed from control of the Third Army to control of the III Corps of the First Army and began movement to its new assembly zone. The 11th Infantry Regiment of the 5th Infantry Division remained in the vicinity of Frankfurt. The 13th Armored Division started moving to its new zone, having been assigned to control of the XVIII Airborne Corps of the First Army.

In the VIII Corps, elements of the 80th Infantry Division relieved some units of the 4th Armored Division north of the VIII and XX Corps' boundary. The 89th Infantry Division captured some important towns, including Rodichen, Waltershausen, Ruhla, Nutha, and Friedrichroda. They gained twenty miles in their day's activities. The 87th Infantry Division relieved parts of the 90th Infantry Division and then continued with its attack to the east, gaining ten miles and capturing Tambach. The 65th Infantry Division prepared to move south to its proper zone. The 6th Cavalry Group remained in assembly throughout the day.

The XII Corps units were deployed on the front, with the 90th Infantry Division on the north, the 26th Infantry Division in the center, and the 11th Armored Division in the south. The 71st Infantry Division (and attached 2d Cavalry Group) mopped up and protected the southern Flank.

In the XX Corps the 6th Armored Division maintained reconnaissance north and east of the captured city of Mühlhausen with Combat Commands "A" and "B." The Reserve Combat Command aided the 76th Infantry Division in the protection of the northern flank along the Werra River. The 80th Infantry Division relieved some elements of the 4th Armored Division and the 89th Infantry Division.

Having a big day and lots of fun, the XIX TAC flew 395 sorties. They claimed 247 motor vehicles, 69 armored vehicles/tanks, 39 locomotives, 340 railroad cars, and 95 planes damaged or destroyed.

The Third Army units regrouped during the day, following changes in the corps boundaries which necessitated the movement of units back to their proper corps' zones.

Reports from the military government indicated that the general feeling among civilians was one of stunned despondency over their misfortunes. The majority of the people blamed the Nazi Party for the continuance of the war, and only a small minority were found who admitted membership in the Nazi Party.

April 8
D-Day +306

On the basis of currently available information, G-2 estimated that the Germans would probably continue to reinforce against the Western Front with a miscellany of low-grade units and hastily conscripted replacements for existing units and that they would continue to commit all available types of Panzer units in both a stopgap and a local counterattack role. Also estimated by G-2 was that there were about 21,200 combat effectives and 110 tanks/assault guns against the Third Army, the equivalent of two-and-a-half divisions.

Both the 5th Infantry and 13th Armored Divisions cleared the Third Army's zone en route to First Army control.

In the VIII Corps control of the 4th Armored Division was passed to XX Corps. The 89th Infantry Division continued to advance and captured Finsterbergen, Catterfeld, Cabarz, Tabarz, and Wolfis, gaining five miles in the process. Six miles were gained by the 87th Infantry Division in the southern portion of the Corps' zone as they captured Dietharz. Both the 87th and 89th Infantry Divisions were closing the gap between themselves and the 4th Armored Division. After operating in the XX Corps for several days, the 65th Infantry Division was relieved by the 76th Infantry Division as it moved south into an assembly area near Berka in the rear of the VIII Corps zone. The 6th Cavalry Group began moving forward to an area near Thal.

In the XII Corps positions were maintained, with the 90th Infantry Division in the north, the 26th Infantry Division in the center, and the 11th Armored Division in the south. The 2d Cavalry Group continued with its screening operations on the southern flank. 2d Cavalry was relieved from control by the 71st Infantry Division, which was sandwiched between the 11th Armored and 26th Infantry Divisions.

In the XX Corps, both the 6th Armored and the 80th Infantry Divisions maintained their positions, preparing to resume their advance. To the rear the 76th Infantry Division's elements were completing a relief of the 65th Infantry Division.

Improved weather conditions allowed air observation posts to increase their activity considerably. This, in turn, enabled the artillery to fire on observed targets—mainly troop concentrations and vehicular movements.

The XIX TAC continued their rudeness toward the Huns, dropping 79 tons of bombs on them, damaged or destroyed were 432 motor vehicles, 41 tanks/armored vehicles, 49 locomotives, and 359 railroad cars. They also destroyed 26 German planes and damaged another 26, while losing only 1 of theirs.

The Third Army had a total of 1,344,670 gallons of V-80 gasoline in supply points east of the Rhine River. To assist in the burning of gasoline, the Third Army was issued a total of 90 new T26E3 tanks, known as Pershing Tanks. Forty of the new tanks were released by the Third Army to the 11th Armored Division and the remainder were held in the Third Army combat vehicle pool.

April 9
D-Day +307

Control of the 5th Infantry Division's 11th Infantry Regiment was passed to the First Army and the regiment remained in Frankfurt. It was the last of the 5th's elements to leave the Third Army control. The 70th Infantry Division continued policing west of the Rhine River.

In the VIII Corps the 89th Infantry Division made a six-mile advance, capturing Mühlberg, Holzhausen, Rudisleben, Bittstadt, and Georgeenthal. The 87th Infantry Division continued to mop up in its zone. Both the 65th Infantry Division and the 6th Cavalry Group were in their assembly areas.

The 90th Infantry resumed its advance in the northern portion of the XII Corps area, capturing Gehlberg and advancing five miles. The 26th Infantry Division cleared Unterneubrunn. The 11th Armored Division, also resuming its attack, entered Rodach and captured Veilsdorf, Grattstadt, Ottonwind, and Drossenhausen. The right flank of the corps was screened by the 2d Cavalry Group.

On the northern portion of the XX Corps, the 76th Infantry Division maintained positions. On the southern portion, the 80th Infantry Division gained up to three miles for the day. The 4th Armored, newly assigned to the corps, remained in its assembly area and prepared for an attack. The area north of Allendorf was cleared by the Reserve Combat Command of the 6th Armored Division.

The XIX TAC flew 549 sorties. Claims for the day included 280 motor vehicles, 34 armored vehicles/tanks, 63 locomotives, 300 railroad cars, and 31 German planes destroyed or damaged.

A gasoline pipeline, a project of ComZ, was completed across the Rhine River at Mainz, with all necessary tanks and pumps installed. The main purpose of the project was to reduce truck traffic across the bridge. Bulk gasoline was transported to Mainz by railway tank car from the end of an existing pipeline at Thionville. At Mainz it was then pumped across the river and discharged in tank trucks on the east bank.

A German food warehouse was captured at Friedberg. The stores inside were released to the Third Army's G-5 for use by the military government.

April 10
D-Day +308

The 70th Infantry Division was still policing in the area west of the Rhine River, dispatching the 275th Infantry Regiment to the Frankfurt area for policing duties there.

The 87th and 89th Infantry Divisions both opened a new attack to the east in the VIII Corps zone and advanced three and five miles respectively. To the rear, the 65th Infantry Division remained in assembly and the 6th Cavalry Group patrolled and picked up German stragglers.

The 90th Infantry Division resumed its attack in the northern portion of the XII Corps zone. The 26th Infantry Division's elements captured Wiedersbach and Giessubel and reached the banks of the Schwarza River. The 11th Armored Division cleared the town of Coburg during their sixteen-mile advance. The 71st Infantry Division, hot on the heels of the 11th Armored, kept mopping up. To the rear, the screening of the southern flank of the corps was continued by the 2d Cavalry Group.

In the XX Corps the 76th Infantry Division went forward five miles, capturing both Gebesee and Ballhausen. The 6th Armored Division, passing through the 76th Infantry Division's zone, jumped off with an attack and gained twenty miles for the day. Passing through the 80th Infantry Division's zone, the 4th Armored Division swept outwardly both north and south of Erfurt. The 80th Infantry Division then captured Thorey, Dietendorf, Frienstedt, and Bindersleben.

The XIX TAC dropped 95 tons of bombs while they flew 535 sorties. They claimed as damaged or destroyed 455 motor vehicles, 59 locomotives, 105 railroad cars, 114 buildings, and 84 German planes.

An experiment was conducted to find possible ways and means of forwarding gasoline. An officer was stationed at an Advance Section ComZ decanting point at Bad Nauheim who stopped all empty trucks on the road that were traveling toward the front and required them to take gasoline to the Third Army transfer point at Alsfeld. At the end of the day, it was discovered that deliveries to the transfer point totalled twenty-five thousand gallons.

April 11
D-Day +309

In the VIII Corps, attacks by divisions were doing as well as could be expected. However, without an armored division to serve as a spearhead, the advances were neither as far nor as rapid as in the other corps in the Third Army. The 89th Infantry Division captured Bad Berka, where a bridge was taken intact. The 87th Infantry Division's attack continued toward the east. The 65th Infantry Division began to move forward from its assembly area. The majority of the 6th Cavalry Group's elements remained in assembly, with the 28th Cavalry Reconnaissance Squadron maintaining contact with the First Army on the northern flank.

The XII Corps' 90th Infantry Division attacked and captured Langwiesen, Breitenbach, and Gehren. The 26th Infantry Division cleared Eisfeld and the 11th Armored Division advanced toward the southwest, clearing Neustadt. The 71st Infantry Division closely followed the 11th Armored Division, and the 2d Cavalry Group continued with its screening of the southern flank.

In the XX Corps, the 4th and 6th Armored Divisions once more let loose with their freewheeling attacks, gaining 40 miles during the operations of the day. The 6th Armored captured bridges across the Saale River, but the 4th Armored Division's advance to the Saale River was stopped by destroyed bridges. The 76th Infantry Division moved forward as quickly as it could, but it could not keep up with the motorized, mobile 6th Armored Division. The 80th Infantry Division, even though encountering stiff opposition at Erfurt, captured the large town of Weimar, fifteen miles further to the north.

The XIX TAC flew 550 sorties and made claims of 539 motor vehicles, 599 railroad cars, 83 locomotives, 53 buildings, and 49 German planes either damaged or destroyed.

The Forward Echelon of Lucky Forward moved from Frankfurt-on-Main to Hersfeld.

April 12
D-Day +310

The Third Army was visited by General Eisenhower and Lieutenant General Omar Bradley. The major purpose of the visit was to verbally order the Third Army to stop at a restraining line running from the Mulde River to the Zwich-Mulde River, and from Plauen to Hoff and Bayreuth.

The 89th Infantry Division continued attacking eastward in the VIII Corps and the 65th Infantry and 6th Cavalry Group remained in reserve. The 87th Infantry Division reached the Saale River and began preparations for crossing. The 28th Cavalry Reconnaissance Squadron maintained contact between VIII and XX Corps.

The order of divisions from north to south in the XII Corps was the 26th Infantry Division, the 11th Armored Division, with the 71st Infantry Division and the 2d Cavalry Group following the 11th Armored Division. All divisions, except the 26th Infantry Division, crossed the Harlach River. The 26th Infantry Division remained behind to clear the towns of Soneburg, Lauscha, and Ernstthal.

The attack of the XX Corps was again spearheaded by the 6th Armored Division on the north and the 4th Armored Division on the south. They were followed by the 76th and 80th Infantry Divisions respectively, while the 3d Cavalry

Group screened both flanks at the same time. The 6th Armored Division's Combat Command "B" captured a bridge over the Weisse-Elster River and both the Reserve Combat Command and Combat Command "A" secured positions southwest of Zeitz. All three combat commands of the 4th Armored Division gained up to twenty miles, bypassing Jena and completing bridges across the Saale River at Maua and Kunitz. In support of the 80th Infantry Division, the artillery fired close to one thousand rounds into the city of Erfurt.

In large-scale attacks, the XIX TAC claimed 588 motor vehicles, 428 railroad cars, 23 locomotives, and 16 armored vehicles/tanks damaged or destroyed. Also claimed were 24 planes destroyed in the air and 32 damaged on the ground.

On April 12 arrangements were made whereby the surgeon of Advance Section ComZ agreed to assume responsibility for captured German hospitals west of the line of Giessen-Gelhausen, within the Third Army's zone of operations. This transfer of responsibility involved approximately 11,786 patients in 23 captured German hospitals or groups of hospitals.

April 13
D-Day +311

The German situation was extremely untenable on all sides. It appeared possible that very shortly the German units could be fighting the Americans and British on the Western Front and the Russians on the Eastern Front at the same time. Although there was a considerable amount of artillery and anti-tank weapons fire received around Zeitz (in the XX Corps area) elsewhere the Germans offered only scattered and ineffective resistance.

In the VIII Corps both the 87th and 89th Infantry Divisions crossed the Saale River. Between them they captured Reinstadt, Kesslar, Rudolstadt, Bad Blenkenburg, and Saalfeld. The 65th Infantry Division had some of its elements mopping up in rear areas, with the remainder in assembly. The northern flank was screened by the 6th Cavalry Group.

The 90th Infantry Division, in the XII Corps, captured Rottersdor, Huberndorf, Ruppersdorn, and Lothra; they also managed to capture two bridges intact. The 26th Infantry Division, making gains up to ten miles, cleared Golsberg, Buchbach, Kulmbach, and Stadt Steinach. The 11th Armored Division continued to capture numerous small towns during its advance. The 2d Cavalry Group moved through the 11th Armored Division's zone, advancing some of its elements as far as forty miles during the day. The 71st Infantry Division screened the southern flank of the corps' zone and provided close support for the 11th Armored.

The 4th Armored Division made some rapid advances—as far as thirty-five miles—in the XX Corps area, seizing three bridges intact over the Zwicker-Mulde River. The 6th Armored Division, paralleling the 4th Armored Division, gained twenty miles and crossed the Weisse-Elster River. Elements of the 76th Infantry Division advanced east, clearing Jena and Eisenberg. The 3d Cavalry continued to screen the flanks.

The XIX TAC lost 3 planes in 242 sorties. They made claims of 24 German planes, 140 motor vehicles, 7 armored vehicles, 240 railroad cars, and 16 locomotives damaged or destroyed.

April 14
D-Day +312

The 87th and 89th Infantry Divisions continued their joint advance to the east in the VIII Corps, some elements gaining up to ten miles during the day. The 28th Cavalry Reconnaissance Squadron (6th Cavalry Group) passed through the 89th Infantry Division's zone and captured a bridge intact across the Weisse-Elster River. The 65th Infantry Division completed its patrolling mission and moved into a forward assembly area.

The 90th Infantry Division, in the XII Corps, advanced twelve miles east of the Saale River and cleared the towns of Schelgel, Bruck, and Goritz. The 26th Infantry Division's three regiments advanced abreast and gained up to fifteen miles. The 11th Armored Division captured the city of Bayreuth before it pulled back into an assembly area. The 2d Cavalry Group assumed positions southeast of Bayreuth and the 71st Infantry Division relieved the 11th Armored Division in both the city and to the northwest.

In the XX Corps the 6th Armored was preparing to cross the river fifteen miles south of Leipzig. The 4th Armored Division's elements drove to points less than fifteen miles west of Chemnitz. The 80th Infantry Division cleared the Germans west of the Zwicker-Mulde River. The 76th Infantry Division cleared the zone behind the 6th Armored Division, and the corps' southern flank was screened by the 3d Cavalry Group.

The XIX TAC flew 279 sorties. They claimed 18 German planes, 190 motor vehicles, 20 locomotives, and 75 railroad cars after dropping 20 tons of bombs and strafing damaged or destroyed.

General Patton attended a ceremony marking the opening of the Roosevelt Memorial Railroad Bridge across the Rhine River in the vicinity of Mainz. During the ceremony General Patton was called upon to officially open the bridge for use by cutting a ribbon with a large pair of scissors which had been handed to him. He handed them back, demanding "...a goddamned bayonet" for cutting the ribbon, saying that he was not "...a goddamned tailor."

Plans were developed to advance the Third Army's transfer point from Eisenach to either Erfurt or Weimar, a forward movement of about 50 miles to the latter points. Eisenach was 145 miles from the Third Army railheads in the Mainz area and forward supply points were another 40 miles further to the east. The front line was already 100 miles beyond the town of Eisenach and the establishment of a new transfer point was vital and urgent. The speed of the Third Army's advance was very much reflected in the current heavy issues of gasoline. During the week of April 8 to April 14, a total of 4,331,087 gallons of V-80 gasoline was consumed. The amount averaged out to a total of 618,727 gallons per day.

April 15
D-Day +313

It was estimated by the Third Army's G-2 Section that there were about 15,500 combat effectives with possibly 65 tanks/assault guns against the Third Army's front lines, the equivalent of 2 divisions.

In the VIII Corps the 87th and 89th Infantry Divisions continued to advance abreast of each other and gained ten miles during the day. The two divisions captured Schleiz, Piesigitz, and Weida. Advancing in front of the two divisions was the 6th Cavalry Group, which crossed the Weisse River. The 65th Infantry Division remained in corps reserve.

The towns of Hoff and Frossen were captured by the 90th Infantry Division in the XII Corps. The 90th also crossed the Saale River at various points north of Hof. The 26th Infantry Division, to the south, captured Munchberg and consolidated positions between Hof and Gefrees. The 71st Infantry Division also consolidated positions, their zone being from Gefrees to Bayreuth. The 11th Armored Division remained in assembly for the day.

The 6th Armored Division remained on the offensive, pushing as far and as fast as it could. They drove north to a vicinity just north of Chemnitz. The 4th Armored Division maintained its positions just west and northwest of Chemnitz. The 76th Infantry Division captured Kayna after advancing to the Zwickauer-Mulde River. The 80th Infantry Division cleared both Glauchau and Crimmitschau, and afterward, began relieving units of the 4th Armored Division. The screening of the corps' southern flank was done by the 3d Cavalry Group.

The XIX TAC flew 364 sorties, registering claims of 562 motor vehicles, 101 locomotives, and 432 railroad cars damaged or destroyed. Three planes were lost during the day's operations, but they destroyed 5 planes in the air and 50 on the ground and also damaged 1 plane in the air and 39 on the ground. The Luftwaffe was being forced to abandon many of its airfields because of the Americans and British advancing on the Western Front and Russians advancing on the Eastern Front. The abandoned fields and pilotless airplanes were excellent targets. During the period of April 1 to April 15, the XIX TAC destroyed a record number of German planes, claiming 111 destroyed, 6 probables, and 49 damaged in aerial activity. They also claimed 321 destroyed, 5 probables, and 306 damaged by bombing as ground targets. During the period the XIX TAC lost only 23 planes.

When the Third Army's units reached the line from the Mulde River to the Zwickauer-Mulde River and from Plauen to Hof and to Bayreuth, the entire army was halted in its advance in conformance with verbal orders of SHAEF.

The 120th Evacuation Hospital moved to Ettersburg to provide medical service for inmates of the large concentration camp there known as Buchenwald. Out of twenty-one thousand persons in the camp, about five thousand needed immediate medical care.

April 16
D-Day +314

Joint advances were the order of the day for the 87th and 89th Infantry Divisions on the VIII Corps' front. The 87th advanced nineteen miles, capturing Oelsnitz, Elsterberg, and Zeulenroda; and the 89th gained nine miles, capturing both Griez and Walddorf. The 6th Cavalry Group preceded the 89th Infantry Division, with some of its elements entering the city of Zwichku.

The XII Corps was well stabilized and acquiescent. The 90th Infantry Division was in the north, the 26th Infantry Division in the middle, and the 71st Infantry Division on the southern flank. The 2d Cavalry Group patrolled for a short time on the southern flank, but later went into an assembly area after being relieved by elements of the 71st Infantry Division.

The divisions in the XX Corps area maintained their positions. Some elements of the 6th Armored Division were relieved by the 76th Infantry Division in place, while at the same time and to the rear, the 65th Infantry Division was assigned to the corps. Other corps units (80th Infantry Division, 4th Armored Division, and 3d Cavalry Group) remained unchanged.

A total of 23 planes were damaged in the air and another 84 on the ground by the XIX TAC. They also accounted for the destruction or damaging of 347 motor vehicles; 319 railroad cars; and 111 locomotives.

The Third Army counted up its daily bag of POWs and the total was 32,269. It was another record day.

The military government estimated that at least 10 percent of the persons in forward areas in the XII Corps were displaced persons. In factory areas, the figure was even higher. A total of 112 thousand displaced persons were placed into camps throughout the Third Army's zone.

April 17
D-Day +315

Letter of Instruction No. 21, received from the Twelfth Army Group headquarters, gave detailed orders for the armies of the army group to launch a powerful attack for the purpose of gaining contact with the Soviet forces in the Danube Valley. Also in the letter were instructions for the group to seize the city of Salzburg. The Twelfth Army Group was to defend the general line from the Erz-Gebirge Hills to the Mulde River and to the Elbe River within its zone of operations and hold the existing bridgehead as a threat to Berlin.

The Third Army was to have a total of four corps placed under its command. They consisted of the III, XII and XVIII Airborne and the XX Corps. In all of the corps, the divisions commanded were the 5th, 8th, 26th, 65th, 70th, 71st, 80th, 86th, 90th, 97th, and 99th Infantry Divisions; and the 4th, 11th, 13th, 16th, and 20th Armored Divisions. At the current time the 70th Infantry Division was in the reserve of SHAEF. The 5th and 8th Infantry Divisions and the 4th Armored Division were in the Twelfth Army Group's reserve. Divisions of the III, VIII, and XX Corps were to remain with their respective corps but were subject to such adjustments as were deemed necessary by SHAEF and/or the Twelfth Army Group to maintain the balance of supporting troops in the armies to which they were assigned.

A directive from the Third Army headquarters indicated the assignment of the new divisions and the new corps. The III Corps (86th and 99th Infantry Divisions and 20th Armored

Division) was to pass control of the 5th Infantry Division to the XVIII Airborne Corps and control of the 7th Armored Division to First Army.

The VIII Corps (76th, 87th, and 89th Infantry Divisions and the 4th and 6th Armored Divisions) was to assume control of the 76th Infantry Division.

The XII Corps (26th, 90th, and 97th Infantry Divisions and the 11th Armored Division) was to move the 71st Infantry Division to relieve elements of the XV Corps and then pass control to the XX Corps.

The XVIII Airborne Corps (5th and 8th Infantry Divisions and the 4th Armored Division) was to assist in the movement of the III Corps to the Third Army zone of operations.

The XX Corps (65th, 71st, and 80th Infantry Divisions and the 13th Armored Division) was to relinquish control of the 4th and 6th Armored Divisions and the 76th Infantry Division. The corps was to relieve the 80th Infantry Division, assume command of the 65th Infantry Division, and assume command of the 71st Infantry Division. Upon arrival into the Corps area, the 71st Infantry Division was to come under control of the corps headquarters.

The XIX TAC flew 500 sorties, and destroyed 51 enemy planes, and damaged another 58. Among other claims were 544 motor vehicles; 176 locomotives, and 186 railroad cars damaged or destroyed.

The Third Army was preparing for the upcoming operation into the National Redoubt area, which existed only in the minds of Eisenhower and his advisors.

April 18
D-Day +316

The III Corps passed from control of the First Army to the Third Army. The 99th Infantry Division passed to control of III Corps and closed at Trabelsdorf.

The control of the northern zone of the XX Corps was passed to VIII Corps, with the VIII Corps assuming command of the 4th and 6th Armored Divisions and the 76th Infantry Division. The 4th Armored, relieved on the line by the 76th

Infantry Division, proceeded to an assembly area. The lineup for the corps was then as follows from north to south: 6th Armored Division, 76th Infantry Division, 89th Infantry Division, 87th Infantry Division, 4th Armored Division, and the 6th Cavalry Group in assembly.

The XII Corps passed control of the 71st Infantry Division to the XX Corps. Also in the XII area, the 90th Infantry Division resumed its advance. In the central part of the Corps area, the 26th Infantry Division's elements resumed their attack, gaining nine miles and capturing Kirchenlamitz. On the southern flank of the corps, the 11th Armored Division made some excellent progress, advancing eleven miles to Tremmersdorf. The 2d Cavalry Group advanced along the northern flank, screening along the Czechoslovakian border.

The XX Corps instituted a general movement to the south. The 65th Infantry Division moved to an assembly area near Bamberg, which had previously been captured by the Seventh Army. The 71st Infantry Division advanced two miles and the 80th Infantry Division moved west and south from its old zone. Some elements of the 3d Cavalry Group closed in zone around Lichtenfels.

The XIX TAC flew 393 sorties and claimed 333 motor vehicles, 67 locomotives, and 383 railroad cars damaged or destroyed. Their toll of German planes was 14.

April 19
D-Day +317

The defenses confronting the Third Army proved to be only a thin crust. It was first penetrated by elements of the Third Army at Grafenwöhr and then penetrated at will at many other places on the Western Front.

The III Corps prepared for occupation of a new area on the Third Army's southern flank. The 86th Infantry Division closed into the new area; at the same time the 99th Infantry Division was in the assembly area near Schwabach.

In the VIII Corps the divisions remained in positions along their restraining line, continued patrolling, and waited for the order to Go.

The XII Corps advanced to the southeast with the 90th Infantry Division to the north, the 26th Infantry Division in the center, and the 11th Armored Division to the south. The divisions gained eleven, twelve, and fifteen miles respectively. The 11th Armored Division captured Grafenwöhr. The 2d Cavalry Group kept in contact with the VIII Corps to the north while patrolling.

The XX Corps in their new zone of occupation, continued to attack with the 71st Infantry Division. The 71st gained eight miles due south of Bayreuth and captured Pegnitz. The 65th Infantry Division began passing through the XV Corps' zone in the Seventh Army. The 80th Infantry Division and the 3d Cavalry Group continued with their movements to their new zone in the south.

The XIX TAC claimed 45 planes destroyed and 10 damaged on the ground and another 7 shot down in aerial combat. The XIX TAC lost only 1 plane. Otherwise, they accounted for the damage and/or destruction of 353 motor vehicles; 39 locomotives; and 125 railroad cars.

During the time that XII Corps attacked to the southeast, other Third Army units regrouped and prepared during the day for the coming operation into the German Redoubt area.

By this date, the Third Army had attained its goal of moving at least one million rations and one million gallons of gasoline to base points at Würzburg and Bamberg before the roads could become congested with troop movements for the new mission to the southeast. Advance Section ComZ planned to establish as quickly as possible a transfer point at Kahl for packaged and bulk gasoline and also a decanting point at the airfield east of Würzburg.

In the 6th Armored Division's area, the general reaction to be found among the German civilians was one of relief that the war was apparently, and for all intents and purposes, drawing to a close. The average citizen claimed to be totally ignorant of the atrocities in Nazi concentration camps, and they laid the responsibility for both the war and their defeat directly on the Nazi leadership.

April 20
D-Day +318

The Third Army forces were making substantial gains in the central and southern portions of its zone against negligible opposition. Although numerous road craters, blown bridges, and roadblocks were encountered, the majority of them were totally undefended.

Amendment No. 1 to an operational directive dated April 17 from the Twelfth Army Group indicated that the XVIII Airborne Corps would not be coming under the control of the Third Army after all. The 5th Infantry Division and the 4th Armored Division were directed to move to an area southeast of Fulda when they were released by the First Army.

The 86th and 99th Infantry Divisions remained in their respective assembly areas in the new III Corps area. The 20th Armored Division passed to control of the corps and assembled in the vicinity of Mainbernheim. The 14th Cavalry Group (also assigned to the corps) closed in the vicinity of Iphofen.

The divisions on the line in the VIII Corps patrolled aggressively and maintained their positions. The 4th Armored Division remained in the assembly area near Crimmitschau. The 76th, 87th, and the 89th Infantry Divisions and the 6th Armored Division were also on the line. The screening of the Corps' southern flank was completed by the 6th Cavalry Group.

In the XII Corps the 90th and 26th Infantry Divisions continued with their advances, gaining eleven miles and capturing Metzenhof, Kemnath, Pressath, Erbendorf, Brand, and Seussen. The combat commands of the 11th Armored Division maintained positions near Grafenwöhr and Eschenbach. The 2d Cavalry Group cleared the town of As during its continued screening of the northern flank. The 97th Infantry Division was assigned to the corps and was en route to the corps' zone.

In the XX Corps the 65th Infantry Division captured Trautmannshoffen and Lauterhofen. The 71st Infantry Division captured Velden and Auerbach. To the rear the 80th Infantry

Division closed near Schesslitz and then initiated a spur-of-the-moment attack which moved them very near to Nürnberg. The 3d Cavalry Group continued to patrol.

A total of 575 sorties were flown by the XIX TAC. They claimed 42 planes destroyed and 22 damaged in addition to 294 motor vehicles, 58 locomotives, and 617 railroad cars damaged or destroyed.

There were some sudden alterations in the tactical plan which made necessary the swift relocation of many heavy ordnance installations, including the main supply depots and the Third Army vehicle pool. The 26th Ordnance Battalion was moved a distance of about 165 miles to Fürth. The vehicle pool was moved to Nurnberg (a total of 150 miles). Many trains of full-track vehicles consigned to the vehicle pool at Hanau were rerouted to the new location. A sufficient number of vehicles to replace current losses was shipped directly to the forward depots from Hanau.

April 21
D-Day +319

Because the Third Army was coming closer to the Eastern Front, specific recognition data concerning Russian vehicles and equipment was issued to corps commanders.

In the III Corps the 86th Infantry Division moved to a forward assembly and the 99th Infantry Division moved to Schwabach. Parts of the 14th Cavalry Group reconnoitered, while at the same time, the 20th Armored Division remained in assembly. The III Corps made preparations for an attack.

The VIII Corps patrolled during the first part of the day. Later on, the 76th, 87th, and 89th Infantry Divisions; the 6th Armored Division; and the 6th Cavalry Group all passed to the control of the First Army at 221200. The 4th Armored Division remained in assembly in the Twelfth Army Group.

In the XII Corps the 26th Infantry Division gained eight miles, capturing Schwarzenbach and Parkstein. The 90th Infantry Division advanced twelve miles, capturing Falkenberg and entering Arzberg. The 2d Cavalry Group, to the north, advanced four miles and captured Haslov.

The 65th Infantry Division, attacking to the south in the XX Corps area, cleared Neumarkt. The 71st Infantry Division attacked and gained seven miles. The 80th Infantry Division had some of its elements relieve elements of the Third Infantry Division (Seventh Army) in Nürnberg, while the other 80th's elements assembled near Schesslitz. The entire 80th Infantry Division passed to the SHAEF reserve during the day. The 2d Cavalry Group attacked through positions of the 65th and 71st Infantry Divisions, making good gains. The 13th Armored Division was assigned to the XX Corps and was en route to the corps' area.

Good weather continued, allowing the XIX TAC to be impolite to the Germans. They bombed airfields, destroying 46 planes and damaging another 19, all on the ground. They also claimed 274 motor vehicles and 182 railroad cars.

The Third Army passed control of the VIII Corps (76th, 87th, and 89th Infantry Divisions; the 6th Armored Division; and the 6th Cavalry Group) to the First Army. In addition, they were required to pass the 4th Armored Division and the 80th Infantry Division to the Twelfth Army Group reserve and the SHAEF reserve respectively.

So far, from April 1 to April 21, the Third Army troops had taken a total of 240,661 POWs.

April 22
D-Day +320

G-2 reports indicated that as Third Army continued to drive to the southeast, gaining momentum each day, advances by the Allies on the Western Front and the Russians on the Eastern Front were creating pockets in all zones of operations. Furthermore, as the days progressed, the pockets developed pockets.

The III Corps took over control of the zone which originally was XV Corps' area, passing control of the 20th Armored Division to the XV Corps and assuming control of the 14th Armored Division. To the south, elements of the 86th Infantry Division passed through the 42nd Infantry Division and went forward. The 99th Infantry Division remained in its assembly area near Schwabach. The 14th Cavalry Group moved to relieve elements of the 65th Infantry along the III-XX Corps' boundary.

In the XII Corps the 97th Infantry Division closed with the 303d, 386th, and 387th Infantry Regiments moving into assembly areas near Hof, prepared, if necessary, to protect along the Czechoslovakian border. The 90th Infantry Division was advancing to the south along the Czechoslovakian border. South of the 90th Infantry Division, the 11th Armored Division continued to make good gains to the southeast. Combat Command "A" advanced to Haag, Reserve Combat Command cleared Hirschau and Schnaittenbach, and Combat Command "B" reached Unttraubenbach. Following on the heels of the 11th Armored, the 26th Infantry Division cleared enemy pockets and gained fifteen miles for the day. The 2d Cavalry Group maintained a reconnaissance screen along the Czech border.

In the XX Corps the 71st Infantry Division advanced southeast and captured Amberg, Illschwang, and Rosenberg during their eleven mile gain. The 65th Infantry Division advanced in a parallel to the 71st, gaining eight miles and clearing both Neumarkt and Kastl. The 80th Infantry Division remained in the reserve of SHAEF in the rear of the corps' area. The 13th Armored Division closed in the vicinity of Eschenau. The 3d Cavalry Group, advancing in front of the 65th Infantry Division, captured a bridge intact over the Naab River near the town of Burgiengenfeld. During the day, some elements of the Third Cavalry gained as many as twenty-four miles while capturing Hormannsdorf, Hohenfels, and Hohenburg.

Poor flying conditions limited the operations of the XIX TAC. They did fly 79 sorties, managing to damage or destroy 113 motor vehicles, 40 locomotives, and 91 railroad cars.

A problem developed in the distribution of balanced A rations to the troops because of long supply lines and congested rail traffic.

The Forward Echelon of Lucky Forward moved 150 miles from Hersfeld to Erlangen.

A total of 134 thousand displaced persons were currently being housed in military government camps throughout the Third Army's zone of operations.

April 23
D-Day +321

After the III Corps had completely assumed the former zone of the XV Corps, their units were disposed as follows: the 86th and 99th Infantry Divisions abreast of each other, preceded by the 14th Armored Division, with the 14th Cavalry Group screening the left (east) flank of the corps' zone. During the day, the Corps units captured Hags-bron and averaged a six mile advance.

The disposition of the XII Corps' divisions was much different. The 11th Armored Division preceded the 26th Infantry Division, 90th Infantry Division, 2d Cavalry Group, and the 97th Infantry Division. All of the units to the rear of the armor were moving south and screening along the Czechoslovakian border. This made up a long, continuous column of three infantry divisions and one cavalry group.

In the XX Corps the 65th and 71st Infantry Divisions were preceded by the 3d Cavalry Group, while the 80th Infantry Division (in SHAEF reserve) and the 13th Armored Division were in the rear areas. The 3d Cavalry Group continued with its spearheading operations, sweeping forward for a twenty-five-mile gain to a point within 5 miles of Regensburg. The 71st Infantry Division cleared Schwandorf, going forward seventeen miles. The 65th Infantry Division captured many small towns against very negligible resistance during its fifteen mile advance.

In the XIX TAC, 158 sorties were flown. They claimed 26 German planes, 247 motor vehicles, 36 locomotives, and 7 armored vehicles damaged or destroyed.

Losses of the Third Army were the smallest of any day in the history of its operations. With only 3 men of the Third Army killed, 37 wounded, and 5 missing, the Third Army took a total of 8,878 POWs.

Reconnaissance units in the vicinity of Grafenwöhr uncov-

ered a large German ammunition dump containing an estimated three million chemical warfare shells.

April 24
D-Day +322

The 5th Infantry Division was passed from control of the
First Army to the Third Army, but was to be kept in SHAEF
reserve. While the 5th was enroute to the Third Army zone,
the 4th Armored Division (in Twelfth Army Reserve) moved
into an assembly area. The 70th Infantry Division continued
with its policing duties around Frankfurt.

The 86th Infantry Division, in the III Corps area, crossed the
Altmühl River at three points, advanced twenty-four miles,
and cleared a number of small towns. The 99th Infantry
Division also crossed the Altmühl River during their seventeen mile advance. The 14th Armored Division set up bridgeheads over the river while keeping parallel with the two
infantry divisions. The 14th Cavalry Group screened the left
flank and at the same time cleared Waldorf and Kelheim,
reaching the Danube River by the end of the day.

The attack of the XII Corps continued to be spearheaded by
the 11th Armored Division. The 11th's Combat Command
"B" advanced twenty-eight miles, cleared Regen, and reached
Schonberg; Combat Command "A" reached the vicinity of
Swiessel. The 104th and 328th Infantry Regiments of the 26th
Infantry Division both crossed the Regen River, gaining fifteen miles and cleaning up after the 11th Armored Division.
The 90th Infantry Division moved south after being relieved
by the 2d Cavalry Group. Along with the 90th Infantry Division and the 2d Cavalry Group, the 97th Infantry Division
assisted in forming a continuous screen for the corps' southern flank.

The 261st Infantry Regiment of the 65th Infantry Division
passed through the 3d Cavalry Group in the XX Corps area.
They advanced twelve miles through Killersried and Rech-
berg, reaching the Danube River to the west and southwest of
Regensburg. Along the northern bank of the Danube, the 3d
Cavalry Group provided screening. In the 71st Infantry Divi-

sion, the 5th and 14th Infantry Regiments crossed the Regen River near Regenstauf and then continued on their way to the southeast toward the Danube River. The 80th Infantry Division remained in the vicinity of Nürnberg immediately after being released to the Third Army for full operational control. In the 13th Armored Division, the elements (plus the 93d Cavalry Reconnaissance Squadron) moved southward from their assembly area at Eschenau, screening the corps' right flank as they went.

A total of 306 sorties were flown by the XIX TAC, with claims of 373 motor vehicles, 31 locomotives, and 510 railroad cars damaged or destroyed.

There were extremely large quantities of foodstuffs, both military and civilian, being captured. The Third Army was directed by higher headquarters that German food supplies were to be used for Allied displaced persons, German civilians, and Allied POWs. The exception to that directive was American and British POWs, who were to receive United States Army rations. Due to a shortage of C and K type rations in ComZ, higher headquarters requested that the Third Army make every effort to utilize A or 10-to-1 type rations to the maximum extent.

The Rear Echelon of Lucky Forward moved from Frankfurt to Erlangen, a distance of 140 miles.

April 25
D-Day +323

The 86th Infantry Division advanced twelve miles along the west flank of III Corps, clearing Eichstätt and Wetistetten and entering Ingolstadt. The 14th Armored Division expanded bridgeheads over the Altmühl River to a depth of 5 miles and the 99th Infantry Division cleared Dietfurt and advanced ten miles along the west bank of the Ludwigs Canal. The 14th Cavalry Group continued to round up stragglers around the junction of the Ludwigs Canal and the Danube River.

In the XII Corps the 11th Armored Division kept up its rapid advances. Combat Command "A" cleared Grafenau and Freyung and Combat Command "B" reached a point five miles southeast of Freyung, only 10 miles from the Austrian border. In the rear the 26th Infantry Division advanced twenty-one miles, clearing Zeitldorn, Steinach, and Falkenstein. To the rear of the 26th Infantry Division, the 90th Infantry Division, 2d Cavalry Group, and the 97th Infantry Division moved south along the Czechoslovakian border.

Bridgeheads were set up in the XX Corps zone by both the 65th and 71st Infantry Divisions. The 3d Cavalry Group was relieved on the line by the 65th and 71st Infantry Divisions. The 3d Cavalry Group then moved east to assume positions on the corps' left flank. In the rear the 13th Armored Division began a forward movement to an assembly area near Velbeurg.

The XIX TAC destroyed 56 German planes and damaged another 66 on the ground in 389 sorties. They also accounted for 516 motor vehicles, 83 locomotives, and 281 railroad cars damaged or destroyed.

A rail regulating point began operation in the Würzburg area to assist in the relief of the Third Army's shipping problem.

April 26
D-Day +324

The 86th Infantry Division assumed a bridgehead over the Danube River in the III Corps, gained four miles for the day, and captured Ingolstadt. Also in the 86th, the 343rd Infantry Regiment completed a treadway bridge near Nigolstadt, crossing and driving six miles south of the Danube River. The 99th Infantry Division's 394th and 395th Infantry Regiments drove south to the Danube.

In the XII Corps the 11th Armored led the way, with the 26th Infantry Division following close behind. The 90th and 97th Infantry Divisions and the 2d Cavalry Group continued with their screening operations along the Czechoslovakian border. Some patrol elements of the 11th Armored Division had crossed the Austrian border, but they came back to assembly areas about 6 miles north of the border.

In the XX Corps area, the 65th Infantry Division reinforced

and expanded its bridgehead over the Danube River, completing a treadway bridge in the vicinity of Lohstadt. Another treadway bridge was completed further east, near Sulzbach, by the 71st Infantry Division. Both the 65th and 71st Infantry Divisions reached a depth of five miles beyond their bridgeheads. The 80th Infantry Division remained in assembly at Nürnberg and the 13th Armored Division moved to a forward assembly area at Velburg. The 3d Cavalry Group patrolled and maintained contact with the XII Corps.

Poor weather did not keep the XIX TAC out of the sky. They flew 465 sorties and claimed 444 motor vehicles, 70 locomotives, and 425 railroad cars damaged or destroyed.

A record amount of V-80 gasoline was issued to Third Army troops with their vehicles using a total of 1,129,675 gallons.

April 27
D-Day +325

A directive from the Twelfth Army Group indicated that the First Army would take over the responsibility for the left flank of the Third Army along the Czechoslovakian border as troops became available. The same directive also changed the boundary between First and Third Armies.

In the XII Corps, the 86th Infantry Division made advances up to fifteen miles south of the Danube River, capturing Neustadt, Eining, and Sittling. The 90th Infantry Division held positions along the north bank of the Danube. The 14th Armored Division relieved some elements of the 86th Infantry Division at Ingolstadt and maintained positions north of the Danube. The 14th Cavalry Group assembled in the vicinity of Buch.

In the XX Corps, the 13th Armored Division crossed the Danube River both east and west of Regensberg, passing all three of its combat commands through the 65th and 71st Infantry Divisions. The 65th Infantry Division captured Regensberg, on the southern bank of the Danube. The 71st Infantry Division increased its bridgeheads to a depth of ten miles, capturing Pfatter in the process. The 80th Infantry Division moved from Nürnberg to the south and prepared to cross the Danube. Patrolling on the east flank was the 3d Cavalry Group.

In a total of 103 sorties, the XIX TAC destroyed 11 German planes and damaged 12 more. The low claims of the day were the result of poor visibility and the lack of targets.

A committee was formed by the military government in Frankfurt. Its purpose was to alleviate the suffering caused by the Nazi discrimination toward the Jews. New and complete ration cards were issued, provisions were made for the homeless, repairs to damaged homes were begun, grants were made to the needy, impartiality was pledged by the chamber of commerce in hiring policies, and two Jews were appointed to the local labor board.

April 28
D-Day +326

A directive from the Twelfth Army Group directed that the Third Army would continue with its drive to join with the Russians in the Danube Valley and to seize Salzburg. The directive also altered the boundary of the Sixth and Twelfth Army Groups.

In the III Corps the 86th Infantry Division continued with its advance to the south along the western flank of the corps' zone, gained eleven miles, and cleared Wolznach. The 99th Infantry Division continued toward the east, with its 393d and 395th Infantry Regiments abreast of each other. The 99th also cleared Neustadt, Abensberg, and Mühlhausen. The 14th Armored Division advanced between the 86th and 99th Infantry Divisions and gained eighteen miles. The 14th Cavalry Group remained in assembly near Buch.

In the XII Corps the majority of the 11th Armored Division remained in assembly, but Combat Command "B" began clearing ground between the Austrian border and the Passau-Rohrnbach Road. The 26th Infantry Division cleared its zone and prepared to strike out across the Austrian border. It advanced seven miles, captured Zenting, and closed with the forward armored units. The 97th Infantry Division passed to control of the First Army.

The 13th Armored Division, still in advance of other XX Corps units, drove south to the Isar River, gained up to twenty miles, and captured Greibing. To the rear of the armor, the 71st Infantry Division cleared Straubing and Taimering and advanced ten miles. On the right flank of the 71st, the 3d Cavalry Group moved south and at the same time policed its zone. The 65th Infantry Division maintained its positions and policed south of Regensburg. The 80th Infantry Division conducted policing actions in the western part of the corps' zone.

Bad weather cancelled flying by the XIX TAC.

Once more, the supply situation had become critical. The Third Army needed gasoline, all types of rations, and had no rail transportation close to them. A very strict rationing of gasoline was imposed on all units. Commanders of all echelons were requested to take measures to inventory, assemble, and guard captured German food stocks.

The problem of collecting and storing captured food supplies became a high priority. The expected liberation of about three hundred thousand Allied POWs and displaced persons in the Third Army's zone required the full exploitation of the captured German foodstuffs. The Quartermaster Field Service Division was allotted an additional service company and a battalion headquarters to complete the task.

Near Deggendorf, on the Danube River, five barges were found that were loaded with about twenty-five hundred gas-filled bombs. The German High Command had left one officer at the site to insure that neither side detonated the bombs and inadvertently create an unintentional gas attack. A neutral zone was established around the area of the Danube where the barges were located.

April 29
D-Day +327

After a thirteen mile advance, the 86th Infantry Division reached the Isar River, with its 343d Infantry Regiment forcing a crossing. Just to the immediate east, the 99th Infantry Division advanced eighteen miles, also reaching the Isar

River. The 14th Armored Division cleared Siegenburg and Pfeffenhausen and captured Moosburg. The 14th's Reserve Combat Command cleared Landshut and the 14th Cavalry Group crossed the Danube River on the east flank, with some elements reaching the Isar River along with the other divisions.

In the 5th Infantry Division, the 10th and 11th Infantry Regiments closed in an assembly area near Grafenau in the XII Corps. The 11th Armored Division cleared up to the Austrian border, capturing both Ulrichstrent and Wilheilmstreut. The 26th Infantry Division cleared the zone to the north of the 11th Armored Division, gained eleven miles, and captured Otterskirchen. In the northern portion of the zone, the 2d Cavalry Group and the 90th Infantry Division patrolled along the Czechoslovakian border.

Along the XX Corps' western flank, the 80th Infantry Division attacked to the south, driving toward the Isar River. The Division's 319th Regiment reached the river in a twenty-six-mile advance and captured many towns in its drive. The 13th Armored Division made assault crossings of the Isar River at Mamming and also at Platting. Immediately after the assaults, construction of bridges at both crossing sites was begun by engineers. The 71st Infantry Division, in a fifteen mile drive, advanced to the south and cleared Leiblfing. The 3d Cavalry Group went into an assembly area and the 65th Infantry Division patrolled and policed.

During a total of 233 sorties, the XIX TAC claimed 452 motor vehicles, 277 railroad cars, 28 armored vehicles/tanks, 60 locomotives, and 9 planes on the ground damaged or destroyed.

An enemy chemical depot at Nieder Leierndort, stocked with about sixty-thousand gas-filled aerial bombs, was captured.

April 30
D-Day +328

From March 26 until April 26, the Third Army captured a total of 183,331 POWs, not including the number of German soldiers who were admitted to the Third Army hospitals. Of the larger total, 1,832 were from Panzer divisions and 9,073 were from infantry divisions. The remaining 173,796 soldiers were from miscellaneous units. The relatively few POWs processed from the Panzer divisions were expected, because the Germans had lost most of their Panzers in the Ruhr Pocket.

The German's replacement system had completely broken down, and it was virtually impossible for the high command to replace any of the troops who were being killed, wounded, or captured by the Third Army. The situation became so critical that the Germans were committing makeshift units to battle which were composed of ersatz soldiers, including cripples of every description, those with mental health problems, young boys and girls, and about 500 women.

According to a directive received from the Twelfth Army Group, the 16th Armored Division was to revert to the Twelfth Army Group Reserve at 301200.

In the III Corps the 86th Infantry Division's elements gained seven miles, patrolled, and prepared to cross the Isar River. Farther to the east, the 99th Infantry Division closed up to the Isar River and established a bridgehead at Moosburg in conjunction with elements of the 14th Armored Division. Also in the 99th, another bridgehead was set up at Landshut by the 393d Infantry Regiment, which also captured Achdorf, south of the Isar River. The 14th Armored Division advanced six and eight miles with its Combat Commands "A" and "B" respectively. The 14th Cavalry Group completed its patrolling and prepared to cross the Isar River at the end of the day.

In the XII Corps the 11th Armored Division was still in the vanguard. Its units drove several miles inside Austria, capturing a bridge intact at Kappel. The 26th Infantry Division drove close into the Austrian border, which was only two miles away at the town of Passau. The 5th Infantry Division gained fourteen miles during the day and prepared to follow the 11th Armored Division into Austria. Both the 2d Cavalry Group and the 90th Infantry Division patrolled and policed along the Czechoslovakian border in the northern part of the corps' zone. The 97th Infantry Division (First Army) relieved some of the elements of the 90th Infantry Division in the north to allow the 90th to side step to the south.

In the XX Corps the 80th Infantry Division made crossings of the Isar River with its 318th and 319th Infantry Regiments. In the 71st Infantry Division, the 14th and 66th Infantry Regiments captured Pilsting and Wallersdorf, crossed the Isar River, and gained about three miles during the day. The 13th Armored Division made some rapid gains from their Platting bridgehead, fanning out in a twenty-five mile advance and completing a bridge across the Isar River strong enough for heavy equipment. The 3d Cavalry Group remained in assembly. The 65th Infantry Division continued occupation and policing of its zone in the vicinity of Regensberg, far to the rear of the XX Corps' zone.

Finishing up the month with 175 sorties, the XIX TAC claimed 107 motor vehicles, 67 locomotives, 588 railroad cars, and 4 planes damaged or destroyed.

The 130th Evacuation Hospital moved to the vicinity of Moosburg to provide care for patients in the Allied POW camp discovered there.

In accordance with orders from General Eisenhower that immediate steps be taken to give decent and reverent burials of all persons of all nationalities who had been victims of Nazi atrocities, Third Army chaplains officiated at hundreds of ceremonies during the last week of April. In some towns military government officers ordered civilians to make coffins, dig up bodies from pits, and rebury them decently in separate cemeteries. At Schwarzenfeld, services were conducted over the graves of two hundred Jews who had been reportedly murdered by SS troops.

General Patton recorded a speech to be broadcast on American radio stations during the upcoming V-E Day celebration.

Now that victory in Europe has been achieved, let us review the Third Army's part in this epic struggle.

From Avaranche to Brest, thence across France, Germany, and into Austria, the Third Army and its equally victorious comrades of the 19th Tactical Air Command have fought their way.

The Seine, the Moselle, the Saar, Rhine, and the Danube, not to mention twenty other lesser rivers have been successfully stormed.

The Siegfried Line has been penetrated at will. Metz, Trier, Koblenz, and Frankfurt and countless other cities and towns have been cleared of the enemy. More than eighty thousand square miles of country have been liberated or conquered.

You have demonstrated your irresistible powers in France, Belgium, Luxembourg, Germany, Czechoslovakia, and Austria. You have captured more than three-quarters of a million Nazi soldiers and have killed or wounded at least half a million others.

But, in thinking of the heritage of glory you have achieved, do not be unmindful of the price you have paid. Throughout your victorious advances, your line of march is marked with the graves of your heroic dead; while the hospitals are crowded with your wounded.

Nor should we forget the efforts of those at home who have invariably provided us with the sinews of war, the means to Victory. To those at home we promise that, with their unremitting assistance, we shall continue so that with the help of Almighty God, and through the inspired leadership or our President and the High Command, we shall conquer not only Germany, but also Japan; until the last danger to life, liberty, and the pursuit of happiness shall perish from the earth.

CHAPTER 10

May, 1945

The Third Army's May combat operations lasted only seven days. May 8 would be Victory-in-Europe (V-E) Day. The Third Army would finish its armor-fisted drive into Germany and Germany's occupied territories by pushing to the Czechoslovakian border, turning southeast in another push across the Danube, Isar, and Inn rivers, and into Austria. Lastly, they would surge into Czechoslovakia to capture Plze. One of the discoveries of the seven days in May would be that SHAEF and Eisenhower, indeed, would be proven to be totally incorrect about the National Redoubt area, which General Patton and his G-2 Officer, Colonel Oscar Koch, had claimed did not exist except in Eisenhower's subconscious fears.

May 1
D-Day +329

Poor roads, roadblocks, and rough terrain were the only defense offered against Patton's Third Army in its advance. In the III Corps the 86th Infantry Division made continuous gains to the southeast and the 16th Armored Division's elements moved swiftly to the vicinity of Wasserburg. The 99th Infantry Division was supplemented by both tanks and tank destroyers which assisted them in more rapid gains. They assembled at the end of the day near Altfraunhofen. The 14th Armored Division's Combat Commands "A" and "B" both advanced about twenty miles, seizing a bridge and a dam intact near Jettenbach. The 14th Cavalry Group crossed the Isar River and continued with its advance to the southeast, on the Corps' left flank.

In the XII Corps the 26th Infantry Division kept moving toward its objective of the Danube River. The 11th Armored Division's elements pushed themselves over poor roads, reached Neufelden, and crossed the Mühl River. The 5th Infantry Division captured bridges across the Mühl River near Schiagel. Some elements of the 97th Infantry Division relieved other elements of the 90th Infantry Division, and at the same time, cleared a wooded area just across the Czechoslovakian border. The remainder of the 97th Infantry Division consolidated its positions. The 2d Cavalry Group maintained contact with the 5th Infantry Division and patrolled. The 4th Armored Division continued its movement to the corps' zone of operations.

In the XX Corps the newly motorized 261st Infantry Regiment of the 65th Infantry Division crossed the Isar River at Platting and moved quickly to the southeast, capturing Sulzbach. The 261st was followed by the 259th and 260th Infantry Regiments (65th Infantry Division). The 71st Infantry Division moved some of its elements into the vicinity of Anzenkirchen. The 80th Infantry Division's 318th and 319th Infantry Regiments moved southeast; at the same time, the 13th Armored Division drove rapidly to the south to the Inn River near Marktl, Braunau, and Neu-Ötting. The 3d Cavalry Group moved south, crossing the Isar River at Dingolfing.

The XIX TAC was restricted from flying by bad weather. They flew only 113 sorties, claiming 13 motor vehicles, 10 locomotives, 93 railroad cars, and 14 horse-drawn vehicles damaged or destroyed.

The supply situation was considered critical. Because of inadequate transportation facilities and extremely heavy demands, supply lines were extremely long. A total of 1,842,959 rations and 821,910 gallons of V-80 gasoline were on hand in the Third Army supply and at reserve points, and 800 long tons of clothing and equipment were in the Third Army's

Class II and Class IV depots. An additional amount of 4,110 long tons of Class II and Class IV supplies were en route to the depots.

May 2
D-Day +330

In the III Corps the 86th Infantry Division remained in place and passed to control of the Seventh Army. The 99th Infantry Division began assembling near the end of the day, and the 14th Armored Division captured a bridge over the Inn River in the vicinity of Frahan. The 14th Cavalry Group moved to an assembly area near Landshut and cleared the enemy from the corps' zone up to the Inn River.

The 5th Infantry Division continued with the job of clearing the woods along the Czechoslovakian border in the XII Corps. The 26th Infantry Division advanced to the east behind the 11th Armored Division, clearing the area to the Danube River. The 90th Infantry Division maintained positions and patrolled to the east. Combat Command "A" of the 11th Armored Division crossed the Muhl River at a fording point near Neufelden and continued to the southeast, traveling over poor roads. Combat Command "B" constructed a treadway bridge over the Mühl River at Starz and succeeded in crossing all troops by the end of the day. The 2d Cavalry Group patrolled and maintained contact with both the 5th and 90th Infantry Divisions. The 4th Armored Division moved into an assembly area in the Deggendorf-Regen area.

In the XX Corps the 65th Infantry Division reached the Inn River, advancing southeast. The 65th's 261st Infantry Regiment crossed the Inn River at Scharding and the 259th Infantry Regiment assembled. In the 71st Infantry Division, the 5th and 66th Infantry Regiments seized dams intact across the Inn River near Ering and Obernberg, respectively. The 80th Infantry Division's 318th and 319th Infantry Regiments reached the Inn River, while at the same time the 317th Infantry Regiment started crossing the river. The 13th Armored Division's elements pushed across the Inn River, captured Braunau and Neu-Ötting, and established bridgeheads at both towns. The

3d Cavalry Group moved south, protected the corps' right flank, and then moved into an assembly area.

The weather situation kept the XIX TAC from flying a great deal. Only sixteen sorties were flown, with no claims made for the day.

Lucky Forward headquarters moved to Regensburg.

The military government initiated various measures to assure maximum spring planting by the local inhabitants. A total of 219 tons of seeds were hauled to the city of Frankfurt from surplus stocks at Erfurt. A total of 385 tons of seeds, which were discovered in railway cars in Frankfurt, were distributed through normal civilian channels. Fifteen hundred tons of nitrogenous fertilizer, which had been stored in the Frankfurt I.G. Farben plant, were released for distribution to civilians.

May 3
D-Day +331

Information obtained by G-2 indicated that the entire German army was on the verge of collapse, hanging by a thin thread of command control. Details were obtained concerning a desperate, last-chance German plot to use amateur airborne saboteurs to blast installations in friendly rear areas. Captured German pilots revealed that they had been given orders to destroy bridges, cut railroad lines, and then proceed to their homes when their missions had been accomplished. In the northwestern sections of Germany, Holland, and Denmark, the German forces were surrendering.

In the III Corps the 99th Infantry Division moved to an assembly area. The 14th Armored Division held positions along the Inn River and secured a bridge in the vicinity of Frahan. The 99th's Reserve Combat Command remained assembled in Bergkirchen.

The V Corps (1st, 2nd, and 97th Infantry Divisions and the 9th Armored Division) was assigned in place from the First Army to the Third Army.

The 5th Infantry Division consolidated and patrolled in the XII Corps. The 11th Armored Division moved east and southeast, reaching Willersdorf. Following the 11th Armored Division, the 26th Infantry Division continued with its advance to the southeast. The 90th Infantry Division was relieved by elements of the 26th Infantry Division and began to reassemble. The 4th Armored Division closed in an assembly area, and the 2d Cavalry Group maintained positions and patrolled.

The 65th Infantry Division completed a bridge across the Inn River at Scharding and continued its advance to the east in the XX Corps area. The 80th Infantry Division completed a bridge over the Inn River at Braunau. The 13th Armored Division moved to a new zone and maintained its bridgeheads. Elements of the 3d Cavalry Group moved southeast and crossed the Inn River at Braunau.

Unfavorable weather again prevented the XIX TAC from a large number of sorties. Flying only 149, they claimed 56 motor vehicles, 4 locomotives, 47 railroad cars, one bridge, and 8 buildings damaged or destroyed.

A test train carrying supplies for the Third Army reached Nürnberg, but operation of the line from Würzburg to Bamberg to Nürnberg permitted only a limited quantity of tonnage to be shipped until double track and special communications could be completed.

May 4
D-Day +332

The very first full capitulation of an entire division occurred when the German 11th Panzer Division surrendered to the Third Army's 90th Infantry Division.

The 99th Infantry Division and the 14th Cavalry Group remained assembled in the III Corps area. The 14th Armored Division's Combat Commands "A" and "B" were relieved by the 86th Infantry Division (XV Corps) from the duty of guarding installations in its zone.

The 9th Armored Division's Combat Command "A" was attached to the 1st Infantry Division (V Corps) while assembling near Marktredwitz. The 2d Infantry Division made advances up to four miles; the 97th Infantry Division attacked to the east, advancing five miles. Other elements of the 9th Armored Division closed in an assembly area near Trausnitz. The 102d Cavalry Group patrolled in the corps' rear area and guarded installations.

The 5th Infantry Division's 2d and 10th Infantry Regiments launched an attack to the northeast in the XII Corps. The 26th Infantry Division consolidated positions and patrolled the corps' right flank. The 90th Infantry Division closed in an assembly area. The 11th Armored Division captured the city of Linz (to the southeast) and a bridge over the Danube River intact (to the northeast). Also in the 11th's area, the towns of Zwettl and Kattstorf were captured. The 4th Armored Division remained in assembly and the 2d Cavalry Group maintained positions.

The 65th Infantry continued with their rapid advance in the XX Corps. The 5th Infantry Regiment of the 71st Infantry Division reached the vicinity of Steyr, capturing bridges intact over the Traun and Ager Rivers at Wels and at Lamback respectively. The 80th Infantry Division captured Schwanenstadt and Vöcklabruck. The 13th Armored Division remained in their assembly area, just west of Braunau. The 3d Cavalry Group crossed the Inn River at Braunau and took up positions on the corps' right flank from Neukirchen to Strasswalchen. The 3d Cavalry Group also succeeded in capturing a bridge intact over the Ager River at Kammer.

The XIX TAC flew 150 sorties, claiming 426 motor vehicles; 10 tanks/armored vehicles, 25 locomotives, 231 railroad cars, 11 gun positions, 16 buildings, 42 horse-drawn vehicles, and 1 roundhouse damaged or destroyed.

Because of the new assignment of the V Corps (with four divisions) to the Third Army plans were made to supply the new units by creating supply lines in a northeasterly direction. An additional transfer point was opened at Regensburg, with the original transfer point at Nürnburg remaining in operation.

The military government in Frankfurt screened and investigated possible appointees to an advisory board whose job would be to fill important civil posts. Assisting them in this endeavor were civil service specialists who were experts in the areas of public health, labor, law, industry, and other fields.

May 5
D-Day +333

When the Third Army units entered the city of Plze in Czechoslovakia, they found it to be controlled by Czech partisans. The German garrison had been confined to its barracks. In the Sixth Army Group's area, the entire German Army Group "G" (consisting of the First and Nineteenth Armies) surrendered.

According to a directive issued by Third Army headquarters to the III Corps, a plan was outlined for occupation. In part, the plan read

> The 38th Antiaircraft Artillery Brigade was to assume responsibility for the Third Army area as directed, coordinating with the Provost Marshal, and Military Government of Headquarters, Third Army, and the Commanding Generals of the 4th and 70th Infantry Divisions. Within the prescribed area, it was to control traffic on main supply routes and to maintain law and order, both military and civil. It was to guard the Third Army's rear command post, railroad and highway bridges, railroad tunnels, the Third Army supply installations, signal installations, Allied POW and displaced persons camps. It was also to administer to Allied POW camps. (The 4th and 70th Infantry Divisions were given similar instructions, with the exceptions being the zones of responsibility).

In the remainder of the III Corps area, the 99th Infantry Division moved to Landshut for assembly and the 14th Cavalry Group remained assembled.

In the V Corps zone, the 1st Infantry Division advanced up to four miles. The 9th Armored Division, passing through some of the 1st Infantry Division's elements, moved to the vicinity of Klingen. The 2d and 97th Infantry Divisions both advanced about six miles in their attacks to the east. Directly after the 16th Armored Division closed in the corps' zone, its Combat Command "B," followed by Combat Command "A," attacked through elements of the 97th Infantry Division and succeeded in capturing Plze. The 102d Cavalry Group patrolled and protected the corps' rear areas.

In the XII Corps the 5th Infantry Division continued with its easterly advance. The 11th Armored Division had elements moving to a point near Helimonso. The 90th Infantry Division launched an attack late in the day, and the 26th Infantry Division closed near Zwettl. The 2d Cavalry Group occupied Klatovy and maintained positions.

In the XX Corps the 65th Infantry Division advanced east, with its 260th Infantry Regiment occupying Linz. Other elements in the 26th advanced to the south along the Enns River. The 71st Infantry Division relieved some elements of the 80th Infantry Division along the Enns River, just south of Steyr. The 80th Infantry Division remained in assembly near Braunau, the 13th Armored Division remained in assembly near Tann, and the 3d Cavalry Group continued to screen the right flank of the corps.

Bad weather cancelled XIX TAC activity.

With the exception of both the V and XII Corps, all of the Third Army's divisions were limited to a daily gasoline ration of 50 percent of their average draw for the period from April 26 to May 4. Divisions that did not require gasoline were not to draw any until further notice.

May 6
D-Day +334

During this week of piecemeal and large-scale surrenders of German troops, G-2 issued significant order of battle facts. G-2 indicated that the collapse of all central control of German forces was reflected by the puncture of the mythical National Redoubt and the sudden disappearance from prominent positions of Nazi Party high officials shortly following the announcement by the Germans of Adolph Hitler's death.

The capture of München, Innsbruck, and Berchtesgaden, against virtually no resistance, indicated that the redoubt fortress was no more than a dream fostered by the Nazi war machine and SHAEF advisors. The overwhelming rapidity of the Allied advances, coupled with the Germans' tremendous logistical problems, smashed whatever plan might have existed to make the redoubt fortress a legend in German military history.

Although German resistance did stiffen a little just north of the Eger River, elsewhere the Third Army met with no aggressive activity whatsoever. German units assembled in compliance with surrender instructions with no complaint. In the VIII Corps zone, patrols advanced against scattered opposition and established contact with Soviet forces in the vicinity of Amstettin.

In the III Corps the 4th and 99th Infantry Divisions, the 14th Armored Division, and the 14th Cavalry Group remained in assembly areas.

The 1st Infantry Division was making good progress in the V Corps area. The 2d and 97th Infantry Divisions continued with their joint advance to the southeast. The 9th Armored Division remained in assembly. The 16th Armored Division's Combat Command "A" and Reserve Combat Command moved up to Plse, to join Combat Command "B." The 102d Cavalry Group maintained the security of corps' installations, with some elements moving up to As.

In the XII Corps the 5th Infantry Division continued with its coordinated advance. The 26th Infantry Division cleared the enemy out of its zone and moved into blocking positions on its divisional right flank. The 90th Infantry Division advanced in its zone. In front of the 90th, the 4th Armored Division reached the restraining line, which was their final objective. The 11th Armored Division patrolled in its zone and maintained positions. The 2d Cavalry Group continued with its clearing of the Germans in zone and screening the corps' left flank.

In the XX Corps the 65th and 71st Infantry Divisions consolidated their positions along the Enns River, with the 71st completing relief of the 80th Infantry Division. Elements of the 80th Infantry Division assembled near Schwanenstadt and Vorchdorf, later sending patrols out to the south. The 13th Armored Division remained in its assembly area near

Tann; the 3d Cavalry Group provided protection for the corps' right flank, patrolling to the south.

Weather conditions made activity by the XIX TAC impossible.

Because of the increasing receipts and the lessening of hostilities, the gasoline situation was improving.

Through all of the Third Army zone of operations, German nationals received copies of the Frankfurt *Presse* newspaper. The publication was greeted with great enthusiasm. A report to the military government stated that the paper was popular both in urban and rural areas, and that in order to achieve maximum circulation, papers were to be posted in prominent places and the people were urged to share their copies with others.

May 7-8
D-Day +335-336

A TWX was received from Supreme Allied Commander General Dwight D. Eisenhower officially terminating the European War.

1. A representative of the German High Command signed the unconditional surrender of all German land, sea, and air forces in Europe to the Allied Expeditionary Force and simultaneouslyto the Soviet High Command at 0141 hours, Central European Time, 7 May, under which all forces will cease active operations at 0001 B hours, 9 May.

2. Effective immediately, all offensive operations by Allied Expeditionary Forces will cease and troops will remain in present positions. Moves involved in occupational duties will continue. Due to difficulties of communication there may be some delay in similar orders reaching enemy troops, so full defensive precautions will be taken.

3. All informed down to and including divisions, tactical air command and groups, base sections, and equivalent. No, repeat, no release will be made to the press pending an announcement by the heads of the three governments.

Only small and infrequent fire fights were encountered by Third Army units. The Germans continued to surrender in large numbers. Patrols of Third Army units made contact with the Soviet troops near Amstettin. The commanding general of the German Army Group South surrendered all troops under his command to the commanding general of the XX Corps. The German garrison located at Lorient surrendered on May 7 and the garrison at St. Nazaire surrendered on May 8.

A Letter of Instruction was sent to the 33d Field Artillery Brigade, stating in part

1. Effective at once the 33d FA Brig, with attached troops, will constitute the army agency responsible for;

a. Collecting, protecting, supplying, administering, and evacuating all Allied Prisoners of War, and civilian internees within the Army area, coordinating with the Army G-1.

b. Collecting, guarding, and protecting displaced persons within the army area, coordinating with the army G-5.

c. Where such responsibilities have been specifically delegated to other commands in designated areas, the 33d FA Brig will supervise, coordinate, and inspect such activities.

2. General Instructions.

a. Allied Prisoner of War installations will be established when necessary and serviced in accordance with Standing Operating Procedure No. 58, 3 April 1945, Headquarters, ETO, US Army, and letter this headquarters, file AG 383.6 GNMCA-4, 26 April 1945, subject:

"Processing of Recovered Allied Military Personnel."

b. Civilian Internment Camps will be established and serviced in accordance with unnumbered publication, this headquarters, subject: "Internment Camps."

c. As follows:

(1) Displaced Persons will be collected and placed in temporary camps when necessary and will be evacuated to permanent camps in accordance with directives of military government.

(2) Camps will be guarded to enforce the "stay put" policy.

(3) Camps will be placed off limits, and the entry of unauthorized persons prevented.

(4) Camps will be supplied and administered where necessary due to the absence of military government personnel and facilities for that purpose.

The 70th Infantry Division continued to police assigned army areas, and the 4th Infantry Division continued with its movement to an area east of Nürnberg.

In the III Corps zone, the 99th Infantry Division, the 14th Armored Division, and the 14th Cavalry Group remained in assembly areas. At the end of the day, the 99th Infantry Division began movement to an area near Würzburg.

In the V Corps the 1st Infantry Division consolidated and maintained positions. The 9th Armored Division assembled near Luket and Horslavkov, the 2d and 97th Infantry Divisions improved their positions, the 16th Armored Division maintained positions near Plze, and the 102d Cavalry Group moved to Plze to guard the V Corps' installations.

In the XII Corps all units (5th, 26th, 90th Infantry Divisions and 4th and 11th Armored Divisions) maintained and consolidated their positions.

In the XX Corps, while maintaining positions, the 66th, 71st, and 80th Infantry Divisions processed large numbers of German troops who had surrendered during the day. The 13th Armored Division remained in assembly near Tann, and the 3d Cavalry Group maintained positions along the corps' southern flank.

The XIX Tactical Air Command flew nine defensive patrol missions over the Third U.S. Army front lines and 5 demonstration missions over POW camps. No claims were made.

The Third Army commanding general held his last operational briefing for officers of the headquarters and talked with the assembled section chiefs.

The upcoming investigation of war crimes engaged the attention of fourteen officers and twenty-nine enlisted men in the capacities of investigating officers, interpreters, stenographers, typists, photographers, and drivers.

With the celebration of Victory in Europe Day on May 8, 1945, Third Army correspondents had many stories to write. They submitted to Third Army censors 1,320 stories, with a total number of 289,052 words. Photographers submitted 325 photographs.

Wire recordings of two *Army Hour* programs; 7 Combat Diary programs, and a victory message from General Patton were disseminated in the United States.

On May 9, 1945, the Third Army received a message from General Dwight D. Eisenhower. The message praised the soldiers and leaders of the Third Army, stating, "Working and fighting together in a single, indestructible partnership, you have achieved perfection in unification of air, ground, and naval power that will stand as a model in our time."

CHAPTER 11

Third Army Operational Summary

In 281 days of fighting, the Third Army achieved a greatness and compiled a record which can be measured only in superlatives. The Third Army gave new meaning to the term *fluid warfare* by following the only real order ever given to them by General Patton: "Kill the enemy."

The Third Army was an army of movement. It was the only fully mechanized army created for the purpose of maneuver, speed, and exploitation. Indeed, the Third Army and its general were literally made for each other.

General Patton was given the command of the Third Army because of his audacity, boldness, and ruthlessness, not in spite of it. In turn, the Third Army had been created specifically as a mobile force, using its twentieth century technology to apply the cavalry concept to seek out, disrupt, and destroy the enemy. It was soldiers such as Generals Patton, Harmon, Walker, and dozens more who were cavalrymen first and tank generals second. They used the tried-and-true (sometimes almost medieval) cavalry methods applied in conjunction with their new fire-belching iron horses to create a type of warfare that surpassed even the best applications of the Germans. These cavalrymen are the ones who took the concept of blitzkrieg (lightning war) and made it into an art form.

The story of the Third Army was also a story of true and

trusting teamwork between the ground forces and the new power of the airplane. The XIX Tactical Air Command became part and parcel of the Third Army, just as surely as General Patton was their commander, too. General Patton and General O.P. Weyland were the best of friends and the best of professional soldiers.

In February of 1944, General Weyland was given command of the XIX Tactical Air Command and was assigned to work with General Patton. General Weyland recalled,

Initially, this was not looked upon as a highly desirable assignment. General Patton had achieved a reputation as being hard to work with, and he had a rather low regard for air power. However, this was to change rapidly as the XIX Tactical Air Command and the Third Army went into battle together. I visited Patton's several headquarters and combat divisions to indoctrinate them in the capabilities of modern tactical air power. In turn, he visited my combat units at their advanced fields. This was something new to him. He watched aircraft armorers load on bombs and refill machine gun magazines, communicators check and tune the all-important aircraft radio, and mechanics repair and service the airplanes. The immaculately dressed army commander frequently got oil and grease on his hands and clothes—but he enjoyed it. He sat in on combat briefings before missions and listened to intelligence debriefings after the missions. He quickly achieved a new respect for air power.

Whereas many ground commanders still believed that tactical air power should be subordinated to the ground force commander, General Patton agreed with me that he would command the ground and that I would run the associated tactical air forces. At the same time we both laid our cards on the table. We planned and executed our respective responsibilities in the closest of coordination. And he always kept his word.

General Patton kept close tabs on the performance of the XIX Tactical Air Command during the first few days of the Normandy breakout, and one day asked me to come over to his living van. He said, "I've never seen anything like the way your planes have cleared the way ahead of my tanks. Goddamnit, we'll stick together and roll right into Berlin. How about a drink, Opie?" General Patton was the greatest army field commander I have ever known—and I've worked with a number in combat. He was audacious, but sagacious. Despite his colorful language, he had his own version of religion. Being a cavalryman, Patton believed in open warfare and in the old cavalry adage of, "When in doubt, attack." His philosophy suited me perfectly, because it enabled the tactical air command to fight most effectively. When friendly ground forces flush the enemy into the open, tactical fighters can hit them mercilessly with rockets, bombs, and machinegun strafing. We were agreed that, if at all possible, we should keep the initiative. We never let the enemy get set. We kept him off balance. Down to the last soldier and airman, the Third Army and the XIX Tactical Air Command considered themselves to be the best battlefield team of our time.

From an early attitude of skepticism, General Patton went to the other extreme. He thought that the XIX Tactical Air Command could do no wrong.

In consideration of speed of advance, in ground liberated or captured, and in losses inflicted on the Germans, there was never anything like the Third Army and its sweep across France.

Even when reduced to cold, statistical figures, the feats and achievements of the Third Army are astonishing. The Third Army liberated or captured 81,522 square miles of territory, including

France	47,828
Luxembourg	1,010
Belgium	156
Germany	26,940
Czechoslovakia	3,485
Austria	2,103

During the greater part of their 281 days of combat, the Third Army maintained a front line averaging between 75 and 100 air miles in length. The longest front line, 200 air miles, existed on April 20, 1945.

An estimated twelve thousand towns and communities were either liberated or captured by the Third Army, including twenty-seven cities of more than fifty thousand.

Third Army Corps

There were a total of six corps assigned to the Third Army during their operations of 1944-1945.

Corps	Time Period	Number of Days
XII	1 Aug 1944 - 8 May 1945	281
XX	1 Aug 1944 - 8 May 1945	281
VIII	1 Aug 1944 - 5 Sep 1944	
	21 Dec 1944 - 22 Apr 1945	160
III	10 Oct 1944 - 11 Feb 1945	
	18 Apr 1945 - 8 May 1945	145
XV	1 Aug 1944 - 24 Aug 1944	
	26 Aug 1944 - 29 Sep 1944	61
V	6 May 1945 - 8 May 1945	3

Third Army Divisions

Five divisions which served with the Third Army for almost the entire period of the its tactical operations.

Division	Time Period	Number of Days
4th Armored	1 Aug 1944 - 22 Apr 1945	
	24 Apr 1945 - 8 May 1945	280
5th Infantry	5 Aug 1944 - 8 May 1945	276
80th Infantry	1 Aug 1944 - 16 Aug 1944	
	24 Aug 1944 - 8 May 194	274
90th Infantry	1 Aug 1944 - 16 Aug 1944	
	26 Aug 1944 - 8 May 1945	272
6th Armored	1 Aug 1944 - 4 Sep 1944	
	17 Sep 1944 - 22 Apr 1945	252

Operational Divisions

A total of forty-two divisions served under control of the Third Army from August 1, 1944, until May 8, 1945. Included were twenty-five infantry, fourteen armored, and two airborne divisions.

Infantry Divisions

1st Infantry Division
2d Infantry Division
4th Infantry Division
5th Infantry Division
8th Infantry Division

26th Infantry Division
28th Infantry Division
29th Infantry Division
35th Infantry Division
42d Infantry Division
65th Infantry Division
69th Infantry Division
70th Infantry Division
71st Infantry Division
76th Infantry Division
79th Infantry Division
80th Infantry Division
83d Infantry Division
86th Infantry Division
87th Infantry Division
89th Infantry Division
90th Infantry Division
94th Infantry Division
95th Infantry Division
97th Infantry Division
99th Infantry Division

Armored Divisions

2d French Armored Division
4th Armored Division
5th Armored Division
6th Armored Division
7th Armored Division
8th Armored Division
9th Armored Division
10th Armored Division
11th Armored Division
12th Armored Division
13th Armored Division
14th Armored Division
16th Armored Division
20th Armored Division

Airborne Divisions

17th Airborne Division
101st Airborne Division

The strength of the Third Army was greatest on May 8, 1945, when there was a total of 437,860 assigned personnel. According to monthly personnel rosters compiled by the Adjutant General's Machine Records Unit, the strength at the end of each month of operation was

1 August	92,187
31 August	220,169
30 September	138,639
31 October	252,512
30 November	247,150
31 December	347,660
31 January	353,981
28 February	304,542
31 March	312,205
30 April	346,839

Replacements for 281 days: 258,924

Prisoners Of War Captured

		per day average
France, Avranches-Brest, to the Moselle: (1 August 1944 - 24 September 1944)	94,199	1,713
Forcing the Line of the Moselle: (25 September 1944 - 7 November 1944)	8,481	193
Capture of Metz and the Saar Campaign: (8 November 1944 - 18 December 1944)	36,489	890
The Bastogne/St. Vith Campaign: (19 December 1944 - 28 January 1945)	23,218	566
Eifel to the Rhine/Capture of Trier: (29 January 1945 - 12 March 1945)	58,781	1,367
Capture of Koblenz/Palatinate Campaign: (13 March 1945 - 21 March 1945)	81,692	8,169
Rhine/Frankfurt-On-Main/Mulde: (22 March 1945 - 21 April 1945)	240,661	9,022
Danube/Czechoslovakia and Austria: (22 April 1945 - 8 May 1945)	221,962	13,057
1 Aug 1944 - 8 May 1945 Total:	765,483	2,724
9 May 1945 - 13 May 1945 Total:	515,205	
Grand Total:	1,280,688	

In contrast with the large casualty list of the Germans who opposed the Third Army, the army itself suffered small numbers of casualties. Total casualties were 160,692. In this figure, 27,104 were killed, 86,267 wounded, 18,975 injured and 28,237 missing in action.

Of the missing in action figure, many were reported to have been captured. The Third Army's casualties included 8,372 officers and 152,324 enlisted men, giving a ratio of about one officer to each 18 enlisted men. Out of the entire casualty total, 33,004 were returned to duty from a previously reported casualty status.

G-2 intelligence troops apprehended 42 enemy agents and/or saboteurs after investigating 337 reports and interrogating 2,500 civilians for tactical information. Both aircraft and artillery bombarded the Germans with a total of 31,552,700 psychological warfare leaflets. A total of 722 combat and military government loudspeaker missions were completed in an attempt to induce the Germans to surrender. At the request of the intelligence units, the XIX Tactical Air Command completed 1,767 tactical reconnaissance missions and 77 photograph reconnaissance missions, resulting in the distribution of 3,205,670 aerial photographs.

The XIX Tactical Air Command completed the following feats.

Missions	7,326
Sorties	74,447
Tons of bombs dropped	17,486
Napalm tanks dropped	3,205
Rockets launched	4,599
German planes destroyed	1,640
Aircraft lost	582

Note: a *sortie* was one airplane flying within a mission. A mission could contain a variable number of sorties (or single airplanes). It could be theoretically possible for a sortie to be a mission, but a mission would not necessarily be a sortie.

The targets either destroyed or damaged by the XIX Tactical Air Command included

Tanks and armored cars	3,833

Motor vehicles	38,541
Locomotives	4,337
Railroad lines cut	2,585
Marshalling yards	974
Towns and villages	816
Factories	3,664
Supply dumps	220
Military installations	1,730
Gun installations	2,809
Highway and railroad bridges	285
Miscellaneous naval vessels	654
Miscellaneous targets	3,010

From August 1st until May 8, the Third Army antiaircraft artillery claimed 1,084 German planes destroyed and 564 probably destroyed out of a total of 6,192 planes which flew over the Third Army area. The total of planes shot down added up to 26.6 percent of all sightings.

Third Army's artillery fired 5,870,843 rounds of ammunition; a total weight of 158,207 tons. Artillery observation aircraft executed 87,002 missions, totaling 93,933 flying hours. Out of those missions, 22,865 were fire missions, 31,191 were reconnaissance and/or patrol missions, and 32,946 were for liaison and miscellaneous missions. Upon becoming operational, the Third Army had 636 field artillery pieces of 105mm or larger. On May 8, 1945, the total number of field artillery amounted to 1,464.

The Third Army's tank destroyers knocked out 648 German tanks and 211 self-propelled guns during the 281 days of fighting. Acting as assault guns and in support of infantry and armored units, tank destroyers knocked out 349 German antitank guns, 175 artillery pieces, 519 machine guns, and 1,556 general purpose vehicles. During the campaigns to breach the Maginot and Siegfried Lines, the tank destroyers succeeded in eliminating 801 pillboxes. Ammunition expended by the tank destroyers amounted to 101,178 rounds for direct-fire missions and 231,998 rounds for indirect-fire missions.

All supplies brought into the Third Army area (by every available means of transportation) totaled 1,234,529 long tons.

Within the Third Army boundary, there were 2,186,792 tons of supplies transported a total distance of 141,081,336 miles by the Third Army's transportation pool. There were a total of 264,606 trucks in convoys, which were issued with 2,242 highway clearances. A total of 3,655,322 vehicles moved through 109 traffic regulating points with supplies for the troops.

Third Army engineers were required to reconstruct 2,092 miles of railway track from St. Germain (France) to the National Redoubt area. Out of a total of 496 railheads surveyed by engineers, two-thirds of them were actively used by supply services of the Third Army headquarters. Supplies received from Quartermaster totaled 774,541.86 long tons. The total amounts of long tons moved by rail and truck were 741,201.56, by air the total was 33,340.3.

The overall total of ammunition received by the Third Army headquarters units during its 281 days of combat was 533,825 long tons with 482,345 tons were issued to divisions other than the Third Army headquarters units. The trucks of the Third Army traveled 14,101,977 miles to haul a total of 1,549,993 long tons of ammunition.

Large equipment issued to the Third Army units:

General purpose vehicles	26,905
Combat vehicles	7,581
Artillery pieces	4,482
Small arms	193,910
Spare parts	47,611

Large equipment repaired by the Third Army included:

General purpose vehicles	99,114
Combat vehicles	21,761
Artillery pieces	11,613
Small arms	125,083
Instruments	32,740

There were a total of 32 major river crossings made by the Third Army from August 1 until May 8. The Moselle River was crossed 5 times in 5 different places. The Seille, Our, and Saar Rivers were each crossed twice. Other principal rivers which were bridged were the Mayene, Sarthe, Yone, Marne, Meurthe, Nied, Blies, Saeur, Sure, Prüm, Kyll, Rhine, Main,

Nahe, Lahn, Altmühl, Danube, Isar, and the Inn. These river crossings and the additional crossing of numerous smaller rivers and streams required the building of 2,498 bridges by Third Army engineers. These bridges had a total footage of 255,520 feet, which is almost 8.5 miles of bridging. Included in this total were 705 assault bridges, with a total footage of 70,169 feet; and 1,793 Bailey bridges, with a total footage of 185,351 feet. In addition, the Third Army Engineers also averaged 2,240 miles of road maintenance during the fighting.

There were 9 chemical mortar companies assigned to the Third Army. They expended a total of 349,097 rounds of 4.2 inch chemical mortar shells, including 189,095 rounds of high explosives, and 160,002 rounds of white phosphorous. Chemical warfare supplies issued to the Third Army units included 32,454 gallons of flame thrower fuel and 335,944 grenades of all types.

The Third Army's Signal Corps was responsible for adequate communication between units. To provide that communication, they laid 3,747 miles of W-110 wire, 8,179 miles of spiral-four wire, and 4,551 miles of open wire in 281 days. Out of this amount, 1,232 miles of W-110 wire and 1,883 miles of spiral-four wire were recovered for further use. Signal troops rehabilitated 3,965 circuit miles of both French and German open wire and 36,338 miles of underground cable. The Third Army Message Center handled a total of 7,220,261 code groups, while both Forward and Rear Echelon switchboard operators handled an estimated average of 13,968 telephone calls daily.

Army ambulances transferred a total of 269,187 patients from divisional clearing stations and similar levels to the Third Army hospitals. The total number of patients evacuated from the army area was 164,810. Of these patients, 28,826 were evacuated by air, 91,005 by road, 1,164 by boat, and 43,815 by rail. The mortality rate of patients in the Third Army hospitals amount to 2.78 percent. The percentage of deaths from all causes (not combat-inclusive) was 1.4 percent. Patients returned to duty without evacuation from the army area numbered 114,024; or 43.5 percent.

Military personnel in the Third Army were paid a total of $240,539,569 from August 1 until April 30, inclusive. Out of this amount, about 43.83 percent went to both family and individual allotments, 7.13 percent went to government insurance, 6.56 percent went to war bonds, 1.9 percent went to soldiers' deposits, 23.99 percent went to personal transfers, 5.49 percent went to other collections, and 11.1 percent was retained.

The Third Army provided Civil Affairs administration in France, Belgium, Luxembourg, and Czechoslovakia. They also provided military government administrations in Germany and Austria, governing about 30,000,000 people. The military government courts tried 1,015 cases involving 1,323 persons. Of these cases, 1,194 people were found to be guilty as charged and 129 were innocent of charges. Total fines of 116,405 reichsmarks were collected and a total of 17,817 days of imprisonment was imposed. The military government took charge of 5 concentration camps formerly operated by the Nazis. In these camps, there were 47,645 political prisoners. A total of 875,000 displaced persons cared for by the Military Government were repatriated by May 9, 1945.

General Patton's code name for his Forward Echelon Headquarters was Lucky Forward. The name was chosen partly due to Patton's great belief in luck and partly because he believed in simplicity. Lucky Forward moved 19 times from August 1 until May 8, traveling 1,225 miles in the process. Their various locations are noted as follows.

Forward Echelon - Lucky Forward

Date	Location	Distance
5-7 July	Nehau, France	
1 August	Lebignard, France	25 miles
2-3 August	Beauchamps, France	36 "
8 August	Poilley, France	32 "
12 August	St. Ouen, France	35 "
14-15 August	La Bazoge, France	67 "
20 August	Brou, France	73 "
25 August	Courcy-aux-Loges, France	68 "
30 August	La Chaume, France	80 "
4 September	Marson, France	99 "

15 September	Braquis, France	68 "
22-28 September	Etain, France	5 "
11 October	Nancy, France	60 "
28 December	Luxembourg City, Luxembourg	90 "
27-28 March	dar-Oberstein, Germany	80 "
3 April	Frankfurt-on-Main, Germany	85 "
11 April	Hersfeld, Germany	85 "
22 April	Erlangen, Germany	150 "
2-3 May	Regensburg, Germany	87 "
	Total Miles	**1,225**

An average of 320 chaplains within the Third Army represented 25 different denominations. Seven of the chaplains were killed in action, 5 were missing in action, 3 were captured, 3 were captured and immediately released, and 45 were wounded in action.

Decorations awarded to the Third Army soldiers totaled 34,840 during campaigns from August 1 to May 8.

Medal of Honor	19
Distinguished Service Medal	44
Distinguished Service Cross	291
Legion of Merit	159
Silver Star	4,990
Soldier's Medal	247
Bronze Star	29,090

There were totals for the three types of promotions within the Third Army breakdown as follows:

Normal promotions	6,464
Battlefield promotions	1,817
Combat appointments	848

News correspondents with the Third Army were very busy writing a total of 7,010,963 words in 30,326 stories about the soldiers of the Third Army. In addition, they submitted to the Third Army censors 7,129 photographs.

Courts-martial cases in the Third Army numbered 325 general, 1,205 special, 6,474 summary tried and reviewed.

Entertainment was a very important and popular item among the Third Army soldiers. Types of shows and their attendance were 11,230,000 at motion pictures, 650,000 at USO shows and 625,000 at soldier's talent shows.

Food was a very important item for the American soldier, and he had many varieties and types available. The five basic types of rations were

A Rations: Very similar to the food served in garrisons, containing about seventy percent fresh foods.

B Rations: Similar to the A Ration, with the exception that some nonperishable items, such as canned meats, canned fruits and vegetables, and dehydrated potatoes and eggs were substituted for fresh items. B Rations contained enough food for ten men for one day. One package could be used to make two hot meals and one cold meal.

C Rations: C Rations were developed just prior to WWII to replace the *reserve* rations of World War I. Included in the package, which could serve ten men for one day, were small cans of meat and vegetables; meat and beans; meat and vegetable stew; meat and spaghetti; ham, eggs, and potatoes; meat and noodles; meat and rice; frankfurters and beans; pork and beans; ham and lima beans; and chicken and vegetables. Additional items in the package included jam, crackers, powdered drinks, sugar, and cereals.

D Rations: The D Ration was for emergencies only. It consisted of a highly concentrated chocolate bar (made of cocoa, oat flour, and skim milk powder) weighing four ounces. It contained 600 calories and was created to replace the World War I emergency iron ration.

K Rations: Originally developed for use by paratroops, the K Ration quickly became popular among all troops on the front lines. A single meal was packaged in a waterproofed, 6 and one-half-inch long, cardboard box. Each box was labeled as breakfast, dinner, or supper. Breakfast consisted of a fruit bar, Nescafe, sugar, crackers, and a small can of ham and eggs. Dinner and supper contained either a can of cheese or potted meat, crackers, a boullion cube, orange or lemon powder, sugar, chocolate (or other candy), and Wrigley's chewing gum.

CHAPTER 12

The Staff

What is staff? is an excellent question, especially in light of the fact that very little has been written for the layman about either staffs or their duties and responsibilities.

The predominant writings concerning staff sections and staff officers have been written by professional soldiers for professional soldiers: men who are officers and who are destined for promotion to higher ranks. Most of the study and education concerning staff officers is done in special environments at military service schools. With this thought in mind, it is the objective of this chapter to outline and explain (in a generalized overview) the organization, structure, and duties of the staff officers of the Third Army.

At the time of the Third Army's entrance into the European Theater of Operations, in 1944, the Staff Officer's Field Manual of the United States Army defined the staff as "...a unit consisting of the officers who assist the commander in his exercise of command." This definition clearly reflects the same thought written some eighty years ago by General Bronsart von Schellendorff in his classic treatise, *The Duties of the General Staff*. Writing about the German Great General Staff, Schellendorff said that they were "...the assistants of the commander."

General Patton considered himself a combat general. He knew that the main function of an army is to destroy the enemy. He also knew that for an army to function, two things, organization and standardization, were required. It is the duty of the staff to manage those two functions of the army. Patton was not a staff officer who worked behind a desk, but he had attended all of the army schools that taught in the area of staff training. Patton had also held various staff positions between World War I and World War II, giving him the necessary experience of staff duty. Therefore, he knew what a staff's job was and what was expected of it.

Patton was fully aware that no single man or single unit can win a war. Winning requires—even demands—the closest of teamwork between all men and all units. Even Patton grudgingly admitted that the staff was a necessity in managing the organization and standardization of the army.

In addition to the *personal staff* of General Patton, there were two other main groups of staff officers. They were the *general staff* and the *special staff*. The *general staff* was organized to handle all of the functions of command. The *special staff* was organized to include the technical specialists. The staff groups of the Third Army were:

G-1 (Personnel)
G-2 (Intelligence)
G-3 (Operations/Training)
G-4 (Logistics)Medical
G-5 (Civil Affairs)
Adjutant General
Antiaircraft Artillery
Artillery
Chaplain
Chemical Warfare
Engineer
Finance
Headquarters Commandant
Inspector General
Judge Advocate
Ordnance
Provost Marshal
Public Relations
Quartermaster

Signal
Special Services
Tank Destroyer

The Third Army was, like other armies, composed of a *four-sectional* organization. This means that the general staff was divided into four sections, with each section having specific duties. This *four-section* concept is based on the idea that all of the duties of a commander can be placed into four distinct and separate functions, which are personnel, military intelligence, operations and training and logistics.

With the general staff divided thusly, each section had an officer in charge known as the chief of the section, or the Chief of Staff. Also, additional sections and special sections may be added according to the particular needs of the specific command. There was a new G Section added to the United States Army's organizational structure in the early 1940's. It was sometimes referred to as Civil Affairs and will be explained later in this chapter.

Duties of the Sections
G-1

The Third Army's G-1 Section (Personnel) was concerned with all matters which pertained to the personnel of the command, including civilians and POWs. This includes the planning and supervision of matters of procurement, classification, assignment, pay, promotion, transfer, retirement and discharge, decorations, citations, honors, awards, religious, recreational, welfare, postal service, morale, stragglers, collection and disposition of POWs, and relations with civil governments and civilians within the theater of operations. Above all, G-1 (and all of the other G Sections) had the prime mission of serving the combat troops. They had to always remember that combat troops, and not the services, are the ones that win battles.

The Third Army's G-1 Section's chain of command, duties, and responsibilities are outlined as follows.

Assistant Chief of Staff G-1
Executive Officer

Administration:
Administrative Checking
Duty Rosters
Files/Reference Material
Correspondence Routing
Morale

Miscellaneous:
Awards and Decorations
Graves Registration
Law and Order
Mail

Personnel:
Appointments
Assignments/Reassignments
Discharge
Leaves, Furloughs, Passes
Personnel Reinforcements
Promotions
Reclassification
Rotation

Post Exchange Activities:
Prisoners of War
Red Cross Activities
Reward and Punishment
Uniform

Reports Section:
Daily Summary of Casualties
Statistical Information
Strengths of Units
Weekly G-1 Report

G-2

The Third Army's G-2 Section was concerned with military intelligence. Although the name is self-explanatory, some comments are needed.

The G-2 Section was responsible for all matters pertaining to the collection, evaluation, interpretation, and distribution of information about the enemy. Also, they were responsible for counterintelligence activities. Generally, it could be stated that this section is responsible for informing the commander regarding the enemy's situation and capabilities, the weather, and the terrain.

Although no one G section is more important than another, and all of them are necessary for the complete administrative capability of an army, the G-2 Section is unique and extremely complex. The activities of G-2 were not inclusive. The G-2 Section, by nature, was required to coordinate with all of the other G sections and all Special sections. G-2 was required to know what everyone was doing, how they were doing it, why they were doing it, where they were doing it, and they needed to know everything all of the time. This information had to be gathered, assessed, assimilated, judged for veracity, and disseminated to all other sections as needed. Additionally, the G-2 section had to know the enemy's situation in as great detail as their own, if possible.

An excellent explanation of G-2's function was given by Colonel Oscar W. Koch, who was the Third Army G-2 chief of staff. Colonel Koch once mentioned a question asked by General Patton concerning an upcoming operation. Patton asked, "If I attack, will I bring on a major engagement?" Colonel Koch answered quickly and very simply, "No, Sir." General Patton responded, "Issue the order." On the surface, this might seem a simple and not very arduous task, but there is much underlying the situation that does not immediately meet the eye. When asked for advice by a commanding general, the intelligence officer must give information quickly and succinctly and take into consideration a country's resources (natural and acquired), detailed political structure, economy, people's attitudes (their ideologies and characteristics), climate, and transportation and communications systems. Factually, the intelligence officer must know that country as well as he knows his own—or better.

General Patton's view of the G-2 Section was that,

> ...[G-2] must be prepared to force information on unwilling recipients concerning an infinity of subjects such as the following. What is the enemy going to do? What is his strength? How is he going to attack? What is the morale of the enemy in front of us? How many rifles are there per yard of front? What is the gauge of the railroad behind the lines? What are

the bridges made of? Are they in repair? Where is his rail-head? What is the condition of the roads behind his lines? Has he many guns? Where are his airfields, etc.

Just a few of the many sources from which G-2 gets answers to the above questions are intelligence summaries from corps and army; prewar study and reports; books of travel; the encyclopedia; statements of deserters, refugees, or prisoners; captured papers, letters, postcards, telegrams, photographs; reports of spies; airplane reconnaissance photographs; inter-cepted radio messages; reports of patrols; insignia of prison-ers; reports from adjoining divisions; and reports from independent units. The G-2 must sift through the information from all of these (and other) sources, checking one item against another and discarding the useless information. G-2's information must be up to the minute or it will be too old.

The Third Army's G-2 Section's chain of command, duties, and responsibilities were as outlined.

Assistant Chief of Staff G-2

(Special Direct Liaison Unit with Third Army Headquar-ters)

Executive Officer

Situation:
    Combat Intelligence
    Situation/Work Maps
    Journal/Work Sheets
    Summaries/Bulletins
    Periodic Reports
    G-2 Estimates
    Target Area Analyses
    Liaison Visits
    Research
    G-2 Briefings
    War Room Organization, Maps, and Charts

Administration:
    Message Center
    Mimeograph Reproduction
    General Files
    Transportation
    Dissemination
    Personnel
    Supplies
    After-Action Reports

Auxiliary Agencies:
    Administration, Supervision, Coordination
    Intelligence Specialists
    Allocation to Corps and Divisions
    Location/Control of Military Intelligence Teams
    Guidance/Supervision of OSS/SI Activities
    Supervision of POW Briefing
    Activities Security Missions
    Evaluation/Dissemination of Files
    Reports from Specialists
    Teams

Security:
    Counter Espionage
    Counter Sabotage
    Counter Subversion
    Counterintelligence
    Directives
    Military Security
    Document Security
    Counterintelligence
    Information
    Passwords/Replies
    Censorship
    Counterintelligence Reference
    Counterintelligence Control Files
    Allied Security Liaison
    Personality Files

Specialized Sub-sections:
    Order of Battle Team
    War Room
    Navy Liaison
    Psychological Warfare
    Enemy Documents
    Office of Strategic Services/Secret Intelligence (OSS/SI)
    Field Interrogation Detachment
    POW Interrogation Teams
    Interpreter Teams
    Evasion and Escapes Units
    Counter Intelligence Corps
    Counter Intelligence Liaison
    Photo Center
    Photo Interpretation Teams
    Air Reconnaissance Coordinating
    Ground Liaison Officers

G-2 Air:
  Map and Model Policies
  Collection/Graphic Representation of Enemy Information
  Air Mission Requests
  Tactical/Photo Reconnaissance
  Vectorgraphs
  Photo Mosaics
  Air Reconnaissance Information
  Dissemination
  Liaison of Air and Ground Headquarters

G-3

The Third Army's G-3 Section was concerned with operations and training. Their responsibility was organization, training, and combat operations. For example, it was the G-3 Section, sometimes just known as *operations*, that translated the commanding general's tactical decisions and orders into issued orders. G-3 was also occupied with explorative studies into future tentative operations, having the need for speculative plans concerning what might occur in any given situation.

The Third Army's G-3 Section's chain of command, duties, and responsibilities were:

Assistant Chief of Staff G-3
  Executive Officer

Operations:
  Outline Plans, Directives, and Orders
  G-3 Periodic Reports
  Situation Reports
  Situation Maps
  Signal Communications
  Coordination
  Operational Diary
  War Room Maintenance (Coordinated with G-2)

Army Information Service:
  Liaison with Front Line Units
  Tactical Information to Headquarters

Air Sub-section:
  Air-Ground Planning
  Air-Ground Training
  Supervision of AF Liaison Squadron

310

Tactical Photo Reconnaissance (with G-2)
Situation Map Record of Air Activities
Priorities Recommendations on Air Coordination
Ground Targets Recommendations

Troop Movements/Organization:
Unit Assign/Attach Orders
Troop Lists/Order of Battle
Units Reorganization/Activation
Unit Location
Unit Movement Orders
Unit Movements Coordination

Troop Movements and Organization:
Unit Assignments/Attachments
Troop Lists/Order of Battle
Units Reorganization/Activation
Location of Units
Unit Movement Orders
Coordination of Unit Movements

Administration:
Message Recording/Distribution
Journal Maintenance
Personnel Rosters
Typing and Filing
Office and Files Security
Office Supplies
Organic Transportation
Section Movement
Field/Office Section Arrangement

Training, Historical, and Miscellaneous:
Training Directives
Training Program
Procurement/Coordination
Army Schools Organization
Training Facilities
Special Training
Historical/Operational Records
Equipment Studies
Army Operational Records
Dissemination of War Department Information
Supervision of Orientation Activities
Army Educational Program; Planning, Administration, and
Supervision
Liaison and Accommodations:

Liaison with Corps and Adjacent Higher Echelons
Coordination/Dissemination of Current Information
Situation Maps
Covered Accommodations
Unit Arrival Accommodations

Passive Air Defense:
Advice to Units on Planning, Operations and Training
Civil Affairs Coordination
Accommodations Inspections
Control Center Establishment (when necessary)

Special Forces Detachment:
Resistance Forces; Coordination/Control
Headquarters Liaison

G-4

The Third Army's G-4 Section was concerned with logistics. The chief of staff of this section advised the commanding general about the amount of supply support which could be given to any plan which had been proposed by G-3 (operations and training). G-4 also controlled all of the arrangements for effecting the supply and evacuation of the troops of the command. In addition to these duties, G-4 was responsible (in coordination with G-1) for the preparation of the actual orders which regulate all administrative functions of the command.

The Third Army's G-4 Section's chain of command, duties, and responsibility were as follows.

Assistant Chief of Staff G-4
(Liaison with Higher Echelons and Corps/Divisions)
Executive Officer

Administration:
Personnel
Publications
Records
Reports
Internal Security
Distribution of orders
Correspondence Control
Section Supply
Reproduction

Supply/Statistics:
  Supply Levels
  Procurement/Distribution
  Allocations
  Unit Equipping
  Equipment Maintenance
  New Equipment
  Salvage
  Captured Material
  Supply of Attached Allied Units
  Supply Summaries
  Periodic Reports

Fiscal:
  Procurement: Policies and Procedures
  General Supplies, Services and Facilities Coordination
  Civilian Labor Allocations
  Funds Sub-Allotment
  Local Resources Exploitation
  Appointments of Purchasing and Contracting Personnel

Operations:
  Movement of Service Units
  Situation Maps
  Administrative Orders Compilation
  Communication Lines
  Army Rear Boundary Plans
  Accommodations for Service Area Units

Transportation:
  Highway Movements
  Rail Movements
  Traffic Control
  Operation of Truck Units
  Railhead Regulating

G-5

The Third Army's G-5 Section was sometimes not referred to as a G section, but simply called Civil Affairs. G-5 Section was established in the army in the early 1940s for the purpose of controlling the civilian population within a country in which the army was fighting.

The Third Army's G-5 Section's chain of command, duties, and responsibilities were as follows.

Assistant Chief of Staff G-5
Executive Officer

Personnel/Administration:
  Internal Arrangement
  Supply Administration
  Personnel Selection/Requisition
  Maintenance of Records
  Coordination with *Plans and Operations* Section for Securing,
    Reinforcing, and Replacing Personnel

Intelligence:
  Information Collection
  Information Dissemination
  Control of Top Secret Documents
  Policy Information Compiliation
  Enforcement of Security
  Publicity and History
  Public Works and Utilities
  Communications

Plans and Operations:
  Movement of CA Troops
  Training Preparations
  Refugees and Displaced Persons
  CA Operational Location List

Relief and Supply:
  Relief Supplies
  Economics (Labor, Agriculture, Training Inspections and
    Local Resources)
  Transportation
  Relief Agencies

Government Affairs:
  Political Activities
  Legal Affairs
  Public Health and Sanitation
  Fiscal Affairs
  Public Safety
  Arts and Monuments

SPECIAL STAFF SECTIONS AND DUTIES

Adjutant General Section

The Adjutant General Section was charged with recording, authenticating, and communicating all orders, instructions, regulations, and personnel records.

Adjutant General
Executive Officer

Miscellaneous Division:
Cables/Message Section
Mail/Records Section
Publications Section
Distribution Section

Executive Division:
Casualty Reports Section
Machine Records Unit
(Data Processing)
Postal Section
Top Secret Section

Personnel Division:
Classification Section
Officer's Status Section
Enlisted Men's Status Section
Morning Report Section

MACHINE RECORDS UNIT

A little-known background function of the Adjutant General's Section was record keeping for Third Army personnel. This proved to be no small task. The average strength of the Third Army during its 281 days of combat was around 250,000 men. How was it possible for such a small number of Adjutant General personnel to keep tabs on that many men? The answer was the Machine Records Unit, which utilized punched card equipment to perform personnel accounting. The process was completed on unit record machines, sometimes called electrical accounting machines (EAM). These machines were the forerunners of modern day computer systems. They worked as follows:

1. Records were punched on the keypunch machine.
2. Punched cards were then sorted on a sorting machine.
3. Using a collator, the sorted cards were merged with Unit Master Header cards (e.g. 39th Machine Records Unit).
4. Lastly, these merged cards were run through the printing & accounting machine, which could perform mathematical functions and print output such as monthly personnel rosters, accident reports, TO&E reports, etc.

To assist the soldiers in reading the holes in the punched cards, they could run them through a machine called an interpreter which would print the data from the card on the top, front edge of the card.

If a card deck became old or worn, it could be completely reproduced onto new cards by means of a Reproducer.

Some of these machines were complex enough to require control boards which had to be hand-wired to perform desired functions. The wires would read data from specific columns of the punched cards and print them in specific output locations on report forms. This hand wiring was the predecessor of modern-day programming.

Antiaircraft Artillery Section

The Antiaircraft Artillery Section was charged with the defense of ground installations by means of firing air bursts of artillery at enemy airplanes.

Commanding Officer
Executive Officer

Section 1:
Administration
Correspondence
Personnel Requisition
Citations
Section Files

Section 2:
Unit Reports Analysis
Weekly Intelligence
Daily Situation Reports
Communications
Radar

Claims (damaged/destroyed)
Aircraft Recognition

Section 3:
Operations Directives
Missions
Defense Priority Lists
Situation Maps
Attachments
Journal Activity
Unit Locations
Order of Battle
History

Section 4:
Supply
Ammunition
Materiel
Transportation

Section 5: (Training)
Attached Instruction Teams

Artillery Section

The Artillery Section was the principal supporting arm for both the infantry and armored forces. The artillery did not fight alone, but was fully equipped to defend itself against direct attack by enemy forces. This support was given to other arms through the firepower of its cannons—known as either guns or howitzers. Guns fire shells which do not curve high into the air, whereas howitzers fire shells which rise high and can reach targets protected by obstacles such as hills or high buildings.

Commanding Officer
Executive Officer

Sections 1 and 4:
Artillery Intelligence; Collection/Evaluation/Dissemination
Aerial Photography and Maps
Counter Battery Procedure/Activities

Section 2:
Ammunition
Supply
Maintenance

Personnel

Section 3:
Training
Operations
Troop Movements
Communications
Liaison

Chief Clerk:
Clerical Operations
Message Center Operation
Drafting

Artillery Air Section:
Training
Operations
Supply
Maintenance
Personnel

Chaplain Section

The Chaplain Section was, of course, charged with the spiritual guidance of the Third Army troops, but additionally (and also importantly) the chaplains were expected to have a good effect on the morale within the Third Army.

In a paper that General Patton wrote in 1919, he indicated that the mission of the chaplains was to "...fight the Devil." In parentheses, he added, "usually unsuccessfully."

Commanding Officer

Executive Assistant:
Plans and Training
Public Relations
Graves Registration

Administrative Assistant:
Correspondence
Personnel
Funds, Equipment, and Supplies

General Duties: (Coordinated by both executive and administrative assistants)

Inspections
Conferences

Correspondence
Religious and Pastoral (personal)

Chemical Warfare Service Section

The Chemical Warfare Service Section was charged with the mission of supplying the necessary equipment to protect the troops against enemy gas attacks to neutralize enemy positions with either gas or burning materials, and to cover the enemy front with smoke screens to hide the movements of the Third Army troops.

Chemical Officer
Executive Officer

Administration:
Administration
Office Supervision
Mail
Records
Statistics
Publications

Supply:
Protective Items
CWS Ammunition
Materiel Maintenance
Materiel Salvage
Requisitions
Reports

Intelligence/Technical Section:
Combat Technical Intelligence
Intelligence Maps/Reports
Study of Chemical Warfare

Operations/Training Section:
Planning, Supervision, and Coordination of Chemical
Operations
Operations Maps/Reports
Chemical Defense Orders
Training Schools

Engineer Section

The Third Army Engineer Section was somewhat of a double-edged sword. Although their initial mission was to furnish technical engineering, if the need arose, the engineer troops could readily go into battle as infantry.

The engineers had multiple tasks. They built, repaired, and maintained bridges, buildings, and structures of all kinds except telephone and telegraph systems. They conducted military mining; blew up bridges, buildings, and roads when necessity dictated; and sometimes destroyed captured weapons. They built and maintained extensive road networks for army use. They operated railways, electric power systems, water supply systems, and all other utilities except those specifically assigned to other branches.

Army Engineer
Executive Officer

Administration:
  Correspondence Files
  G-1 Personnel Liaison
  Supply
  Office Operations/Movements
  Military Discipline
  Message Center Operation
  Technical Publications
  Transportation

Intelligence:
  G-2 Liaison
  Technical Reference Library
  Situational Maps
  Technical Intelligence Teams
  Reconnaissance Reports
  Collection, Evaluation, and Dissemination of Intelligence
    Data

Operations/Training:
  Training Planning
  Tactical Planning
  Training Supervision
  Training Inspections
  Troop Disposition Lists
  Drafts Engineer Field Orders

Supply:
  Computes Supply Requirements
  Supply Procurement
  Supply Records Maintenance

Equipment Maintenance Plan

Technical:
  Construction Estimates
  Projects Specifications/Plans
  Development of Plans for Repair, Maintenance, and
    Operation
  Construction Standards
  Technical Inspections
  Collection of Engineering Data for Fortifications,
    Mine-Fields, Demolitions, etc.
  Road Net Reconnaissance
  Maintains Schedules, Progress Charts, and Operations Maps
  Technical Consultations
  Real Estate Acquisitions and Disposals

Topographical:
  Supervision of Map Control
  Topographic Surveys
  Artillery Officer Liaison
  Army Map Preparation (with G-2 approval)
  Reproductions for Army Hqts.
  Maps and Surveys

Finance Section

The Finance Section had the mission of disbursing and ac-counting for all of the the Third Army's funds. It paid salaries and amounts due for army purchases.

Finance Officer
  Administrative Fiscal Officer
  Disbursing Officer
  Chief Clerk

Administrative/Fiscal Section:
  Fiscal/Report Branch
  Filing Branch
  Distribution Branch
  Stenographic Branch

Disbursing Section:
  Commercial Accounts Branch
  Pay and Allowances Branch
  Accounting Branch
  Cashier

Headquarters Commandant Section

The Headquarters Commandant Section was responsible for running the Third Army's headquarters unit. It was not a command section of the Third Army, but it had the mission of supplying the necessities for the personnel in the command echelon.

Commanding Officer
Executive Officer

Commandant's Office:
Planning and Training
Mess Operations
Supply
Billeting
Purchasing and Contracting
Utilities
Automotive and Transportation

Special Troops:
Adjutant
Special Services
Post Exchange
Surgeon
Headquarters Company
Headquarters Band

Inspector General Section

The Inspector General Section conducted inspections and investigations other than those which related to actual combat. They reported with strict impartiality on all irregularities and deficiencies that they might observe. Additionally, the Inspector General was required to make suitable recommendations to rectify any discrepancies that were observed.

Inspector General
Executive Officer

Investigations:
Conducts Investigations
Prepares Reports

Administration:
Executes Reports

Maintains Army Regulations, War Dept. Circulars, and ETO
    Circulars
Filing of Reports and Records

Inspection:
    Inspects All Army Units
    Prepares Inspection Reports
    Reports Deficiencies and Irregularities

Judge Advocate Section

The Judge Advocate Section was the legal branch of the
Third Army. Because of the indigenous legal system of the
military, this section was required to carry out military justice
and punish military criminals. The judge advocate also ex-
amined records of trials by courts-martial and advised General Patton and his staff concerning legal matters.

Judge Advocate

Executive Branch:
    Administration
    Personnel
    Claims Processing
    Legal Library Maintenance

War Criminals Branch:
    Investigation of Charges
    Report Preparation
    Military Commissions Trials
    Liaison to Staff Sections

Legal Assistance Branch:
    Civil Advice
    Military Advice
    Wills Preparation
    Powers of Attorney
    Miscellaneous Legal Papers

Military Justice Branch:
    Charges/Actions Processing
    General Courts Martial Trials
    Trials Record Review
    Supervision of Military Justice

Military Affairs Branch:
    Legal Advice to Commanding General and Staff Sections

Medical Section

The Medical Section was charged with the health of Third Army soldiers and the care of the sick and wounded. The Medical Section gave advice on soldier's clothing, food, drinking water, bivouac areas, billets, and the hours and conditions under which he must survive on the battlefield. This section also directed the control of disease-bearing insects, sanitary measures, venereal disease, and treatment of psychoneurosis.

Surgeon General
  Executive Officer
  (Liaison with the Twelfth Army Group)

Administration/Personnel:
  Message Center
  Medical Files
  Classified Documents
  Correspondence
  Personnel Administration

Preventive Medicine:
  Prevention/Control of Disease: Epidemics, Potable Water,
    Sewage/Waste Disposal, Medical Intelligence and
    Venereal Diseases (Prevention)
  Special Investigations
  Medical Laboratory Supervision
  Monthly Reports
  Statistical Charts

Operations/Training:
  Operational Planning
  Evacuation Procedures
  Hospitals
  Medical Unit Inspection
  Reinforcements
  Operations Map
  Administrative Records

Supply/Finance:
  Liaison with Staff Sections
  Technical Supervision
  Purchasing/Contracting
  Inspection of Captured Medical Equipment and Supplies
  Medical Supplies/Requisitions

Consultant:
Training
Qualifications
Capabilities
Performance
Neuropsychiatry
Nursing Service
Medical Supply Coordination
Civilian Contagious Diseases (with G-5)
Chemical Warfare Casualties

Dental:
Training
Qualifications
Performance
Inspections/Supervision
Dental Records
Procedures

Veterinary:
Food Inspections
Sanitary Mess Inspections
Dehydrated Food Inspections/Supervision
Special Army Rations Inspections/Supervision

Ordnance Section

The Ordnance Section designed, obtained, and distributed the weapons and ammunition which were supplied to the troops. These items were coded as Class V Supply. These Class V supplies were not controlled by the Quartermaster Section. Ordnance was also involved in improving older weapons and developing new weapons.

Army Ordnance Officer
Assistant Ordnance Officer

Administration:
Message Center
Correspondence
Documents Control
Personnel Records

Operations:
Daily Ordnance Lists
Operational Map
Troop Lists

Administrative Orders
Captured Material Reports
Destroyed/Lost Material Reports

Supply:
Procurement
Distribution
Contract Procurement
Equipment Standardization

Maintenance:
Supervision
Research/Development
Local Manufacture Contracts

Ammunition:
Class V Supply Administration
Allocation Procurement
Ammunition Distribution

69th Ordnance Group:
Combat Troop Support
Major Equipment Reclamation
Replacement Parts/Assembly
Supplies
Supervision of Subordinate Battalions

70th Ordnance Group:
Major Equipment Supply
Major Equipment Replacement
Major Equipment Maintenance, Reclamation, and Evacuation
Supervision of Subordinate Battalions

82d Ordnance Group:
Ammunition supply
Supervision of Subordinate
Battalions

Provost Marshal Section

The Provost Marshal Section was the police department of the Third Army. Like its civilian counterpart, the Provost Marshal Section was autonomous, yet it worked closely with the judicial (Judge Advocate) branch of the military justice system for the enforcement of military law.

Provost Marshal
Executive Officer

Administration:
Correspondence
Report Submission
File Maintenance
Records Maintenance
Message Center
Policies
Statistics

Investigation:
Investigation of Crime Reports
Offender Apprehension
Preparation of Crime Reports
Liaison with Other Staff Sections
Completed Investigations Reports

Traffic:
Traffic Control
Traffic Policies
Liaison with Other Staff Sections
Road Net Reconnaissance
Convoy Control
Liaison with Civil Agencies

Law And Order:
Law Enforcement
AWOL and Straggler Control
Prisoner Stockage Control
Summary Courts Control
Liaison with Other Staff Sections
Disciplinary Reports

Prisoners of War:
POW Control
Internment Camps Control
Control of Allied POW
Camps Overrun by the Third Army

Defense:
Communication Lines
Signal Communications
Command Post

Public Relations Section

The Public Relations Section was responsible for the liaison between the Third Army and the news correspondents from

America's newspapers, radio networks, and wire services. Part of their mission was the censoring of information prior to its dissemination to the United States.

Public Relations Officer

Camp Commandant:
Housekeeping, Movement, Supply, etc., of Press Camp.

Administration:
Maintenance of records, supply, and procurement.

Service Group:
Transportation, mess, and housekeeping of press camp.

Correspondents:
Procurement of copy and pictures for news and radio release.

Press:
News dissemination from army channels.

Copy Room:
Copy Control; to censors and transmission agencies.

Photo:
Pictorial coverage within the Third Army.

Radio:
Material production within the Third Army.

Information:
Operations of the Press Camp War Room.

Press Censors:
Security censorship of all copy from army level.

Communications Platoon:
399 Radio Operator and Teleprinter to ETO Headquarters, Paris, and the United Kingdom.

Radio Mackay:
Copy transmission direct to United States via Continuous Wave and telephone.

NOTE: In the Official Third Army After Action Report, this section was sometimes referred to as a G-6 Section. At other times it was simply listed as Public Relations. There is no definitive answer as to whether or not it was considered a "G" Section.

Quartermaster Section

The Quartermaster Section was responsible for the primary supplies that a soldier needs to enable him to fight a war. These items were classified as follows:

Class I: Items generally used up at a regular rate (e.g. food).

Class II: Items of specific issue to units and individuals (clothing, weapons, etc.).

Class III: All types of gasoline (petrol), oils, and lubricants (referred to as POL).

Class IV: Miscellaneous items not covered elsewhere.

Class V: See Ordnance Section.

Quartermaster Section was also responsible for the operation of all rail and road transportation not specifically assigned to combat units.

Quartermaster
Executive Officer

Administrative Functions

Administration:
Purchasing
Contracting
Personnel Supervision

Graves Registration:
Evacuation from Collecting Points
Identification
Burial
Cemeteries Operation

Field Service:
Troop Units Supervision
Labor Units Operation/Assignment
Laundry Operation
Fumigation and Baths
Salvage Equipment Repair Facilities
Captured Enemy Supplies: Collection/Disposition

Supply Functions

Operations:
Movement Regulation
Movement Expediting
Supplies

Class I:
    Ration Supply
    Gratuitous Post Exchange

Class II and IV:
    Sales Stores Operation
    Sales Stores Distribution
    Post Exchange Sales Supply
    Red Cross Supplies

Class III:
    POL Products Supply
    Solid Fuel Supply

Signal Section

The Signal Section of the Third Army was responsible for all signal communications. They used almost anything that was available, including motorcycle, airplane, telephone, telegraph, and radio transmission. Signal Section was also given the mission of producing photographs and motion pictures for purposes of both training and historical records.

The Signal Section was classified as a combat arm of the army because its members often had to repair wire during firefights and therefore wore pistols to defend themselves. Additionally, the Signal Section was required to intercept enemy radio messages and to locate enemy radio stations.

Signal Officer
    Executive Officer

Headquarters:
    Supervision of Hqts
    Coordination of Hqts

Administration/Personnel:
    Signal Files Maintenance
    Reinforcements: Procurement/Assignment
    Reproduction/Distribution of other than Signal Documents
    Supervision of Rear Echelon Communications

Communications:
    Tactical Planning
    Signal Systems Information
    Line Route Maps
    Circuit Diagram

Radio Net Diagram
VHF Radio Relay Diagram
Equipment and Procedures
Training
Equipment Procurement
Call Sign Allocations/Codes
Operation Circulars

Plans/Operations:
Signal Units Coordination
Situation Maps
Operational Units Location
Troop Lists
Unit Histories
Investigations
Inspections
Billeting and Bivouac Areas
Visitor Reception

Photo:
Photo Assignment Coordination
News/Tactical
Photo Print Control
Transmittal of War Department Film to Army Pictorial
Laboratories

Signal Intelligence:
Liaison with G-2 Staff Section
History Radio Counter Measures
Captured Intelligence Documents
POW Interrogation
Intelligence Dissemination
Cryptographic Maint./Control
Codes/Ciphers Distribution
Code/Cipher Preparation
Weather Detachment Supervision
Message Center Supervision

Supply:
Procurement
Storage and Issue
Maintenance
Signal Depot Supervision
Repair Supervision
Record Maintenance
Equipment Salvage
Equipment Reports

Enemy Equipment Intelligence:
    Enemy Equipment Collection
    Enemy Equipment Evaluation
    Enemy Equipment Disposition
    Technical Reports

Special Services Section

The Special Services Section was given the primary mission of entertaining the troops. Through stage shows, motion pictures, orchestras, and in liaison with USO Shows, the American soldier was given a little bit of home away from home, whenever possible.

Chief of Section
Executive Officer

Third Special Service Co:
    Soldier Stage Shows
    Motion Pictures
    Orchestras

Supply/Distribution:
    Requisitions
    Distribution of Equipment
    Athletic/Recreational Supplies

American Red Cross:
    Red Cross Supervision
    Coordination
    Field Service
    Hospital Service
    Club Service
    Clubmobiles

Army Exchange Officer:
    Exchange Set-up Supervision
    Policies
    Operations
    Local Purchases

Cinema Sub-Section:
    Receives Films
    Distributes Films
    Controls Film Library

Athletic/Recreational Sub- Section:
    Plans Special Athletic Events

Supervises Entertainment Programs
Advises Subordinate Units

Repairs/Services:
Radios and Projectors

Tank Destroyer Section

The Tank Destroyer Section was originally created as a blocking factor to the German blitzkrieg style of fighting. In the hands of the Third Army commanders the tank destroyers evolved into more of an aggressive force, with three objectives; to seek, to strike, and to destroy German armor.

Commanding General
Executive Officer

S-1 and S-4 Sections:
Record Maintenance
Equipment Maintenance
Personnel
Supply Maintenance

S-2 Section:
Technical Data Updates
Information Maintenance: German Armor Status, Quantity, and Location

S-3 Section:
Maintaining Unit Locations
Equipment Reports
Training
Personnel
Combat Fitness
Methods Analyses
Plans Recommendations
Plans/Orders for Tactical Operations

NOTE: For units the size of a division or larger, staff sections are designated by a prefix of "G." For smaller tactical units, staff designations are prefixed by "S." For that reason, the Tank Destroyer Section refers to its sections as; S-1, S-2, S-3, and S-4.

HEADQUARTERS
THIRD UNITED STATES ARMY
APO 403

9 May 1945

GENERAL ORDERS - NUMBER 98

Soldiers of the Third Army, Past, and Present

During the 281 days of incessant and victorious combat, your penetrations have advanced farther in less time than any other army in history. You have fought your way across 24 major rivers and innumerable lesser streams. You have liberated or conquered more than 82,000 square miles of territory, including 1,500 cities and towns, and some 12,000 inhabited places. Prior to the termination of active hostilities, you had captured in battle 956,000 enemy soldiers and killed or wounded at least 500,000 others. France, Belgium, Luxembourg, Germany, Austria, and Czechoslovakia bear witness to your exploits.

All men and women of the six corps and thirty-nine divisions that have at different times been members of this Army have done their duty. Each deserves credit. The enduring valor of the combat troops has been paralleled and made possible by the often unpublicized activities of the supply, administrative, and medical services of this army and of the Communications Zone troops supporting it. Nor should we forget our comrades of the other armies and of the air force, particularly of the XIX Tactical Air Command, by whose side or under whose wings we have had the honor to fight.

In proudly contemplating our achievements, let us never forget our heroic dead whose graves mark the course of our victorious advances, nor our wounded whose sacrifices aided so much to our success.

I should be both ungrateful and wanting in candor if I failed to acknowledge the debt we owe to our Chiefs of Staff, Generals Gaffey and Gay, and to the officers and men of the General and Special Staff Sections of army headquarters. Without their loyalty, intelligence, and unremitting labors, success would have been impossible.

The termination of fighting in Europe does not remove the opportunities for other outstanding and equally difficult achievements in the days which are to come. In some ways the immediate future will demand of you more fortitude than has the past because, without the inspiration of combat, you must maintain—by your dress, deportment, and efficiency—not only the prestige of the Third Army but also the honor of the United States. I have complete confidence that you will not fail.

During the course of this war I have received promotions and decorations far above and beyond my individual merit. You won them; I as your representative wear them. The one honor which is mine and mine alone is that of having commanded such an incomparable group of Americans, the record of whose fortitude, audacity, and valor will endure as long as history lasts.

G.S. Patton, Jr.,
General

The End of an Era

In September of 1945, General Patton turned over command of his beloved Third Army to an old friend of his, Lieutenant General Lucien K. Truscott.

In 1947, the Third Army returned to the continental United States. Upon arrival at the military installation now known as Fort McPherson, Georgia, the Third Army reverted from being a *combat* Army to its old job of being a *training* army.

The United States Third Army was inactivated on October 1, 1973.

The following is a list of all of the commanding generals of the Third Army from its inception to its inactivation.

Chronological List of

United States Third Army Commanders

7 Nov 1918 - 19 Apr 1919	MG Joseph T. Dickman
20 Apr 1919 - 2 Jul 1919	LTG Hunter Liggett
15 Sep 1932 - 30 Sep 1933	MG Edwin B. Winans
4 Oct 1933 - 27 Feb 1936	MG Johnson Hagood
4 Apr 1936 - 30 Sep 1936	MG Frank Parker
1 Oct 1936 - 30 Sep 1938	MG George Van Horn Moseley
1 Oct 1938 - 30 Sep 1940	MG Stanley D. Emdick
1 Oct 1940 - 15 May 1941	LTG Herbert J. Brees
16 May 1941 - 2 Feb 1943	LTG Walter Kreuger
16 Feb 1943 - 25 Jan 1944	LTG Courtney H. Hodges
26 Jan 1944 - 7 Oct 1945	GEN George S. Patton, Jr.
8 Oct 1945 - 15 Apr 1946	LTG Lucien K. Truscott, Jr.
16 Apr 1946 - 9 Jan 1947	LTG Geoffrey Keyes
10 Jan 1947 - 14 Mar 1947	MG Ernest N. Harmon
15 Mar 1947 - 14 Apr 1947	LTG Oscar W. Griswold
15 Apr 1947 - 18 Jun 1947	LTG Edward H. Brooks[*]
19 Jun 1947 - 31 Aug 1950	LTG Alvan C. Gillem, Jr.
1 Sep 1950 - 7 May 1952	LTG John R. Hodge
8 May 1952 - 21 Aug 1952	MG William A. Beiderlinden[*]
22 Aug 1952 - 31 Jul 1955	LTG Alexander R. Bolling
1 Aug 1955 - 30 Apr 1958	LTG Thomas F. Hickey
1 May 1958 - 17 Feb 1960	LTG Clark L. Ruffner
18 Feb 1960 - 4 Mar 1960	LTG Robert F. Sink[*]

5 Mar 1960 - 30 Sep 1960	LTG Herbert B. Powell
1 Oct 1960 - 16 Oct 1960	LTG Thomas J. H. Trapnell*
17 Oct 1960 - 2 Oct 1961	LTG Paul D. Adams
3 Oct 1961 - 30 Nov 1962	LTG Thomas J. H. Trapnell
1 Dec 1962 - 1 Feb 1963	LTG Hamilton H. Howze*
2 Feb 1963 - 15 Jul 1964	LTG Albert Watson, II*
16 Jul 1964 - 31 Jul 1964	LTG John W. Bowen*
1 Aug 1964 - 23 Jun 1965	LTG Charles W. G. Rich
24 Jun 1965 - 14 Jul 1965	MG William C. Bullock*
15 Jul 1965 - 31 Jul 1967	LTG Louis W. Truman
1 Aug 1967 - 31 Jul 1969	LTG John L. Throckmorton
1 Aug 1969 - 19 Jun 1972	LTG Albert O. Connor
20 Jun 1972 - 14 Jun 1973	LTG Melvin Zais
15 Jun 1973 - 30 Jun 1973	LTG John H. Hay*
1 Jul 1973 - 1 Oct 1973	MG Warren K. Bennet

* Denotes Acting Commander